A COMMUNITY BUILT ON WORDS

A COMMUNITY BUILT ON WORDS

The Constitution in History and Politics

H. Jefferson Powell

THE UNIVERSITY OF CHICAGO PRESS

Chicago & London

H. Jefferson Powell is professor of law at Duke University. He served as deputy assistant attorney general and deputy solicitor general in the Clinton administration. Among his books are *The Moral Tradition of American Constitutionalism* (1993) and *The Constitution and the Attorneys General* (1999).

The University of Chicago Press, Chicago 60637
The University of Chicago Press, Ltd., London
© 2002 by The University of Chicago
All rights reserved. Published 2002
Printed in the United States of America
11 10 09 08 07 06 05 04 03 02   1 2 3 4 5
ISBN: 0-226-67723-0 (cloth)

Much of section VII originally appeared in Walter Dellinger & H. Jefferson Powell, Marshall's Questions, 2 Green Bag 2d 367 (1999), © 1999 The Green Bag, Inc. Reprinted by permission of Professor Dellinger and The Green Bag.

Library of Congress Cataloging-in-Publication Data
Powell, Jefferson, 1954–
     A community built on words : the constitution in history and
politics / H. Jefferson Powell.
         p.   cm.
     Includes index.
     ISBN 0-226-67723-0 (cloth : alk. paper)
     1. Constitutional law—United States. 2. Constitutional
history—United States. 3. United States—Politics and
government. I. Title.
KF4550 .P66 2002
342.73'02—dc21

                                                          2001008037

To the memory of
the Reverend Dr. W. D. Davies,
a great scholar, a great teacher, a great soul,
with love and admiration.

CONTENTS

PREFACE

The importance of understanding the political system of the United States is clear. The United States is the world's richest country, its preeminent military power, and (in some respects) its dominant cultural influence. How it governs itself is of great moment, not only to Americans but to all the planet's inhabitants as well. For several reasons, however, it is not easy to describe the American political system. Like all social orders, American politics reflects both intersection and discontinuity between its official self-understanding and its actual practice, and untangling those relationships is difficult and often controversial. Unlike many societies in history, moreover, American politics takes place in a legal, and perhaps legalistic, framework that Americans call constitutional law. The United States is a republic or representative democracy, we say, but it is also a constitutional democracy, governing itself through and under the world's oldest written (national) constitution. My interest in this book is in understanding how in practice Americans have sought to create out of, or on the basis of, the Constitution a legal framework for their political life. (Because American constitutionalism was in its origins and early years a political culture that transcended state and federal–state boundaries, I have made considerable use of state constitutional materials.) For reasons that will become apparent, the book's chronological ordering is intrinsic to the argument I am making. My ultimate concern, however, is not only historical but contemporary: What does it mean today to label the United States a constitutional republic?

In revising earlier drafts of this book, I have received the most extraordinary support from many friends. Soon after I finished the manuscript Paul

Carrington, Girardeau Spann, Joseph Vining, and James Boyd White took the time to give it careful attention and to make many valuable comments throughout. David Currie and Jed Rubenfeld authored reader's reports for the University of Chicago Press that were extremely helpful. Among others who provided special encouragement or counsel, I should mention David Lange and Burke Marshall. Fran Hamacher handled the manuscript with her customary care and good humor—even when a third of it vanished inexplicably from my computer and had to be retyped from the hard copy! At the Press, John Tryneski gave me the greatest gift an editor can provide, a deep and critical understanding of the author's goals, and comments designed to advance those goals. I am also indebted to David Bemelmans for his superb copyedit of the manuscript. Whatever its faults, this book is a far better work as a result of the generosity and guidance of each of these good people, and I am profoundly grateful.

Long before I knew anything about the law of the Constitution, I had the privilege to study a far older and deeper law with the Reverend Dr. W. D. Davies. Dr. Davies's seminar on the Gospel of Matthew was one of the most intellectually challenging experiences I have ever had. Years later, W. D. and Eurwen Davies took my daughter Sara and me into their home and hearts and greatly enriched our lives in so doing. Dr. Davies always insisted that I should seek the truth of what I was studying, and that my Welsh ancestry placed on me a special obligation to care about justice. I talked with him many times about the themes of this book and asked (and received) his permission to dedicate it to him. To Sara's and my great sadness, Dr. Davies died before the book could appear. I hope that with his characteristic generosity of spirit he would think it an acceptable (if inadequate) tribute.

December 9, 2001

INTRODUCTION

Americans talk a lot about the Constitution. We often do so, however, without realizing it may not be clear what the subject of our conversation is. There is, of course, an historical document that everyone calls "the Constitution of the United States." There is no dispute over which document it is or what its content is. (To be exact, there isn't *much* dispute—some people claim not to believe that the twenty-seventh amendment is part of the Constitution because it was proposed by Congress in 1789 and approved by the last state necessary to make up the required supramajority in 1992.) Except in the case of demonstrable error (or the twenty-seventh amendment) no one gets confused or argues over the Constitution in this sense. You can read it.

Furthermore, and quite remarkably from the perspective of world history, the historical document that you can take out of your pocket and read actually lays out many of the basic ground rules about how to set up and change Congress and the presidency. How often we elect these officials, when they take office, how many senators each state may choose, how many votes in Congress it takes to override a presidential veto, the eligibility of someone who has been elected president twice to be elected again—these and other housekeeping details are settled, and settled beyond serious dispute, by the words of the document. "The Constitution" in this sense has been an enormous historical success: only in situations of catastrophic political breakdown or outright chicanery has there been any question about following these housekeeping rules or what the outcome of doing so would be. (I would count the Civil War and associated events in the first category and the election of 1876 in the second.) Anyone may find some part or another of the Constitution's housekeeping details bizarre or wrong-headed, but there is no question that within the scope of these details the document lays out the ways the United States as a political entity conducts this part of its business.

When people talk about "the Constitution," however, they sometimes have in mind neither the document nor our practice of abiding by its housekeeping details. What is in view, more often than not, is constitutional law, and by that Americans usually mean a political practice they associate with the courts, and especially the Supreme Court of the United States. As all foreign observers of American politics are acutely aware, American courts wield enormous political power. In subtle and usually unacknowledged ways, ostensibly "apolitical" tasks such as statutory construction afford the opportunity for courts to exercise political choice, but the central and most blatant form in which the courts participate in governing the Republic is through their power of judicial review in the name of the Constitution. This power can be seen at its starkest when the Supreme Court undertakes to dictate what policies and procedures Congress or the president may, or more often may not, follow, but it runs throughout our governmental system and is exercised at all levels of the federal and state judiciaries. Whatever one may make of this feature of American government, either as a theoretical proposition or with respect to its consequences, it is a social reality that one can ignore only at, literally in some situations, one's peril. Courts issue rulings, the Supreme Court announces decisions, and the other political actors in the system, to a remarkable extent, obey or at least pretend to do so. (Periodically a researcher announces with an air of shocked discovery that judicial decisions that run contrary to political preferences are often evaded or disregarded. The far more interesting question is how it happens that they are so often accepted.)

"The Constitution" in this latter sense stands in an ambiguous relationship to the historical document. On the one hand, the courts do not claim to trump elective officials' decisions out of simple disagreement with those officials' policies: "We are not concerned . . . with the wisdom, need, or appropriateness of the legislation" is a refrain the courts have recited innumerable times since the founding.[1] Instead, a court exercising the power of judicial review invariably asserts that it is doing so on the basis of the Constitution. Judicial review rests on the assumption that constitutional law—argument about the interpretation of "the Constitution" not as a mere historical artifact but as law that binds the interpreter—can be done, that it is more than just a charade. But it is precisely this assumption—on the truth of which judicial review's legitimacy rests entirely—that seems questionable when we look honestly at what is called constitutional law. Unlike the housekeeping rules, which usually

2

work so well that they produce little controversy over their meaning, the issues that occupy the courts and others under the rubric of constitutional law are highly contentious. The answers given are, from many perspectives, entirely political, in the sense that the answers are determined not by legal argument, but by policy preference. Consider the following indictment.

The dominant opinion among political scientists is that the justices of the Supreme Court regularly vote in accordance with their preferences rather than on the basis of precedent or some other supposedly apolitical metric for decision. While lawyers often complain that the political scientists wrongly slight the importance of legal reasoning in the Court's decisions, the great majority of constitutional lawyers would agree that on the most contentious issues that come before the Court, most justices' votes have more to do with their fundamental orientation—call it jurisprudential perspective, if you like—than with a dispassionate evaluation of the relative merits of the legal arguments they are presented. There are justices less firmly wedded to a consistent orientation, and issues on which any individual justice may waver, but as a general rule no one expects Justice Clarence Thomas to vote for broad federal power or a broad right of privacy in hotly contested cases, or for Justice John Paul Stevens to vote the reverse. Furthermore, the justices' "jurisprudential" orientations are, once again as a general matter, congruent with the political orientations of the two major political parties. Much as many legal scholars dislike admitting it, the evening news is only slightly oversimplifying when it talks in terms of liberal and conservative wings on the Court. Nor is this merely a current or recent phenomenon: despite all of the complications that careful study reveals, John Marshall's Supreme Court still looks significantly different from Roger Brooke Taney's, and the constitutional-law inclinations of many justices sitting on the Court in, say, 1945, were at marked variance from those of many of their predecessors ten years earlier.

A less heated way of putting my point is that constitutional law is a thoroughly historical phenomenon: as L. H. LaRue wrote several years ago, "the most important fact about a case is its date."[2] The sort of issues taken seriously, the range of views seriously in play on those issues, the relative weights of legal argument and policy preferences in the decisions of judges and other actors, the extent of consensus and, conversely, serious discord on constitutional matters—these are all demonstrably related to the era about which one is thinking. In 1984, for example, Charles L. Black gave a lecture in which he summarized the "practical truth" about American federalism in the following manner: "the national government" is "adequately empowered for meeting national needs as these are perceived from time to time, while the smaller constituent entities—the States—are empowered to deal with all matters that for the time being are not perceived as requiring national action."[3] At the time, to be sure, Professor Black's statement was (in his words) a "'$\pi = 3.1$ approximation'" rather than an exact calibration of the state of constitutional law, but he was certainly right in viewing it as a close practical recapitulation of the Court's decisions on congressional power and federalism for the half-century preceding his lecture. Today, in contrast, no one would give the same answer: the practical truth as I write is that a Supreme Court majority believes that the Constitution puts limits of as yet indeterminate magnitude on the federal government's power to meet "national needs." The difference of course is time: the same arguments for and against judicial imposition of federalism limitations on congressional power existed and were as well understood in 1984 as today. What has changed is the makeup of the Court and the political and intellectual climate in which it makes its decisions.

The fact that constitutional law is historically conditioned tends to make people nervous. As I noted above, our shared understanding of judicial review assumes that something else is going on when a court invalidates a statute or executive action on "constitutional" grounds besides the displacement of elective officials' preferences by the preferences of other officials—in the case of federal courts, unelected and life-tenured officials. The nineteenth-century humorist Finley Peter Dunne did not intend a compliment when his character Mr. Dooley remarked that "th'supreme coort follows th'iliction returns."[4] The historicity of constitutional law suggests the possibility that at the heart of the Republic, behind the trappings of representative democracy and the rule of law, we in fact will find a judicial oligarchy ruling great areas of our common life by fiat.

There are two main responses to the anxiety this provokes. One is to deny that the historically conditioned nature of *contemporary* constitutional law is necessary or intrinsic to the enterprise when it is properly understood and undertaken. "The Constitution"—the real one, not the ersatz product peddled by judicial activists of whichever side you don't like—does not allow for judicial politics. As this story usually is told, at some point in the past (exactly when depends on the storyteller), virtuous judges interpreted the Constitution in accordance with its true meaning. Sometimes that meaning is an original intent suspiciously close to the policies advocated by Republican presidential candidates, sometimes it is the egalitarianism of Earl Warren and his colleagues; but whatever and whenever the era of constitutional fidelity was, it is past. The heretics are in the temple, which is the bad news, and the way to oust them is clearly to return to the days of virtue, which is the good news. The problem with this cure for constitutional historicity is that it depends on ignorance about our constitutional past. American constitutionalism was wracked with deep, principled (at least politically principled) disagreement from the beginning. When in 1801 a frustrated citizen complained about the Constitution's makers that "neither two of them can agree to understand the instrument in the same sense,"[5] the comment was an exaggeration, but no more, of the extent to which the founders themselves argued about the meaning of what they had done. There never was an age of constitutional virtue, if by that one means a time when constitutional controversies were resolved by judges (or others) without recourse to contestable political judgments.

The other popular means of allaying concern over the historicity of constitutional law (popular in the academy, at any rate) is to develop a theory about constitutional law. "The Constitution"—the real one, mind you—directs judges and other interpreters to the correct political choices. At various times, including today, constitutional law has gone astray to a greater or lesser degree by neglecting its true theory, but that can be solved if judges and others will simply heed its principles . . . as interpreted by the theorist. The problem with this cure is not that it is intellectually bankrupt—some of the theorists are extraordinarily gifted scholars—but that each theorist prescribes a different nostrum, and the courts generally pay little or no attention to any of them. And like the fall from virtue story, much constitutional theory is an evasion, not an explanation, of constitutional law's close connection with political and cultural history. Neither ersatz history nor sophisticated theory provides a sure foundation for thinking that there is anything to "constitutional" law beyond the historical contingencies of changing judiciaries and shifting political climates.

Neither of these evasions of the history-bound nature of American constitutional law is plausible. That is one conclusion this book attempts to substantiate. At the same time, I believe that a clear-eyed understanding of our constitutional history shows that we need not seek to escape the historicity of our constitutionalism. It is indeed possible to understand and practice constitutional law, on and off the Supreme Court, as something other than a second round of legislative or executive decisionmaking conducted with ritual gestures toward "the Constitution." Constitutional law, viewed across time, displays continuity and intellectual coherence as well as individual choice and narrow partisanship. Its integrity and distinctiveness rest, however, not on some extrahistorical foundation, but in large measure on the very processes of constitutional argument that make us anxious by their malleability and openness to the influence of political predisposition and preference. Constitutional law is an historically extended tradition of argument, a means (indeed, a central means) by which this political society has debated an ever-shifting set of political issues. At any given point in time—including the very beginning of the Republic itself—there are disagreements, often sharp, sometimes fundamental, over what the Constitution means and requires. Not infrequently, the disagreements encompass the very terms of debate: what counts as a constitutional argument has often been a central matter of contention in our constitutional history. On the issues of sharpest disagreement, and in especially rambunctious eras on a great many lesser ones, most contributors to constitutional discussion plainly have found that the Constitution, as they understand it, generally ordains what they think best and forbids what they fear. Constitutional law is historically conditioned and politically shaped.

At the same time, our shared commitment to debate some political issues in constitutional terms profoundly affects the role of historical contingency and political predilection. "The document establishes a vocabulary, and we use these words to talk about our political institutions and our political problems."[6] The formulation of issues, the range of considerations that can be considered or at least openly acknowledged, even one's own thinking about which political outcomes are best, are shaped by the constraint of fitting them within whatever terms and concepts currently are counted as constitutional (or by the need to change those terms and concepts to accommodate different forms of argument). Some issues that were debatable at an earlier point cease to be arguable: "conservative" and "liberal" justices today disagree vehemently and for the most part predictably on a wide range of issues involving freedom of expression, but they do so on the basis of agreement on the Constitution's solicitude for the freedoms of speech and press that did not exist a century ago. There is, to be sure, no guarantee that this agreement will last forever—the issue of federalism and congressional power I mentioned earlier is one on which a half-century constitutional consensus may be on the point of unraveling—but if that half-century's wisdom is undone, it will be dismantled through people making arguments that in form and logic resemble those by which it was built. However counterintuitive it may seem, the integrity and coherence of constitutional law are to be found in, not apart from, controversy.

The historicist interpretation of American constitutionalism that I believe most persuasive leads to a more modest vision of constitutional law than that of more theoretical accounts. It sees constitutional law as a servant of American political life rather than its master, and denies the sharp line between law and politics that other interpretations sometimes propose. It accords more constitutional significance to the actions of elected officials and sees less that is

unique about judicial decisions. If judges accepted it, they would take a somewhat more modest approach to their role in the constitutional order than is
customary, at least among justices of the U.S. Supreme Court. If the rest of us
took it seriously, the historicist account would demand of politicians and citizens alike that they recognize their, our, responsibilities in maintaining a constitutional order that is open to and inclusive of all.

This book is an argument, although the form of the argument may seem to
some readers rather peculiar. My purpose is to commend to the reader what I
call the "historicist" interpretation of constitutional law—specifically, that
constitutional law is thoroughly historical, dependent throughout on the contingencies of time and political circumstance, and that it is a coherent tradition of argument. I seek to do so through examining a series of controversies
with a constitutional dimension stretching from 1790, the year after federal
government under the Constitution began, to 1944. Although I do not ignore
the substantive issues in each controversy, I am particularly interested in the
light each sheds on the ongoing developments and changes in the forms of
constitutional argument—*how* things were said as much as *what* was said. I
also give some brief attention at the end of each section to the possible relevance of the historical controversy to contemporary constitutional discussion.
Both the historicity of constitutional law and the continuities across time of
the tradition will, I hope, become clearer in this manner than they might remain if the arguments for them were presented in abstraction from the actual
historical development of the tradition.

As the readings progress, a third theme in addition to history and tradition
will emerge: a claim that an important connecting thread in the constitutional
tradition is a concern with how to maintain the political community across
conflict and to extend the community to those who are excluded from it, what
I think of as the Constitution's fundamental democratic ambition. There is, of
course, no necessary connection between this claim and my two basic assertions. The reader may find the historicist account persuasive but be unmoved
by my interpretation of constitutional democracy. An interpretive argument
of the type I offer is necessarily rhetorical in the sense that it seeks to persuade
the reader's judgment, not to produce a quasi-mathematical proof for his or
her logical review. Such arguments, and disagreements over them are, if I am
correct, the lifeblood of American constitutionalism.

PART ONE

Among the American founders, Gouverneur Morris had a special vantage point from which to think about the Constitution of the United States. A skilled lawyer and eloquent public speaker, Morris was one of the most active participants in the Philadelphia convention that framed the Constitution. Years later, Morris explained in correspondence that his immersion in the business of making the Constitution had precluded him from keeping a journal of the convention's debates. "My faculties were on the stretch to further our business, remove impediments, obviate objections, and conciliate jarring opinions." Morris's close involvement in the convention's work culminated in his designation as the final draftsman and stylist of the document, and he was convinced with evident pride that the convention's handiwork was as well crafted as humanly possible. "That instrument was written by the fingers, which write this letter. Having rejected redundant and equivocal terms, I believed it to be as clear as our language would permit."[1] Even so, Morris entertained no illusions that textual clarity could avoid the necessity of interpretive debate. Soon after the Philadelphia convention reported the draft Constitution to the Confederation Congress, Morris is reported to have been congratulated by a friend: "You have given us a good Constitution," which he accepted with a warning: "That depends on how it is construed."[2]

Morris's intimation that drafting and even adopting the Constitution would begin rather than end the process of securing constitutional meaning was richly confirmed in the years immediately following ratification. The creation of written constitutions sharply distinguished the constitutionalism of the young Republic from that of the United Kingdom, but not in precisely the ways that a contemporary political theorist might advance on the basis of a priori reasoning. The authority of the constitutional text as a legal instrument, to be construed through the traditional tools of documentary interpretation, became at once an axiom of American political culture, but it by no means followed that the first interpreters of the new constitutional instruments were narrow literalists with regard to the text. Over the course of the federal Constitution's first decade, Thomas Jefferson acquired a reputation as a strong advocate of close attention to constitutional language, but Jefferson's first sustained exercises in constitutional interpretation exemplified the founding generation's recognition that a constitutionalism based on a text is not circumscribed within the four corners of that text. In 1790, and again in 1791, Jefferson presented President George Washington with advice on constitutional issues that unhesitatingly invoked arguments resting on premises beyond the text, not out of disloyalty to the Constitution but from a conviction that such arguments are a necessary part of a viable constitutional culture. Like his great rival in Washington's cabinet, Alexander Hamilton, Jefferson implicitly portrayed constitutional interpretation as an activity necessarily involving ideological and political commitments. In contrast to both Jefferson and Hamilton, Attorney General Edmund Randolph cast himself, and by implication the faithful constitutionalist, as an evenhanded and neutral interpreter of the fundamental law. (See sections I and II.)

In the long term, one of the most important institutional consequences of the American decision to commit the state and federal constitutions to paper was the occasion it created for courts to set their own judgments on matters of fundamental law against those of legislatures. Despite the fact that contemporaneous English legal orthodoxy denied the judiciary the authority to disregard the dictates of the sovereign Parliament, during the 1790s the practice of judicial review assumed its place as a regular feature of an American constitutional system. As the 1794 Virginia decision in *Kamper v. Hawkins* revealed, lawyers and judges disagreed over the scope and rationale of the practice more than they did over its existence in some form, which almost everyone granted. Their disagreements in this period, furthermore, like those of nonjudicial constitutionalists often revolved around the relationship between contentions based on text and constitutional arguments drawn in part or whole from other sources. In *Kamper,* Judges Spencer Roane and St. George Tucker linked a high view of the role of judicial review with vigorous resort to extratextual fundamental principles. In their opinions of the previous year in *Chisholm v. Georgia,* federal Chief Justice John Jay and Justice James Wilson had argued against the legitimacy of importing the notion of state sovereignty into constitutional debate, but any apparent disagreement with Roane and Tucker was superficial: Jay and Wilson's ultimate purpose was not to commend literalism but to link the interpretation of the federal Constitution to a different and, in their judgment, more appropriate set of principles. (See sections III and IV.)

A decade after the Philadelphia convention adjourned, constitutional discussion in the United States on both state and federal levels was richly infused with moral, political, and prudential considerations, considerations that were treated as equally integral to the task of interpreting a constitution as reasoning from its text. This did not mean, however, that the constitutionalists of the 1790s had simply collapsed the distinction between constitutional and nonconstitutional debates over principle. Respect for the axiomatic authority of the text structured and sometimes controlled constitutional reasoning. Justice William Paterson's opinion in the U.S. Supreme Court's decision in *Calder v. Bull* is a striking example of the role of technical legal construction in judicial interpretation of the Constitution. (See section V.)

I. 1790: Secretary Jefferson and the Foreign Affairs Power

The Constitution of the United States, like all American constitutions since the Revolution, is a document. Indeed, founding-era Americans congratulated themselves on having devised what Chief Justice John Marshall called "the greatest improvement on political institutions—a written constitution." It is the written Constitution, and nothing else, which is "the fundamental and paramount law of the nation." Constitutionalism in the American mode is defined by the text and by the text's identity as the Constitution. Albert Gallatin no doubt thought he was stating a truism when he told the House of Representatives in 1799 that Americans' "liberties are only protected by a *parchment*—by *words*."[3] The central aspiration of two centuries of American constitutionalism is this attempt to bind power by words, to govern government with a text, to prevent tyranny and ensure liberty through a written document.

Our identification of a specific and discrete text as *the* Constitution is so familiar that we can easily think it simple as well as obvious. And that is wrong. To be sure, the Constitution (and its amendments), and nothing else, is the specific and discrete text. Constitutional law therefore is—or ought to be—law derived from the document and nowhere else. Many years ago Justice Owen Roberts described judicial review as involving "only one duty: to lay the

article of the Constitution which is invoked beside the statute which is challenged and to decide whether the latter squares with the former."[4] Roberts is
usually quoted in order that the writer may scoff at his simple-mindedness,
but the mockery is misplaced: if the "fundamental and paramount law of the
nation" is a *written* constitution, then constitutional law (whether enforced by
courts or applied by other actors) must be in some sense an evaluation of what
government is doing by what the constitutional text states. But there is nothing
simple about this task of comparison and evaluation.

The complexities of making a specific document the nation's Constitution did not steal upon Americans unaware, nor are they the discovery of a
(post)modernity more sophisticated than the Constitution's creators. The difficulty and ambiguity of equating constitutionalism with a text were well
known in the founding era. In the speech quoted above, Gallatin immediately
went on to warn the House that we need suffer no monarchist plot or military
coup to lose our constitutional liberties: "they may be destroyed whenever it
shall be admitted that the strict and common sense of words may be construed
away." A written constitution, Gallatin and his contemporaries recognized,
unavoidably brings with it the threat of its own destruction or subversion. The
words on the parchment protect liberty and govern government only insofar
as there are people who take the words seriously and act, intelligently and in
good faith, to make their commands a reality. The central internal threat to
the project of a written constitution stems from the fact that, as the founders
universally expected, the Constitution must govern all sorts of issues that the
letter of the text does not address in any direct sense. In order to apply the
Constitution to matters not literally within its wording, we must construe it,
and derive meanings from it that cannot be found simply by repeating the
words on the parchment. But as Gallatin warned, construction of the Constitution's meaning, however necessary, poses the risk that its meaning will be
"construed away," inadvertently or otherwise, and that the interpreter will
substitute his or her own thoughts for the fundamental and paramount law.
Constitutional law, in the sense we now use the term, originates in the felt need
to demonstrate a relationship of fidelity between assertions of constitutional
meaning and the meaning of the authoritative text.

Written constitutionalism, as the founders understood it, thus requires the
creation of other texts, whether written or not, that connect the written Constitution with the propositions and commands attributed to it. The recurrent
impulse throughout our nation's history to disavow the creation of these other
texts in the name of allegiance to the Constitution alone is not in fact a return
to the founders but a repudiation of their own practice. To see this point, let us

turn to one of the earliest written interpretations of the Constitution as a governing document, a 1790 opinion by Secretary of State Thomas Jefferson. The opinion is of special interest not only because of its date but also because of its author. Jefferson was a highly skilled lawyer as well as a distinguished statesman; in a 1790 letter, his cousin John Marshall described him as one of "the ablest men & soundest lawyers in America." Marshall later changed his mind about Jefferson's soundness, but not about his ability, and well understood what modern lawyers often forget, that Jefferson's views on constitutional matters helped to define the boundaries within which subsequent constitutional debate would take place. Among those views was an emphasis on the threat to the Constitution posed by the interpretive process: "Our peculiar security is in the possession of a written Constitution. Let us not make it a blank paper by construction."[5]

Jefferson wrote his opinion for President George Washington on a question of great importance to the president. In his first annual address to Congress, Washington had asked the legislature to appropriate "a competent fund designated for defraying the expenses incident to the conduct of foreign affairs." He went on to indicate, however, that the task of conducting foreign affairs lay in other hands. "The interests of the United States require, that our intercourse with other nations should be facilitated by such provisions as will enable me to fulfil my duty in that respect, in the manner, which circumstances may render most conducive to the public good."[6] Washington's reference to foreign relations being *his* duty and his suggestion that it included the authority to determine the manner of conducting those relations touched off a buzz of argument in the House of Representatives. A variety of issues and positions surfaced, including skepticism on the part of some about the need for permanent diplomatic relations of any sort. But as the debate developed, the central question to emerge was who has the authority to decide what level or grade of diplomatic representation the United States should employ in a given foreign state. The question was no mere nicety: in addition to its bearing on the cost of the diplomatic establishment (the higher the level minister the greater the expense), the power to choose among the grades of diplomat recognized at international law could in itself affect the options and objectives of American dealings with the foreign power.[7]

Led by Washington's fellow Virginian Richard Bland Lee, one group of congressmen sought to include in the appropriations legislation a requirement that the president's determination of the level of diplomat to employ receive the approval of the Senate, which by the plain text of Article II would already be involved in approving the appointment of American diplomats. Lee and his allies expressly rejected Washington's clear suggestion that foreign affairs were uniquely the president's responsibility. United States representatives, Lee claimed, "were the joint servants of the president and senate."[8]

> [A]s no appointments can be made but by and with the advice of the Senate—that no treaties can be formed without their concurrence, it appears incongruous that they should have no voice in determining the salaries of persons which they may appoint to make treaties, or to carry on the intercourse between the United States and foreign nations. This will give an undue influence to the President in forming treaties—and, superceding the interference of the Senate in a business to which they are equally competent, with the President, is contrary to the Constitution.[9]

Lee's motion to require Senate approval was defeated, but its opponents were divided in their reasons and the question of the Senate's direct constitutional authority in the matter clearly was open when the House decided to delay adoption of a bill pending the arrival of Secretary Jefferson.

Jefferson had returned only the previous December from his post as U.S. minister to France, and some members of the House believed that his recent European experience would enable Congress to estimate with greater precision the sum needed to finance American diplomacy. Jefferson was not in New York (the temporary national capital); indeed, he did not even accept appointment as secretary of state until a couple of weeks after the House tabled the bill. When he did arrive, in late March, one of the president's first duties for him was to prod Congress into adopting a satisfactory foreign relations bill. Jefferson did so, informing a House committee that the president would be as economical as feasible while suggesting to a group of senators that the important issue was the adequacy of the funding (the amount of which all agreed was within congressional control) rather than the issue of constitutional authority that had split the House.[10] At the same time Jefferson was attempting to soothe ruffled feathers, Washington was seeking reassurance that the Constitution safeguarded his power to "to fulfil [his] duty" as to foreign affairs. Washington had conversations with Chief Justice John Jay and Representative James Madison, who advised the president orally that the Senate had no constitutional authority to interfere with his decision about where and at what grade the United States should establish diplomatic missions, "their powers extending no farther than to an approbation or disapprobation of the person nominated."[11] From Jefferson Washington requested a formal, written opinion "whether the Senate has a right to negative the *grade* he may think expedient to use in a foreign mission, as well as the *person* to be appointed."[12] Jefferson's conclusion was the same as that of Jay and Madison. Our interest, however, is in how Jefferson arrived there.

Before turning to what Jefferson wrote, consider first what he had to work with. The Constitution's text is surprisingly vague about the allocation of authority over foreign affairs. There is no provision explicitly assigning the authority, in contrast to the related area of military matters, which receive considerable (if ambiguous) attention in Articles I and II. Indeed, only one provision has unequivocal bearing on the question Jefferson was asked, the appointments clause of Article II, section 2:

> The President . . . shall have Power, by and with the Advice and Consent of the Senate to make Treaties, provided two thirds of the Senators present concur; and he shall nominate, and by and with the Advice and Consent of the Senate, shall appoint Ambassadors, other public Ministers and Consuls, Judges of the supreme Court, and all other Officers of the United States, whose Appointments are not herein otherwise provided for, and which shall be established by Law . . . .

The appointments clause makes it clear that the president's power to make the final appointment of "Ambassadors, other public Ministers [meaning diplomats below the grade of ambassador] and Consuls" depends on some form of Senate concurrence, presumably by simple majority rather than the two-thirds required for ratifying treaties. Taken literally and by themselves, however, the clause's words do not answer the question Washington posed but are capable of bearing several constructions: that the president selects the person, destination, and grade and the Senate's only role is to approve or disapprove the individual nominated (the view of Jay and Madison); that the Senate's authority extends to approving or perhaps even designating the diplomatic grade to which the individual is appointed (the view of Lee and his allies); that Congress may vest the authority through legislation in either the president or the president and Senate (a position suggested by John Laurance of New York in the House); or even that Congress as a whole must "establish by Law" a specific diplomatic office before the president and Senate can approve an individual to hold it (a view floated during the House debates by, among others, James Jackson of Georgia).[13] The text by itself does not resolve which of these or perhaps other possible interpretations is correct.

With no clear answer in the words of the appointments clause, or elsewhere, Jefferson began his discussion with an observation about the overall structure of the constitutional text. "The Constitution has divided the powers of government into three distinct branches, Legislative, Executive & Judiciary, lodging each with a distinct magistracy." The separation, Jefferson conceded, is not perfect, for the Constitution submits "special articles of it [the antecedent is "the Executive powers"] to a negative by the Senate," and makes "certain exceptions [to the grant of judicial power] in favor of the Senate." (Jefferson had in mind the Senate's "sole Power to try all Impeachments," Article I, section 3.) However, as the careful reference to *special* articles and *certain* exceptions indicate, the inference Jefferson wished President Washington to draw was that the norm the Constitution establishes is one of division and distinction between legislative, executive, and judicial authority. Understood at a high enough level of generality, this was hardly a controversial assertion in 1790, but it immediately suggested a means for resolving the text's apparent silence about Washington's question. One can decide the location of the power to determine the destination and grade of American diplomats by ascertaining whether the power is essentially legislative, executive, or judicial.

Once again, the materials available to Jefferson provided no self-evident answer. The greatest eighteenth-century dictionary begs the question: according to Dr. Johnson, "executive" means "[a]ctive; not deliberative; not legislative; having the power to put in act the laws," but none of these definitions tell one whether the matter of diplomatic grade involves the creation or activation of "the laws." Are decisions about our level of diplomatic representation deliberations about the rule that is to govern the American diplomatic establishment, or the activity of carrying out American diplomacy? Political theory was equally unhelpful. John Locke, whose essay on civil government Jefferson knew well, denied that diplomatic power was either legislative or executive in nature. In contrast, the English constitutional precedent was clear. Sir William Blackstone's already classic treatise on English law informed the reader that "[w]ith regard to foreign concerns, the king is the delegate or representative of his people," and in that capacity "has the sole power of sending embassadors to foreign lands."[14] The English background thus might be seen as supplying content to Dr. Johnson's tautology that "executive" means "not legislative." Parliament has nothing to do with foreign affairs; those matters must be "not legislative" and thus are "executive." The Constitution's adoption of this background into its grant to the president of the "executive Power" (Article II, section 1) would be then confirmed by the express parallels it creates between the president and Blackstone's king: like the king, the president appoints diplomatic ministers, makes treaties, and commands the army and navy.

But was George III really the model for George Washington and his republican successors? During the debates over the Constitution's ratification, which Jefferson missed but knew in part, the Constitution's supporters had insisted that the president was not an elected version of the monarch; indeed, although this fact was not generally known, the Philadelphia framers until late in their convention were working with a draft constitution giving the power to make treaties and appoint ministers to the Senate. While this flat rejection of the English model disappeared from the final version, as adopted the Constitution retained some form of Senate involvement with both treaties and diplomatic appointments and expressly gave Congress a variety of war-related powers that Blackstone and English practice accorded to the king and his ministers. If, as Alexander Hamilton wrote in *The Federalist* No. 67, it is a "deliberate imposture and deception" to claim "the gross pretence of a similitude between a King of Great-Britain and a magistrate of the character marked out for that of the President,"[15] reliance on English precedent in defining the powers of the president would seem risky at best.

Risky or not, Jefferson followed his general remarks on separation of powers with an unmistakable (if unacknowledged) echo of Blackstone's statement that the king represents the people of his kingdom "in all" "this nation's intercourse with foreign nations."[16] "The transaction of business with foreign nations is Executive altogether; it belongs then to the head of that department, *except* as to such portions as are specially submitted to the Senate. *Exceptions* are to be construed strictly." Jefferson's assertion here was indeed a very strong one in at least three respects.

(1) The "transaction of business" that is "Executive altogether" goes far beyond the president's role as the conduit of communications between foreign states and the United States through nominating ministers, receiving foreign diplomats, and the like. The sentence itself indicated this by treating the power to make treaties (involving as it does the making, not the mere communication, of policy) as a "portion" of the "business with foreign nations" that is as a general matter committed to the president. Later in his opinion, Jefferson eliminated any doubt that he saw the president as primarily responsible for foreign policy in a discussion of why the Senate would be ill suited to play a role in determining what sort of diplomatic representation the United States should maintain with foreign states:

> [T]he Senate is not supposed by the Constitution to be acquainted with the concerns of the Executive department. it was not intended that these should be communicated to them; nor can they therefore be qualified to judge of the necessity which calls for a mission to any particular place, or of the particular grade, more or less marked, which special and secret circumstances may call for. All this is left to the President. They are only to see that no unfit person be employed.

The picture Jefferson sketched here of U.S. foreign relations is entirely centered on the president. Foreign relations are "the concerns of the Executive department," not by presidential self-aggrandizement but by constitutional design. It is the president alone who is to have access to the information needed to determine where and in what manner the United States should be represented, and it is the president alone who is envisioned as deliberating about the benefits and dangers of diplomacy.

(2) The "business with foreign nations" that is part of the distinct magistracy lodged with the executive belongs, furthermore, "to the head of that department." The point here would have been clear to Jefferson's contemporaries, who sometimes referred to the Senate as belonging to the executive when acting on appointments and treaties.[17] In Jefferson's view, this was loose and inexact language. Article II of the Constitution vests "[t]he executive Power" in the president, not the president and Senate; in constitutional terms, to refer to a power as "Executive altogether" is to refer to the authority of the president alone, except insofar as the Constitution has "specially submitted" some portion of it to the Senate. The Senate is no more a part of the executive branch in approving an appointment or treaty than it is part of the judiciary when it tries an impeachment.

(3) Someone could agree with Jefferson up to this point and yet think that the president's power to determine the proper grade or destination of a diplomat is a part of or implied by the Senate's undeniable role in giving its advice and consent to the diplomat's appointment. Jefferson's response to this possibility was to insist that the Constitution's exceptions to the president's exclusive authority over executive functions were "to be construed strictly." But why? In part Jefferson was relying on the old common-law maxim that *expressio unius est exclusio alterius* (in essence, that mention of one or more of several related matters implies that the others not mentioned are not included). If as a general principle foreign business is a presidential responsibility (points one and two), and yet the Constitution has created exceptions to that principle, the exceptions must not be expanded by interpretation lest they improperly encroach on the principle. In the case of the Senate's role in appointments, furthermore, Jefferson argued that "the Constitution itself . . . has taken care to circumscribe [the Senate's "special" power] within very strict limits" by defining it with reference only to a specific point in the process. The observations we read earlier about the Senate being unacquainted with the "special and secret circumstances" of foreign affairs come into Jefferson's overall argument here. Given the premise that foreign business is as a general matter within the president's purview, the Senate will lack the information and involvement nec-

essary to make wise use of the power to disapprove the president's decisions about the destination and grade of diplomats. It would be irrational to assume that the Constitution nonetheless gave it the power.

Secretary Jefferson gave President Washington a much broader answer than the president's inquiry whether the Senate can "negative the grade" of diplomatic nominees seemed to request. According to Jefferson's opinion, the entirety of foreign "business" is a presidential responsibility, and the president is under no general duty to inform the Senate (or, perforce, Congress) about the issues and information shaping *his* foreign policy "concerns." The Constitution's treatment of the Senate's advice and consent power with respect to diplomatic nominations "shap[es] it into a right to say that 'A. or B. is unfit to be appointed,'" nothing more, which suggests in turn that the Senate's role in making treaties is similarly limited. The most zealous modern defender of the president's preeminent role in foreign policy could hardly ask for more, and all this from Thomas Jefferson, the patron saint of strict construction of the Constitution's text. Presumably Washington was pleased. In the end, however, he avoided the need to confront the Senate or Congress over the issue: Congress appropriated a general sum for foreign intercourse and the Senate made no effort to control Washington's decisions on the destination and grade of his appointees.[18]

Jefferson's 1790 opinion tells us a great deal about the project of written constitutionalism as understood in the founding era. The topic of the opinion, it should be noted, related to the written Constitution in the strictest sense: Washington's question concerned the correct administration of one of the processes that make up (constitute) the federal government delineated by the text of the Constitution. In no obvious sense did Washington's inquiry require Jefferson to consider the general principles of republicanism, or the unalienable rights of man, or the rule of law, or any of the other nontextual domains of political thought that might be thought to make up constitutionalism in a broader sense. Washington's question was about the specific text's meaning and application. And as we have seen, and Jefferson recognized, it was unanswerable in purely textual terms. No amount of staring at the words of the Constitution could possibly have generated *the* answer to the question because the words will support several different answers.

In answering the president's question, Jefferson strove to fashion a line of reasoning that would invoke or allude to pertinent features of the text of the Constitution: the distribution of the power-granting provisions in Articles I–

III; the initial clause of Article II providing that "[t]he executive Power shall be vested in a President"; the location of the provisions concerning the Senate's advice and consent role within the enumeration of presidential powers in Article II, section 2; the wording of the appointments clause. The *expressio unius* maxim, which Jefferson employed to cabin in the implications of the Senate's textually granted advice and consent power, is in form an observation about the interpretive significance of the Constitution's wording. Jefferson's own text, in short, implicitly but skillfully affirmed the paramount authority of the constitutional text and in doing so signaled or enacted its (and his) fidelity to the written Constitution.

At the same time, however, Jefferson's opinion hinged on his premise that foreign business is "Executive altogether," and that assertion is not straightforwardly textual at all. The premise is a possible *construction* of the text's meaning in eighteenth-century English, not a necessary one. But that is the most that could have been said for the opposite premise, or indeed any other. The words on the page do not supply what is necessary to answer Washington's inquiry, and the interpreter must look elsewhere, not out of disregard for the authority of the written Constitution but precisely so that it may be brought to bear on a question its words do not literally address. Even Jefferson's specifically textual points derive their significance in his reasoning from his extratextual premise. The *expressio unius* argument, for example, is persuasive only if one agrees that the president's authority ought to be seen as (presumptively) general and exclusive. The maxim would make no headway with someone who believes, for example, that the Constitution vests the Senate (or Congress) with the power to determine foreign policy.[19]

Jefferson did not give an express explanation for his assumption that foreign business is "Executive altogether," probably thinking it unnecessary to belabor a point that he shared with Washington. He is likely to have shared with Madison and Alexander Hamilton (among others) a conviction that presidential energy and responsibility are essential to the system as a whole and especially necessary in the pursuit of foreign policy—as is suggested by his brief depiction in the opinion of the president juggling foreign intelligence and the public good in deciding alone "the necessity which calls for a mission to any particular place."[20] However that may be, what is most instructive for our purposes is how Jefferson responded to a constitutional question without a determinate textual answer, not by declaring it unanswerable, but by supplying a premise that would enable him to determine which possible construction of the Constitution's words is the better one. Jefferson was driven beyond the words of the text precisely because of the need to address a question presented by the text. Textualism demands nontextual sources of argument.

Jefferson concluded his opinion by responding to a possible objection, that the Senate could exercise a de facto veto on the president's choice of destination and grade simply by refusing to give its advice and consent to individual nominees. Jefferson rejected the objection as based on the unacceptable assumption that the Senate would use its constitutional power to do one thing (rule on the fitness of individual nominees) in order to accomplish another (determine the nature of U.S. representation in foreign states). "[T]his would be a breach of trust," Jefferson wrote, "of which that body cannot be supposed capable." Where the Constitution does not directly grant a power, that power cannot legitimately be exercised "thro the abuse of another." The issue of abuse of constitutional power, like the question of the identity and source of the interpreter's extratextual constitutional premises, is one we shall encounter again.

II. 1791: The National Bank and the Point of Interpretation

The one constitutional dispute of importance in the early Republic that all American law students invariably study in some detail is the question whether Congress has the power to incorporate a national bank. This is not, to be sure, out of any historical interest in national banks on the part of most constitutional lawyers, or out of any present-day concern over the constitutionality of the Federal Reserve, "to question which would be to lay hands on the Ark of the Covenant."[21] Students study the issue because Chief Justice John Marshall wrote about it in 1819, memorably and for a unanimous Supreme Court, in *M'Culloch v. Maryland*. At present, however, our concern is with the beginnings of the dispute, in 1791.

Early in his opinion in *M'Culloch*, Marshall summarized the 1791 debate in an interesting manner:

> The power now contested was exercised by the first congress elected under the present constitution. The bill for incorporating the Bank of the United States did not steal upon an unsuspecting legislature, and pass unobserved. Its principle was completely understood, and was opposed with equal zeal and ability. After being resisted, first, in the fair and open field of

debate, and afterwards, in the executive cabinet, with as much persevering talent as any measure has ever experienced, and being supported by arguments which convinced minds as pure and as intelligent as this country can boast, it became a law.[22]

As Marshall noted, the constitutional issue raised by Hamilton's proposal to create a national bank was fully debated in the First Congress, where the opposition was inspired by the "zeal and ability" of James Madison. After Madison and his allies were defeated, and the bill sent to President Washington, Washington turned to his foremost constitutional advisors—Secretary of State Jefferson, Secretary of the Treasury Hamilton, and Attorney General Edmund Randolph—for their views on the issue. (He also asked Madison to draft a veto message for possible use.) Jefferson (who by 1819 Marshall loathed, but whose "persevering talent" he could not deny) and Randolph advised Washington that the bill was unconstitutional, Hamilton that it was within Congress's authority. In the end Washington, the principal "mind as pure and as intelligent as this country can boast," was persuaded to sign it into law.

As Marshall had written long before *M'Culloch*, the constitutional positions of those defending *and* those attacking the validity of a national bank were alike influenced by considerations beyond the text of the Constitution. "The judgment is so much influenced by the wishes, the affections, and the general theories of those by whom any political proposition is decided, that a contrariety of opinion on this great constitutional question ought to excite no surprise."[23] Jefferson's constitutional judgment fit nicely with his Virginia agrarianism, his suspicions about Hamilton's supposedly monarchical views, and his dislike of banks, just as Hamilton's contrary position reflected his convictions about the need to integrate commerce, industry, and government and, of course, his authorship of the idea. (Randolph, as we shall see, tried to stake out a different and ostensibly apolitical position.) The role of political sentiment in the debaters' thinking did not, however, render their arguments a sham. Indeed, in *M'Culloch* Marshall portrayed the 1791 dispute as a virtual paradigm of good constitutional argument, with the principles at stake fully understood and presented under near-perfect conditions of "fair and open . . . debate," and the controversy ultimately resolved by the closest imaginable living approximation to an "ideal audience."[24] We have it on high authority, therefore, that the arguments advanced in 1791 should be taken seriously as exemplars of constitutional reasoning, even as they also reflect "wishes, affections, and general theories."

The written opinions Washington solicited are of particular interest because they reflect, at a remarkably early point in our constitutional history, the existence of deep disagreement about the fundamental presuppositions of constitutional argument. Their disagreements, to be sure, emerged out of a common allegiance to the written Constitution. In this respect the opinion writers differed somewhat from the bank's greatest defender in Congress, Fisher Ames, who denied any "desire to extend the powers granted by the constitution beyond the limits prescribed them" and yet cheerfully contended that Congress had already "adopted it as a safe rule of action to legislate beyond the letter of the constitution."[25] In contrast to Ames's palpable impatience with finely drawn expositions of the Constitution's words, Jefferson, Hamilton, and Randolph all paid careful attention to the text, and each claimed for his argument the virtue of superior fidelity to it. Each, however, approached the text in a distinctive manner, and in doing so implicitly expressed sharply divergent accounts of the proper stance to take as an interpreter of the Constitution.

Randolph, who reported to Washington first, actually presented the president with two opinions. As he explained in his cover letter, the reasoning in the longer opinion "go[es] as far as I am able to discover, to the substance of the dispute," while "paper No. 2" contained arguments that Randolph found inconsequential but provided the president "lest I may have depreciated them below their value."[26] In these brief remarks, Randolph sketched out the portrait of himself as a constitutional reasoner he wanted to project: modest, evenhanded, and dispassionate. His language is dry, methodical—again and again Randolph ticks off a series of points, "1st . . . 2d . . . 3d . . ."—and free of any obvious attempt at elegance. The interpreter, as Randolph portrayed him, ought to be free of any predisposition on the question either way, as ready to dismiss "minor" arguments "against the bill" as "inferior" ones "in favor of the bill" whenever either are unpersuasive. The interpreter's concern is entirely with the "just interpretation of the words contained in" the Constitution.

Randolph's textualism was by no means an exacting literalism. As he elaborately explained to Washington, the correct approach to construing the language of a legal instrument depends heavily on the nature of that instrument:

> There is a real difference between the rule of interpretation applied to a law & a constitution. The one comprises a summary of matter, for the detail of which numberless laws will be necessary; the other is the very detail. The one is therefore to be construed with a discreet liberality, the other with a closer adherence to the literal meaning.

But when we compare the modes of construing a state and the federal constitution, we are admonished to be stricter with regard to the latter, because there is a greater danger of error in defining partial than general powers.

On the one hand, the federal Constitution must be "construed with a discreet liberality"—in other words with a wise or prudent refusal to lose sight of its overall meaning through overnice arguments about its wording. The document's exact language was the product of hard-fought political debate within a large body. "To argue, then, from its style or arrangement, as being logically exact, is perhaps a scheme of reasoning not absolutely precise." Indeed, at times the text may contain language that is in effect meaningless: the "necessary and proper" clause of Article I, section 8,[27] which supporters and opponents of the bill both invoked, in Randolph's opinion neither expands nor contracts the scope of the powers otherwise granted and is in fact "surplusage" included by the framers through "inattention."

The federal Constitution, on the other hand, requires a "stricter" construction than the state constitutions because it is not, like the latter, a grant of all powers conceivably relevant to the polity it governs. With respect to a state's individual concerns, the state legislature enjoys "all authority which is communicable by the people, and does not affect any . . . paramount rights" of the people. In contrast, as the tenth amendment[28] points out, Congress "claims no powers which are not delegated to it" by the text. "Discreet liberality" in the interpretation of the U.S. Constitution thus is limited by the need to respect the limited nature of congressional power, and it was on that point that Randolph found the arguments for the bank bill fatally flawed. "But, in truth, the serious alarm is in the concentered force" of the arguments on behalf of the bill's validity. If these arguments were accepted, Randolph warned, "it may without exaggeration be affirmed that a similar construction on every specified federal power, will stretch the arm of Congress into the whole circle of state legislation." A bill that can only be supported by arguments dissolving the distinction between the limited federal and the unlimited state constitutions is by that very token unconstitutional.

The task of constitutional interpretation, as Randolph portrayed it in his opinions, is fundamentally unconcerned with political goals and purposes. It does not matter from the interpreter's perspective whether the bank bill will be good or bad for the country. The Constitution, to be sure, was drafted and adopted on the belief that it would serve the common good, but whether it does so is not the interpreter's responsibility or concern. Neither fears over the survival of federalism nor concerns over the inadequacy of national power are germane except insofar as they relate to the "just interpretation" of the text. As a constitutional matter, Congress may exercise any power that "reasoning" may identify as belonging to "the subject, to which [an express] power relates," and Randolph was dismissive of reliance by Madison and other opponents on the representations about the Constitution's respect for state autonomy made during the ratification process. Randolph delicately informed Washington that ratification was a political process of persuasion quite different from the apolitical task of constitutional interpretation: "observations were uttered by the advocates of the Constitution, before its adoption, to which they will not and, in many cases, ought not to adhere." He was equally unimpressed by arguments based on national need. "While on the one hand, it ought not to be denied that the federal government superintends the general welfare of the states, it ought not to be forgotten, on the other, that it superintends it according to the dictates of the Constitution."

Three days after Randolph submitted his ostentatiously evenhanded analysis of the arguments for and against the constitutionality of the bank bill, Jefferson turned in a passionate denunciation of the bill.[29] Unlike Randolph, who avoided literary form or flourish, Jefferson made significant use of his great rhetorical skills, embedding a sharp-edged presentation of the legal arguments against the bill's validity within a state paper cleverly designed to appeal to Washington's fundamentally nonlegal mind. The specifically legal arguments largely paralleled those made by Randolph and others, although Jefferson departed sharply from the attorney general at one point: Jefferson found probative the framers' decision not to include an incorporation power in the text of Article I, an argument Randolph ridiculed as an antitextual resort to "an almost unknown history." The rhetorical packaging, in contrast, was uniquely Jefferson's own. In the place of Randolph's self-portrait of the constitutional interpreter as a disinterested servant of the text, Jefferson implicitly invoked an image of the interpreter—in the first instance himself, but ultimately, he hoped, Washington—as the defender of freedom, concerned with the authority of the constitutional text precisely because that text is the thin parchment line separating liberty from tyranny.

With the exception of its last two paragraphs, Jefferson's opinion is a closed rhetorical unit bounded at beginning and end by reference to the state laws that, according to Jefferson, the bank bill would abridge or permit the national bank to violate. (The final paragraphs discuss the president's options in handling the bill rather than the constitutionality of the bill, and thus appropriately lay outside the rhetorical as well as the substantive scope of the main discussion.) Jefferson began the opinion by listing those laws. "The bill," he writes, "undertakes, among other things:"

1. To form the subscribers into a corporation.
2. To enable [the bank's shareholders] to receive grants of land; and so far is against the laws of mortmain.
3. To make alien subscribers capable of holding lands; and so far is against the laws of alienage.
4. To transmit these lands, on the death of a proprietor, to a certain line of successors; and so far changes the course of descents.
5. To put the lands out of the reach of forfeiture or escheat; and so far is against the laws of forfeiture and escheat.
6. To transmit personal chattels to successors in a certain line; and so far is against the laws of distribution.
7. To give them the sole and exclusive right of banking under the national authority; and so far is against the laws of monopoly.
8. To communicate to them a power to make laws paramount to the laws of the states; for so they must be construed, to protect the institution from the control of the state legislature; and so, probably, they will be construed.

The national bank, as this list portrays it, would create an unfamiliar and privileged elite, competing with ordinary citizens over land and other wealth without being subject to the rules and political processes that govern everyone else. The bank, in short, poses a direct threat to the pursuit of financial security and personal honor and stature in the community that is a central concern of respectable citizens of Virginia such as one George Washington, Esq.

On returning to this theme at the end of his opinion, Jefferson shifted his emphasis from the bank as a potential threat to individual prosperity and freedom to Congress as a present danger to the settled order of society:

Can it be thought that the Constitution intended that . . . Congress should be authorized *to break down the most ancient and fundamental laws of the several states . . .* [to decree] such a *prostitution of laws, which constitute the pillars of our whole system of jurisprudence . . .* [to] *pass over the foundation laws of the state government . . .* (emphasis added).

Congress's passage of the bank bill is a fundamental assault on the political and legal structures of Washington's social world, and the bill's fundamental injustice a significant element in evaluating its constitutionality. Constitutional interpretation, far from being Randolph's evenhanded weighing of conflicting perspectives on the meaning of a text, is at its heart a defense against the encroachments of tyranny.

Underlying Jefferson's heated language, and his none-too-subtle appeals to Washington's predispositions as a planter and landowner, lay a profound discomfort about the tendencies of political power. For all his genuine belief in popular republicanism (Hamilton once wrote disparagingly that Jefferson "is too much in earnest in his democracy")[30] Jefferson possessed a strain of deep pessimism about the uses to which even republican governments are likely to put their authority. Power, for him, was in some sense fundamentally the power of doing wrong, and as a consequence Jefferson had a marked tendency to assume that the Constitution's fundamental purpose is negative or prohibitory. (Even the 1790 opinion, which made sweeping claims for presidential power, was written for the most part in terms of the Constitution's circumscription of the Senate's authority.) After his list of endangered state laws, Jefferson continued by stating this assumption as a general proposition about the nature of written constitutionalism:

> I consider the foundation of the Constitution as laid on this ground: That "all powers not delegated to the United States, by the Constitution, nor prohibited by it to the states, are reserved to the states or to the people." To take a single step beyond the boundaries thus specially drawn around the powers of Congress is to take possession of a boundless field of power, no longer susceptible of any definition.

As with other examples of Jefferson's approach to constitutional interpretation, this short paragraph relies on the vivid imagery it evokes—in this instance of real property, buildings, and fields—in order to convey fully its complex message. The Constitution is a fence, confining a force that is otherwise illimitable within metes and bounds "specially drawn" by the text. Breach the fence in the slightest and no constraint will remain on Congress: it will cease to be the custodian of some limited territory of delegated responsibility and become instead the master of a boundless domain.

The bank's defenders claimed that it was "safe" to maintain that "Congress may do what is necessary to the end for which the constitution was adopted" because in doing so Congress would be limited to legislation that is in fact for "the good of society."[31] According to Jefferson, such a claim required one to ignore, whether willfully or not, the plasticity of the notion of the common good, and the intrinsic connections between power and arbitrary will. The Constitution's carefully drawn boundaries on federal power are no mere administrative convenience: reducing the Constitution "to a single phrase, that of instituting a Congress with power to do whatever would be for the good of the United States" is a simple invitation to oppression and misrule. "[A]s they would be the sole judges of the good or evil, it would be . . . a power to do whatever evil they please." In contrast, the purpose of the real Constitution, and therefore the task of the Constitution's interpreter, is "to lace them up straitly," to keep the restless beast of congressional power penned within its proper, limited field. The presidential veto, he told Washington, "is the shield provided by the Constitution to protect against the invasions of the legislature," likely as it is to be "misled by error, ambition, or interest."

A week later, the author of the bank bill defended his handiwork. Alexander Hamilton's opinion was a juggernaut, many times longer than either of the other cabinet opinions and filled with repeated demonstrations of Randolph's and Jefferson's alleged errors, general and specific.[32] (Toward the end, Hamilton remarks that he presumes "that nothing of consequence in the observations of the Secretary of State and Attorney General has been left unnoticed" . . . and then proceeds to refute Jefferson for another several pages.) The effect is to leave the reader overwhelmed, and inclined to think that every conceivable issue has been aired. But despite the almost endless detail, Hamilton (like Jefferson) made it clear to President Washington that what was at stake in the bank dispute went far beyond the correct exegesis of a legal instrument. For Hamilton, however, the threat was not that Washington would unintentionally set loose a potential congressional tyranny, but that he would sanction a view of the Constitution "fatal to the just & indispensable authority of the United States." According to Hamilton, the fundamental purpose of the Constitution is not the binding of power but its creation. That power, Hamilton readily admitted, is limited to the federal government's "declared purposes & trusts," and further constrained "by restrictions & exceptions specified in the constitution." But within the compass of national authority, Congress's powers are adaptive and expansive:

> [T]he powers contained in a constitution of government, especially those which concern the general administration of the affairs of a country, its finances, trade, defense &c ought to be construed liberally, in advancement of the public good. . . . The means by which national exigencies are to be provided for, national inconveniences obviated, national prosperity promoted, are of such infinite variety, extent and complexity, that there must, of necessity be great latitude of discretion in the selection & application of those means.

Less colorfully than Jefferson, Hamilton too outlined a picture of the danger against which the Constitution is a guard—but for Hamilton this was the danger of national impotence, of collective inability to advance the public good.

As Hamilton saw it, Jefferson and Randolph had turned proper constitutional interpretation on its head. The tenth amendment, cited by Jefferson as the Constitution's "foundation," is simply a restatement of the "republican maxim, that all government is a delegation of power." And that, in the end, is precisely the point: the federal government is a delegation of *power,* by the people, to achieve the people's purposes "to the *best* & *greatest advantage.*" Constitutional interpretation should proceed not from Jefferson's premise of suspicion and hostility to power, but out of a fundamentally optimistic view of government's ability to serve "the welfare of the community." Randolph's fretting about the "danger of error" in interpreting Congress's powers is equally beside the point, refuted by his own (correct) rejection of constitutional literalism. "The moment the literal meaning is departed from, there is a chance of error and abuse. And yet an adherence to the letter of its power would at once arrest the motions of government." The "variety & extent of public exigencies" that are "objects of National [rather] than of State administration" counsel the wise interpreter to more expansive, not stricter, readings of congressional power. Hamilton's constitutional interpreter thus carries on the efforts of the framers and ratifiers of the Constitution, Washington chief among them, to give the United States a government equal to the needs of the nation.

I believe it abundantly clear that the legal analyses in Jefferson's and Hamilton's bank opinions are secondary in importance to their radically different understandings of the nature of the Constitution and of constitutional interpretation. Both men were lawyers of the first rank, and both made skillful use of the available legal arguments. Their disagreement, however, stemmed from deeper sources than the "rules of construction" they both invoked. The real point at which the constitutional issue was joined, as so often in later American constitutional history, was not in their arguments over the scope of the commerce power or the meaning of the necessary and proper clause but in their respective visions of the fundamental purpose of the Constitution and, thus, of constitutional interpretation. They speak to us, if they do, not because we find one legal argument better crafted than the other, but because we find one or the other vision compelling.

Randolph, in contrast, offered no broad vision of constitutional purpose.

He was almost ostentatiously uncommitted on the value—or danger—of the bank bill, his stated purpose solely that of serving as an honest broker between the written Constitution and the contentious world of politics. Randolph did not deny that the Constitution incorporates political values, but he assumed that those values are to be found, ex ante, in the text read intelligently. They are not to be brought to the text by the interpreter. Within the presumably broad range of political decisions permitted by the text, the Constitution, and hence the constitutional interpreter, are neutral as to the goals that government pursues. Randolph speaks to us, if he does, because he expressed a deep strain in American constitutional thought—namely, the wish to avoid or escape entanglement in the world of politics, to elevate constitutional debate and constitutional decisionmaking above the realm of expediency and partisanship.

Neither Jefferson nor Hamilton would have seen Randolph's position as tenable in the long run, if indeed it is possible to state it in a coherent fashion. For them constitutionalism, and loyalty to the written Constitution, are inextricably intertwined with political beliefs and commitments (Marshall's "wishes, affections, and global theories"). To be sure, neither would have thought of what he was doing as importing politics into the Constitution. For both the Constitution's specific language is to be read in the light of its overall purpose, a purpose that cannot be stated in purely intratextual terms, and interpretive cruxes are to be resolved by reference to that purpose. Jefferson and Hamilton radically disagreed, of course, about what the Constitution's fundamental purpose is, and this gave their specific disagreements a much sharper edge than Randolph's gentlemanly quibbles with the "friends" and "enemies" of the bank bill. The bank question, for them, was a war over the meaning of the Republic, and not merely a debate over the just interpretation of the constitutional text.

Subsequent constitutional debate has often assumed Randolph's neutrality as an ideal, while adopting a Jeffersonian or Hamiltonian posture in practice. Indeed, during the long half-century between the Supreme Court's acceptance of the New Deal and its decision in *United States v. Lopez,* the Court managed to combine a full-throated Jeffersonian pessimism in its individual rights cases with a profoundly Hamiltonian optimism in its construction of federal power.[33] The 1791 bank opinions show that disagreement over the role of political commitment in constitutional interpretation is coeval with the establishment of the present constitutional order.

III. 1793: The Supreme Court and the Metaphysics of Sovereignty

The Supreme Court's first great constitutional decision, indeed its first important decision of any sort, was also its first great misstep. On February 18, 1793, the Court held in *Chisholm v. Georgia* that Article III of the Constitution gave it jurisdiction over an action for damages brought against a state by a citizen of another state.[34] The Court's decision provoked swift and decisive repudiation. Less than a year after the Court announced its judgment, Congress approved a constitutional amendment intended to overturn *Chisholm,* and within a year the necessary supermajority of states had concurred in Congress's proposal.[35] In February 1798, five years after *Chisholm,* the Court took note of the eleventh amendment, and held that it eliminated the Court's jurisdiction over all actions against states, including those like *Chisholm* itself that were filed before the amendment's ratification.[36] *Chisholm*'s continuing significance, one might well argue, is limited to the light it sheds on the amendment that overruled it, and indeed that is how the justices of the current Court, and most constitutional lawyers, understandably view it.[37]

In his great treatise on the Constitution, Justice Joseph Story suggested that there was more to be found in *Chisholm* than a mirror image of the eleventh amendment. The amendment directly reversed *Chisholm*'s holding, he conceded, but nonetheless he commended the justices' opinions to his reader: "Although the controversy is now ended, the opinions deserve a most attentive perusal, from their very able exposition of many constitutional principles."[38] Following Justice Story's hint, we will focus our attention on a constitutional principle discussed interestingly and at length by two members of the *Chisholm* Court: federalism and the place of the states in the American constitutional system.

The reader will have noted Justice Story's use of the plural in referring to "the opinions." As they frequently did in the 1790s, in *Chisholm* the justices delivered individual ("seriatim") opinions in which each expressed his individual views on the question before the Court. With one exception, they were in agreement that the Court had jurisdiction over an action brought by Alexander Chisholm, a citizen of South Carolina suing as executor of another citizen of the same state against Georgia. Justice James Iredell dissented, arguing that the Court could not proceed in the absence of congressional legislation regulating such actions and hinting (at least) that even with such legislation the action would be barred by the state's sovereign immunity.[39] Justices William Cushing and John Blair rested their opinions in favor of the Court's jurisdiction primarily on the plain language of the Constitution. "The case," Cushing wrote, "seems clearly to fall within the letter of the Constitution." Article III, section 2 provides that "[t]he judicial Power shall extend . . . to Controversies . . . between a State and Citizens of another State." "A dispute between *A.* and *B.* is surely a dispute between *B.* and *A.*," Blair reasoned, and since in other places the Constitution necessarily contemplates that states may be sued (Article III, for example, extends federal jurisdiction over "Controversies between two or more States"), both he and Cushing thought the Court's jurisdiction clear.

Justice James Wilson and Chief Justice John Jay did not disagree with this textual argument, but in somewhat different respects each found it insufficient. Wilson was well known for his (largely justified) claims to legal scholarship—Attorney General Randolph cuttingly referred to Wilson as "the Professor" and Chief Justice Jay as "the Premier"[40]—and he delivered an elaborate opinion that purported to examine the question of the state's suability "from every possible point of sight . . . [b]y the principles of general jurisprudence . . . the laws and practice of particular states and kingdoms . . . and chiefly . . . by the Constitution." Cloaked within a parade of learning and insufferably grandiloquent language (he twice referred to the interpretation of the Constitution as "the legitimate result of that valuable instrument"), Wilson delivered a broadside attack on the legitimacy of talking about state sovereignty in the American constitutional order.

Justice Wilson's initial point was conceptual: the notion of sovereignty is largely incoherent and, in a republic, perverse:

> The perverted use of genus and species in logic, and of impressions and ideas in metaphysics, have never done mischief so extensive or so practically pernicious, as has been done by states and sovereigns, in politics and jurisprudence; in the politics and jurisprudence even of those who wished and meant to be free. In the place of those expressions I intend not to substitute new ones, but the expressions themselves I shall certainly use for purposes different from those, for which hitherto they have been frequently used.[41]

In "the natural order of things," Wilson argued, it is clear that the political organization of the state is inferior in moral and political significance to the individuals who make it up. "Man . . . is the workmanship of his all perfect Creator: A state, useful and valuable as the contrivance is, is the inferior contrivance of man; and from his native dignity derives all its acquired importance." The language of sovereignty carries with it notions of preeminence and high moral right that properly belong to humanity itself, not to the political institutions through which "free men" act together "for their common benefit." But political waywardness has turned this natural order on its head:

> As the state has claimed precedence of the people; so in the same inverted course of things, the government has often claimed precedence of the state; and to this perversion in the second degree, many of the volumes of confusion concerning sovereignty owe their existence. The ministers . . . have wished, and have succeeded in their wish, to be considered as sovereigns of the state.[42]

The mistaken elevation of a magistrate to the rank of "sovereign" is the "old world" error of monarchy, but it is equally erroneous to award the title to the state, for in doing so we elevate the people's servant over the people themselves. "Hence the haughty notions of state independence, state sovereignty, and state supremacy." Free individuals can claim no independence from the claims of justice and no supremacy over the rule of law; how then can the mere servants of an "aggregate of free men" assert such supremacy? "[A]ll arbitrary doctrines and pretensions concerning the supreme, absolute, and incontrollable power of government," including the argument that an American state government is immune from the processes of justice, thus degrade the individual "from the prime rank, which he ought to hold in human affairs."

Even by the standards used in European jurisprudence, Wilson argued, American states are not "sovereign." In discussing internal political relationships the term serves to distinguish monarch from subject, but that distinction is nonexistent in the United States, where "there are citizens, but no subjects." In discussions of the law of nations, "every state, which governs itself without any dependence on another power is a sovereign state," but by that definition, Wilson asserted, to call Georgia "sovereign" is doubly mistaken. As a republic, Georgia the state is dependent on the "supreme power" of its people, who retain the moral and political right to alter or abolish the state's powers and organization. "[A]s to the purposes of the union," furthermore, the people of Georgia "retained . . . to themselves" "the supreme or sovereign power" altogether, and acting "as a part of the 'People of the United States'" delegated national governmental power to federal institutions. "As to the purposes of the union, therefore, Georgia is not a sovereign power." Within the scope of national authority, to assert the sovereignty of the state is to misunderstand the nature of the national constitutional order. "[T]he people of the United States intended to form themselves into a nation for national purposes." The people having acted on this purpose, "[i]s it congruous that . . . any man or body of men, any person, natural or artificial, should be permitted to claim an entire exemption from the jurisdiction of the national government?"

Chief Justice Jay's opinion paralleled Wilson's in part. American independence, Jay wrote, was a repudiation of European notions of sovereignty, which rest on "feudal principles":

> No such ideas obtain here; at the revolution, the sovereignty devolved on the people; and they are truly the sovereigns of the country, but they are sovereigns without subjects (unless the African slaves among us may be so called) and have none to govern but themselves; the citizens of America are equal as fellow citizens, and as joint tenants in the sovereignty.[43]

In the United States, sovereignty, "the right to govern," belongs solely to the people who create constitutions and through them institutions and officers to administer government. In the federal Constitution, "we see the people acting as sovereigns of the whole country; and in the language of sovereignty, establishing a constitution by which it was their will, that the state governments should be bound."

All of this said, however, Jay conceded that one could speak of "the residuary sovereignty of the state" as the power of the state's people to organize their own, nonnational affairs (a point Wilson did not deny in substance). That being the case, the Chief Justice continued, one must ask whether the sovereignty of the people of Georgia over their affairs and, specifically, their collective monies, rendered those affairs and that money immune from suit in federal court. Jay's answer to the question of state suability requires a full quotation:

> Suability, by whom? Not a subject, for in this country there are none; not an inferior, for all the citizens being as to civil rights perfectly equal, there is not, in that respect, one citizen inferior to another. It is agreed, that one free citizen may sue another; the obvious dictates of justice, and the purposes of society demanding it. It is agreed, that one free citizen may sue any number on whom process can be conveniently executed; nay, in certain cases one citizen may sue forty thousand; for where a corporation is sued, all the members of it are actually sued, though not personally, sued. In this city there are forty odd thousand free citizens, all of whom may be collectively sued by any individual citizen. In the State of Delaware, there are fifty odd thousand free citizens, and what reason can be assigned why a

free citizen who has demands against them should not prosecute them? Can the difference between forty odd thousand, and fifty odd thousand make any distinction as to right? Is it not as easy, and as convenient to the public and parties, to serve a summons on the Governor and Attorney General of Delaware, as on the Mayor or other Officers of the Corporation of Philadelphia? Will it be said, that the fifty odd thousand citizens in Delaware being associated under a State Government, stand in a rank so superior to the forty odd thousand of Philadelphia, associated under their charter, that although it may become the latter to meet an individual on an equal footing in a Court of Justice, yet that such a procedure would not comport with the dignity of the former? In this land of equal liberty, shall forty odd thousand in one place be compellable to do justice, and yet fifty odd thousand in another place be privileged to do justice only as they may think proper? Such objections would not correspond with the equal rights we claim; with the equality we profess to admire and maintain, and with that popular sovereignty in which every citizen partakes.[44]

This paragraph is a remarkable anticipation of Justice Oliver Wendell Holmes's insistence that "[w]e must think things not words, or at least we must constantly translate our words into the facts for which they stand, if we are to keep to the real and the true."[45] What then, is the translation into fact of the claim that a state enjoys sovereign immunity from a legal action to enforce a contract it allegedly has breached? Simply this, according to Jay: that a group of citizens organized in a certain way, under a certain title, claims to be free of the political and legal obligations that attach to each of them individually, and to the same group of citizens, or any other, when organized differently and under a different label. Such a claim, in Jay's view, is flatly contrary to the express purpose of the Constitution to "establish Justice," as well as to the "great moral truth, that justice is the same whether due from one man or a million, or from a million to one man." No magic attaches to the term "state." Whatever unique powers a group of citizens organized as a state has—Jay was not arguing, obviously, that states as political entities have no place in the constitutional order—they are to be judged in the light of the Constitution's language and purposes, not by the abstraction of state sovereignty.

Perhaps without intending to do so, Justice Wilson and Chief Justice Jay collaborated in *Chisholm* on one of the more daring undertakings in U.S. constitutional history, the elimination or (at least) neutralization of the language of state sovereignty. If their views had prevailed, reference to the states as sovereigns would play no role in constitutional argument. It would still make sense to refer to the *United* States as a "sovereign" in the context of international law and international relations, and the essentially preconstitutional notion of "popular sovereignty" could still serve as a reminder that even the Constitution is subject to change or repudiation, but state sovereignty would have no analytical significance. It is, I think, worth considering briefly what difference this would make.

One answer, which has considerable force, is that the deletion from briefs and judicial opinions of talk about state sovereignty would make no real difference at all, because the language is purely instrumental and without any real substance. The Supreme Court's practice lends considerable weight to this argument, for the Court's invocations of state sovereignty often stay on the level of political-convention rhetoric ("Mr. Chairman, the sovereign state of North Carolina casts fifty-one votes . . ."). Most if not all of the apparent exceptions are cases in which the Court's decision can be explained on other grounds. A particularly helpful example can be found in the Court's decision in *New York v. United States,* the case that inaugurated the Court's current line of federalism decisions by holding that Congress cannot commandeer state legislatures by requiring them to legislate on congressionally prescribed issues. Writing for the Court, Justice Sandra Day O'Connor noted that in some cases involving the line between federal and state authority,

> the Court has inquired whether an Act of Congress is authorized by one of the powers delegated to Congress in Article I of the Constitution. In other cases the Court has sought to determine whether an Act of Congress invades the province of state sovereignty reserved by the Tenth Amendment. In a case like these, involving the division of authority between federal and state governments, the two inquiries are mirror images of each other.[46]

New York (and other cases of the same ilk), in other words, could be analyzed entirely in terms of the appropriate scope of the commerce clause, or whatever provision of the Constitution is at issue. Doing so, moreover, would have the arguable advantage of drawing attention to the relevant constitutional text or texts and thus connect the discussion to the written Constitution.

As we have already seen, however, fidelity to the written Constitution is not defined by a narrow textualism in constitutional argument. "Behind the words of the constitutional provisions are postulates which limit and control," the Court once wrote in a state sovereign immunity case, and this assertion is, I think, undeniable.[47] As Secretary Jefferson found in 1790, constitutional interpretation sometimes cannot avoid resort to premises lying beyond the four corners of the document. The question of whether to use the language of state sovereignty in constitutional discussion is answered not by asking whether it is found in the Constitution (it is not) but by asking what we mean by the language, and then, what our reasons are for attributing this meaning to the Constitution. Consider the following possible responses.

(1) State sovereignty language safeguards the basic principle that the federal government possesses only those powers the Constitution grants it. As the tenth amendment states, "[t]he powers not delegated to the United States . . . are reserved to the States respectively, or to the people." The principle, to be sure, is not in dispute, but can be observed directly by inquiring into the affirmative scope of federal authority. Talking about state sovereignty is neither necessary to that task nor a guarantee that the principle will be preserved.

(2) State sovereignty language serves the constitutional and democratic goal of devolving power away from the center and closer to the people. Leaving to one side the question of whether the Constitution should be read to incorporate this goal, the Supreme Court's recent experiments with a broad doctrine of state sovereignty give us no reason for great confidence that talking about the states as sovereigns advances it. American-style federalism does not devolve power to a local or popular level; instead it locates power in the states, none of which resembles a New England town meeting, and many of which are larger and more populous than most independent nations. At the same time, the Court's state sovereignty doctrine shows little sign of affecting the substantive range of the national government's authority. Instead, it is mainly confined to shielding state governments from federal interference. Perhaps a different approach would do more to foster democracy, but the language of sovereignty will not help you devise one.

(3) State sovereignty language provides a justification for constraining the use of national power in circumstances that on their face are within the scope of delegated national authority. But why should we wish to do that? What are the constitutional realities (remember Justice Holmes) that make it appropriate to deny the existence of federal power when an affirmative reading of the Constitution seems to create it? There may at times be good arguments for recognizing nontextual limitations on national authority, but the response that "the states are sovereign, that's why" is mere assertion.[48]

In *Chisholm,* Justice Wilson recommended that we avoid using terms in constitutional debate that have no determinate meaning, and Chief Justice Jay intimated that we should address great constitutional questions in the light of the impact our answers will have on the human beings whom the Constitution was created to serve. Both suggestions seem sensible.

IV. 1794: *Kamper v. Hawkins* and the Role of the Judiciary

One of the more puzzling aspects of the constitutional history of the early Republic is the lack of debate over judicial review of legislation. The claim that courts have the power to disregard or annul a statute if, in the court's opinion, it violates the Constitution was flatly contrary to mainstream English legal thought in the late eighteenth century: Blackstone had written that Parliament "can, . . . do every thing that is not naturally impossible; and therefore some have not scrupled to call its power, by a figure rather too bold, the omnipotence of parliament. True it is, that what they do, no authority upon earth can undo."[49] In contrast, during the last decade of the eighteenth century American lawyers, judges, and (what is most remarkable) legislators alike came to agree, almost universally, that some form of judicial review was a feature of the American constitutional order. By the time John Marshall had the opportunity to discuss the issue in *Marbury v. Madison*, the issue was essentially settled and Marshall's discussion of it evoked virtually no attention. (The modern legend that *Marbury* invented judicial review is simply that—a legend.)

Marshall, to his credit, did not pretend that he was making a radical or innovative claim. The issue, he wrote, while "deeply interesting to the United States," is "happily, not of an intricacy proportioned to its interest."[50] The issue, indeed, had arisen earlier in his home state of Virginia, and in one instance, the 1794 case of *Kamper v. Hawkins*, an able court gave it considered attention, with interesting results.[51] The issue in *Kamper* involved a Virginia statute that attempted to confer on state district courts some of the powers previously exercised solely by the state's chancery court. The legislature's purpose was, doubtless, entirely directed toward improving the efficiency of the state judicial system: the chancery court had at this point but a single judge, and the statute's effect was to make certain forms of relief available more swiftly and at less expense to all the parties. Nonetheless, six months after the statute's enactment, the Virginia General Court (which was made up of the district court judges sitting en banc) unanimously held that the legislature had violated the state constitution and that, as a consequence, the district courts were not obliged to follow the statute.

The seriatim opinions delivered by the General Court's members expressed a wide variety of views on the role of the judiciary under an American written constitution. At one extreme sat Judge James Henry, who did not in fact think the statute in itself was unconstitutional; the problem, he thought, was that neither he nor his colleagues had received appointments and commissions as equity judges. Without such a personal conferral of authority, Henry believed he would be personally unjustified in exercising equity powers. More broadly, Henry appeared to think of judicial review as defined by, and perhaps limited to, situations in which the legislature had in effect asked the individual judge to act against his conscience. That being so, Henry suggested, the judge was entitled to weigh his personal qualms against other factors. "The case cannot often happen; it is exceedingly disagreeable to be faulting the legislature; and, perhaps, one particular mischief had better be submitted to, than a public inconvenience."

Two members of the *Kamper* court expressed a perspective that was a polar opposite to Henry's. Judges Spencer Roane and St. George Tucker each defended judicial review as an essential and important part of a governmental system created by a written constitution. The heart of the judicial function is the interpretation of the law—"[i]t is the province of the judiciary to expound the laws" (Roane); "this exposition it is the duty and province of the judiciary to make" (Tucker). In the absence of a constitutional text, however, a court could have no firm basis on which to conclude that the legislature had violated constitutional norms, since those norms themselves "could only be collected from what the government had at any time done." Judicial review was impossible due to a lack of proof, as it were: "the judiciary, having no *written constitution* to refer to, were obliged to *receive* whatever *exposition* of it the legislature might make."

The American written constitution solved this problem and put an end to the "solecism" of parliamentary omnipotence: "with us . . . [the constitution's] principles can be ascertained from the living letter, not from obscure reasoning or deductions only." Argument over what is "constitutional" thus becomes a form of that most commonplace of judicial actions, the construction of a legal instrument. In turn, rather than being an assumption of political power over the legislature, judicial review of the constitutionality of legislation falls within the familiar realm of claims involving conflicting legal texts. As Roane explained, "the judiciary may clearly say, that a subsequent statute has not changed a former for want of sufficient words, though it was perhaps intended it should do so." In a strictly analogous fashion, when faced with a conflict between the text of the constitution and the text of a statute, a court must determine which to apply. "In expounding laws, the judiciary considers *every* law which relates to the subject; would you have them shut their eyes against that law which is of the highest authority of any?" Judicial review is possible because the Constitution is written, and thus amenable to judicial interpretation; judicial review is unavoidable because courts have a duty to decide cases based on the "just exposition" of "what the law is" and in doing so cannot ignore "that which is the supreme law."

The idea that judicial review is a reflex of the judicial duty to decide cases according to the relevant law was not unique to Roane and Tucker. They were probably influenced by the comparable line of reasoning Alexander Hamilton presented in *The Federalist* No. 84, and their colleague William Nelson made a similar argument in *Kamper* itself. Chief Justice Marshall, in turn, probably made use of both *The Federalist* and *Kamper* in writing his opinion in *Marbury*. Agreeing on this argument as a justification for judicial review does not, however, guarantee agreement on the function of the judiciary in exercising the power. According to Judge Nelson, judicial review's justification is also its function, to ensure that the court decides the individual case according to law. "I do not consider the judiciary as the champions of the people, or of the Constitution, bound to sound the alarm, and to excite an opposition to the legislature.—But, when the cases of individuals are brought before them judicially, they are bound to decide."[52]

For Roane and Tucker, this seemingly modest understanding misunderstood the full implications of the American decision to administer a written constitution through a system of divided governmental power. Because the legislative, executive, and judicial branches are separate, "neither [may] exercise the powers properly belong[ing] to the other. Now since it is the province of the legislature to make, and of the executive to enforce obedience to the laws, the duty of expounding must be exclusively vested in the judiciary."[53] By putting constitutional interpretation within the judiciary's competence, the written Constitution makes its own exposition uniquely the responsibility of the courts, which thereby become a "barrier against the possible usurpation, or abuse of power in the other departments."

Judicial review thus stands on a different and higher ground than constitutional interpretation by other organs of government. A decade later Roane remarked in an opinion that "legislative exposition" of the Constitution always ("more or less") "contravenes that principle requiring a separation of the legislative and judicial departments," and in any event "must yield to that of the judiciary."[54] It is only judicial interpretation of the Constitution that makes the supremacy of the Constitution a reality. Without courts exercising the power of judicial review, the principle that the Constitution limits the legislature "would become a dead letter." Litigation involving the constitutionality of a statute thus makes the court "the proper . . . tribunal" in a "controversy . . .

between the legislature on one hand, and the whole people of Virginia (through the medium of one individual [the constitutional claimant]) on the other." The judiciary is, indeed, the champion of the people and the Constitution.

If Judge Nelson's view of judicial review is correct—that the existence of the written Constitution permits a court to disregard a statute on constitutional grounds when the court must do so in order to decide the case before it according to law—a court might conclude that respect for separation of powers and the constitutional role of the legislature should make it chary of exercising the power. "[T]he violations must be plain and clear," Judge John Tyler (who shared Nelson's view) remarked in *Kamper,* a comment echoed on many later occasions and by many judges, including John Marshall. If, on the other hand, Judges Roane and Tucker have the better view—that the judiciary is the special guardian of the Constitution by virtue of its power to expound the law—such hesitance might well be a cowardly refusal to carry out its assigned duty. For courts to confine their exercise of judicial review to those presumably rare cases where a statute clearly violates the constitutional text is to leave the Constitution vulnerable to subtle or disguised erosion. The constitutional order that courts must protect is a matter not just of the instrument's words but of what Tucker called "the fundamental principles which the framers. . . had an eye to." Judicial review must safeguard these principles.

In *Kamper,* Roane attempted to explain what this entails:

> [T]he judiciary may and ought to adjudge a law unconstitutional and void, if it be plainly repugnant to the letter of the Constitution, or the fundamental principles thereof. By fundamental principles I understand, those great principles growing out of the Constitution, by the aid of which, in dubious cases, the Constitution may be explained and preserved inviolate; those land-marks, which it may be necessary to resort to, on account of the impossibility to foresee or provide for cases within the spirit, but without the letter of the Constitution.[55]

Exactly what Roane and Tucker had in mind in referring to "fundamental principles" is unclear; at different points in their opinions these "principles" appear to include the basic idea of separation of powers, their view of judicial review as essential to the preservation of the Constitution, and various inferences from the constitutional text. They were not, of course, advocating judicial lawmaking, as they saw it. Roane's "great principles" guiding judicial review are ones that grow out of the Constitution, not ones that are imported into it. But they saw no difficulty in a court's imposing on the legislature its judgment as to what these principles are and how they are to be applied, because in the area of law exposition the courts are not coordinate with the legislature but supreme. "This exposition it is the duty and office of the judiciary to make." What is clear, however, is their rejection of any narrow textualism, and their acceptance of the legitimacy of judicial invalidation of statutes on grounds that are fairly disputable and, indeed, disputed. For Roane and Tucker, the power of judicial review stems from the written Constitution but its exercise is not bounded by the Constitution's letter.

Constitutional law in the third century of the U.S. Constitution is heir to each of the major themes that emerged in the early state case of *Kamper v. Hawkins*. The adoption in the twentieth century by American law schools of *Marbury v. Madison* as *the* case on judicial review has canonized Marshall's version of the justification for judicial review that all the *Kamper* judges except Henry shared. In consequence the ambiguity that Marshall thereby inherited is built into the education of every contemporary lawyer and judge. Federal courts long ago abandoned the claim that they invalidate statutes only in cases where a constitutional violation is indisputable, but Nelson's and Tyler's concern that courts avoid unnecessary exercise of the power of judicial review remains a central theme in the language of Supreme Court decisionmaking. At the same time, in practice the views of Roane and Tucker have won out. The law of the Constitution is viewed, as a practical matter, as equivalent to what the Supreme Court says it is. The justices and their academic observers endlessly debate *which* "fundamental principles" the Court should rely on in order to "explain and preserve inviolate" the Constitution, but for the most part they agree on the legitimacy of broad judicial power to uphold whichever principles are the right ones—in the view of a majority of the justices.

With this in mind, we might pause to consider the possible significance of the observation that the Roane–Tucker viewpoint relied on the writtenness of the Constitution to justify judicial review while defining the scope and purpose of judicial review in a manner not limited to textual argument. We have, of course, met (in section I) the apparent paradox that administering a written constitution drives one beyond the four corners of the instrument. What *Kamper* highlights is the further development in our constitutional tradition endorsing the right of courts to rely on their understanding of extratextual "principles" in asserting the power to disregard the acts of the coordinate legislature. Given the role that political vision and ideology can (must?) play in determining which principles to apply (see section II), is judicial decisionmaking likely to be any more a matter of adherence to something called "law" than the products of legislative or executive deliberation? If the constitutional judgments of the Supreme Court are similar to political-branch decisions in their connection to the decisionmaker's political commitments, does it make sense to accord the courts the supremacy in constitutional interpretation that Roane and Tucker claimed for them? The courts, they believed, must safeguard constitutional principle against political-branch infringement. *Sed quis custodiet ipsos custodes* (But who will watch the watchers)?

V. 1798 (1): Justice Paterson and the Missing Fundamental Principle

Only one of the Supreme Court's decisions prior to the appointment of John Marshall as Chief Justice has enjoyed much significance as a precedent in later decisions. The exception, *Calder v. Bull,* has turned out to be of permanent significance to the Court and, for different reasons, to the legal academy.[56] *Calder's* judicial importance stems from the fact that at a very early stage, and over Justice William Johnson's somewhat later protests, the case has been taken to settle an important question about the meaning of the ex post facto clauses of Article I, sections 9–10. The clauses forbid the passage of any "ex post facto Law" by Congress or a state, respectively; the standard view of *Calder* treats it as holding that the clauses apply only to penal legislation, and thus do not affect retroactive legislation that has civil effects only. (Justice Johnson vigorously, and perhaps persuasively, argued that the true holding of the case was that the state legislative act in question was in constitutional terms a judicial decision rather than a "law.")[57]

Academic lawyers have been more interested in another feature of *Calder*—namely, the appearance in two of the justices' seriatim opinions of what can be read as a debate over the legitimacy of judicial review based on extratextual considerations. In his opinion concurring in the Court's unanimous judgment, Justice Samuel Chase announced that

> I cannot subscribe to the omnipotence of a state Legislature, or that it is absolute and without control, although its authority should not be expressly constrained by the constitution, or fundamental law, of the state. . . . There are certain vital principles in our free Republican governments, which will determine and overrule an apparent and flagrant abuse of legislative power . . . . To maintain that our federal, or state, Legislature

possesses such powers, if they have not been expressly restrained, would, in my opinion, be a political heresy, altogether inadmissible in our free republican governments.[58]

Justice James Iredell's opinion contains a passage often seen as a direct contradiction of Chase:

> If . . . the legislature of the union, or the legislature of any member of the union, shall pass a law, within the general scope of their constitutional power, the court cannot pronounce it to be void, merely because it is, in their judgment, contrary to the principles of natural justice.[59]

It is unclear historically whether Iredell intended his remarks as a response to Chase, and in any event Chase's comments need not bear the meaning usually attributed to them. His statement is that American legislatures are not limited merely by what some written constitution "expressly" prohibits, but also by "certain vital principles in our free Republican governments." This language need mean nothing more than the assertion—familiar to the reader—that the legal meaning of a written constitution cannot be limited to its literal wording. Iredell's rejection of a judicial power to invalidate unjust laws without regard to constitutional text or principle is not, of course, to the contrary.

My present interest in *Calder*, however, has to do neither with the correct application of the ex post facto clauses nor with the Chase–Iredell "debate," but instead, with a passage from Justice William Paterson's opinion. Paterson agreed with the argument that the Connecticut legislature had exercised an appellate judicial function sanctioned by the state's constitutional practices, and thus that the federal Constitution's ban on ex post facto *laws* was inapplicable. Paterson nevertheless went on to discuss the meaning of the phrase "ex post facto," and concluded that "[t]he words . . . when applied to a law, have a technical meaning, and in legal phraseology, refer to pains and penalties." Paterson made this assertion against a considerable background of debate, some of which would have been familiar to him as a member of the Philadelphia convention.

Madison's notes of the proceedings in Philadelphia record a debate on August 22, 1787 over a motion to insert a clause providing that Congress "pass no bill of attainder nor any ex post facto law." There was general agreement on the value of the bill of attainder prohibition but several members argued against a prohibition on ex post facto laws as unnecessary or improper without indicating their view of its scope. By a divided vote the convention decided to include the phrase. The next day, the convention considered a motion to prohibit states from interfering with private contracts. During the discussion,

George Mason mentioned some examples of valuable state laws dealing with civil matters that he feared such a clause would prohibit, and was answered by James Wilson (the justice-to-be) and James Madison.

> Mr. Wilson. The answer to these objections is that *retrospective* interferences only are to be prohibited.
>
> Mr. Madison. Is not that already done by the prohibition of ex post facto laws, which will oblige the Judges to declare such interferences null & void.

After this exchange, the convention voted to insert among the restraints on the states a prohibition on bills of attainder and ex post facto laws parallel to that already approved with respect to Congress.[60]

At this point, the most plausible understanding of the convention's work would be that the framers assumed a prohibition on ex post facto laws would cover civil as well as penal legislation. The next day, however, John Dickinson "mentioned to the House that on examining Blackstone's Commentaries, he found that the terms 'ex post facto' related to criminal cases only; that they would not consequently restrain the States from retrospective laws in civil cases, and that some further provision for this purpose would be requisite." Madison reported no response to Dickinson's remarks and, indeed, no further discussion of the clause of any sort until September 14, when George Mason made some sort of motion with respect to it. Mason, who thought it wrong-headed to ban civil retrospective laws, explained that he "thought it not sufficiently clear that the prohibition meant by this phrase was limited to cases of a criminal nature." Elbridge Gerry seconded the motion for a purpose diametrically opposed to Mason's—"with a view to extend the prohibition to 'Civil cases,' which he thought ought to be done."[61] The motion was defeated overwhelmingly, with no state delegation voting in its favor.

The subsequent debates over the ratification of the Constitution show that there was no universal agreement over the meaning of "ex post facto Law." A version of Mason's final speech at the convention explaining his refusal to sign the Constitution soon appeared and was understood by most readers to show that Mason thought the term covered civil legislation. Some proponents of ratification replied that the clauses were limited to criminal laws, while others agreed with Mason on the meaning of the term but praised the Constitution for prohibiting retrospective civil laws.[62] During the Virginia state convention, Mason responded to the argument, made to the convention by Edmund Randolph, that the phrase "ex post facto Law" had a technical meaning that would and should control the interpretation of the clauses:

> But the Honorable Gentleman has called to his aid technical definitions. He says, that *ex post facto* laws relate solely to criminal matters. I beg leave to differ from him. Whatever it may be at the bar, or in a professional line, I conceive, that according to the common acceptation of the words, *ex post facto* laws, and retrospective laws, are synonymous terms. Are we to trust business of this sort to technical definitions? The contrary is the plain meaning of the words. . . . Whatever may be the professional meaning, yet the general meaning of *ex post facto* law, is, an act having a retrospective operation. This construction is agreeable to its primary etymology. Will it not be the duty of the Federal Court to say, that such laws are prohibited?[63]

Other commentary from the ratification period confirms Mason's belief that the phrase was at best ambiguous.[64] As Justice Chase remarked in *Calder* a few years later, "the words . . . have not any certain meaning attached to them."

It was, then, against this background of ambiguity and disagreement that Paterson concluded that the ex post facto clauses were limited to criminal laws. After doing so, he made the following comments:

> I had an ardent desire to have extended the provision of the Constitution to retrospective laws in general. There is neither policy nor safety in such laws; and, therefore, I have always had a strong aversion against them. It may, in general, be truly observed of retrospective laws of every description, that they neither accord with sound legislation, nor the fundamental principles of the social compact. But on full consideration, I am convinced, that *ex post facto* laws must be limited in the manner already expressed; they must be taken in their technical, which is also their common and general acceptation, and are not to be understood in their literal sense.[65]

Paterson was one of the most active and influential members of the Philadelphia convention that framed the Constitution, and the reference to his "ardent desire "to have extended the provision" presumably alludes to his agreement with Dickinson, Gerry, and others who unsuccessfully sought to ensure that the Constitution banned retrospective legislation on civil as well as criminal matters. Paterson's construction of the clauses in *Calder v. Bull* thus contradicted what he thought the Constitution should have provided.

The question I wish to ask is why Paterson did not come to the opposite conclusion, that the Constitution means what in his view it ought to mean— given the fact, as I will attempt to show it to be, that doing so would have been entirely possible. Start with the words (we are construing a written Constitution, after all). The Latin expression "ex post facto" means "from what is done afterwards" and the Oxford English Dictionary (OED) records uses of it in English writing from the seventeenth century on with the general sense of "after the fact" or "retrospective"; three of the OED's citations are of early nineteenth-century legal texts referring to noncriminal matters. In Paterson's day, the "literal sense" of the Constitution's words, as he acknowledged, would encompass any law, civil or criminal, that could be viewed as enacted after the matter the law concerned. Even if, as Paterson believed sincerely but (it seems) erroneously, the phrase had a fixed technical meaning in English legal writings, it by no means followed that the interpretation of the people's Constitution should be governed by esoteric professional learning. In *The Federalist* No. 83, for example, Hamilton had reassured the reader that "[i]n relation to such a subject"—he was discussing the proper interpretation of a "constitution of government"—"the natural and obvious sense of its provisions, apart from any technical rules, is the true criterion of construction."[66] Paterson would have been in good company had he declined to treat as controlling the common-law presumption that phrases with an established legal construction should be read in that manner.

In his opinion, Paterson argued that the ex post facto clause of Article I, section 10 ought to be read as limited to criminal matters because if it extended to civil laws the following clause, prohibiting state interference with the obligation of contracts, would be rendered superfluous. Such arguments were not universally convincing to founding-era lawyers—Randolph and Hamilton both interpreted phrases of the Constitution as unnecessary in their bank opinions, while Chief Justice Marshall's opinion in *M'Culloch* presented an elaborate argument intended to show that Congress's authority to wield implied powers would be the same even in the absence of the necessary and proper clause. In any event, the argument could be turned on its head. Both ex post facto clauses are preceded by a prohibition on bills of attainder, which are necessarily ex post facto; the bill of attainder clauses are, as a result, superfluous. In his later attack on the idea that *Calder* settled the meaning of the ex post facto clauses, Justice Johnson pointed out this and other flaws in the argument from superfluity.[67]

It is difficult, furthermore, to see how Paterson could have seen the equivocal discussion of the clauses during the ratification struggle, to the extent he was familiar with it, as requiring him to interpret the phrase "ex post facto law" in a narrower than literal sense. Perhaps one could simply dismiss the anti-Federalists' apparent unanimity in reading the clauses to encompass civil legislation as the expedient argument of men bent on defeating ratification, although by the same token they must have believed that the argument was sufficiently plausible to be worth making, even if they were not in fact convinced that it was the better reading. (And Mason, at least, seems clearly to have been sincere in his concern over a constitutional prohibition on state enactment of retrospective civil laws.) The fact that some (but not all) Federalists gave the clauses their broader, literal reading suggests that the issue of which was the expedient construction to propound was murky, at least to supporters of ratification, which in turn suggests that the argument over the clauses' interpretation was a genuine one not controlled by calculations about how to sway the public.

At first glance, Paterson's knowledge of the Philadelphia convention's proceedings seems a clear basis for his narrow reading of the clauses. Paterson just happened to know, as it were, the meaning the document was intended to have at these points, and it would have been peculiar, if not a dereliction of duty, for him to have interpreted it in any other way. Once again, however, Paterson could have made a strong contrary argument, in two parts. First, while founding-era constitutionalists occasionally invoked the proceedings in Philadelphia as probative of constitutional meaning, doing so was by no means uncontroversial. The convention, of course, was not the body that gave the Constitution legal force: It was the state ratifying conventions, not the Philadelphia framers, that stood in relation to the Constitution as a legislature does to a statute. At this point, furthermore, neither the convention's official journal nor Madison's extensive notes of its debates were public—in 1791, the reader may recall, Randolph referred to the convention's deliberations as "an almost unknown history." Perhaps most important, placing interpretive weight on the convention's proceedings went against widely shared views on the proper rules of legal interpretation. When Jefferson referred to the convention's decision not to include an express power to grant corporate charters, Hamilton attacked Jefferson's argument as poor history and bad law. As an historical matter, Hamilton claimed, the reasons for the convention's actions were uncertain and, indeed, might have stemmed from differing motives on the part of different framers. As a legal matter, he continued, "whatever may have been the nature of the proposition or the reasons for rejecting it concludes nothing in respect to the real merits of the question":

> The Secretary of State will not deny, that whatever may have been the intention of the framers of a constitution, or of a law, that intention is to be sought for in the instrument itself, according to the usual & established rules of construction. Nothing is more common than for laws to express and effect, more or less than was intended.[68]

In a similar fashion, Paterson would have been on firm ground in concluding that "the usual & established rules of construction" did not require him—indeed, arguably forbade him—to subordinate the Constitution's literal meaning to some unexpressed intention on the part of the convention, whatever his personal sense of that intention might have been.

Furthermore, Paterson had a second reason for dismissing the framers' proceedings as a reason to limit the clauses to criminal matters: at least as far as the surviving records show, those proceedings did not demonstrate any settled agreement that the clauses were to be so limited. Dickinson and Gerry indicated that they thought (or feared) that the words would be read to apply only to penal laws, Madison and Mason the opposite; the clearest suggestion of a general view on the interpretation of the phrase is the fact that the convention decided to repeat it in the section restraining the states *after* the colloquy among Mason, Wilson, and Madison in which Madison implied that ex post facto laws include civil legislation. Paterson, of course, knew far more than we about what was said and thought at the convention, and perhaps we simply lack the evidence that would show that most framers accepted Dickinson's citation of Blackstone as proving that the term had a technical and controlling meaning at law. Paterson's own language, however, strongly suggests that his assertion about the framers' intentions was an inference from their language rather than a claim of special knowledge.[69]

There seems, then, to have been no insuperable obstacle preventing Paterson from construing "ex post facto laws" to include civil legislation. In contrast, as his concluding remarks in his *Calder* opinion made clear, he had a powerful reason to read the phrase expansively. The illegitimacy of retrospective legislation was for Paterson a political principle of the deepest significance: "There is neither policy nor safety in such laws . . . retrospective laws of every description . . . neither accord with sound legislation, nor the fundamental principles of the social compact." This sounds like the sort of fundamental principle that the constitutionalists we have been reading would have thought a prime candidate for inclusion in constitutional argument *in the absence of a text embodying it.* Paterson, in contrast, had a text for his principle, the ex post facto clauses read literally. He need only have said something to this effect:

> It is true that some English law writers, including the celebrated Blackstone, have construed the expression "ex post facto law" to refer only to laws affecting criminal cases, and suggestions have been made that this is the meaning of the Constitution of the United States as well. But our Con-

49

stitution is meant to guarantee the fundamental principles of the social compact, and wherever possible its words should be construed to achieve that end. In the present instance, the words the Constitution employed and the great end it sought to achieve are in complete accord, and we would err if we separated them by imposing a forced construction on the words "ex post facto."

My point in all this is not Justice Johnson's, which was to prove that *Calder's* construction of "ex post facto law" was both dictum and erroneous, but only to show that Paterson could have read the clauses to have the meaning he thought best without straining in any way the information and modes of legal argument available to him. And in earlier sections we have repeatedly observed a willingness on the part of prominent founding-era constitutionalists to consult "fundamental principles" in interpreting constitutional texts. And yet in this case Paterson went out of his way to endorse the reading of the clauses that was contrary to his understanding of fundamental principles. Even if the Constitution ought to prohibit retrospective civil laws—even if concluding that it does not meant that the Constitution leaves unprotected a fundamental principle of a free society—Paterson limited the ex post facto clauses to the meaning he believed the phrase had acquired at law. Perhaps, like Randolph in 1791, Paterson wanted to draw a sharp distinction between (politically neutral) constitutional interpretation and (politically charged) arguments over "policy and safety." Perhaps he thought it important as a judge to demonstrate, and to act on, a scrupulous adherence to the forms of legal argument. Whatever his underlying motive, in *Calder* Paterson found the existence of a formal legal reason for choosing one interpretation of the Constitution over another conclusive.

From the perspective of some modern constitutional theory, what Justice Paterson did in *Calder v. Bull* made no sense at all. Ronald Dworkin's argument that it is part of the task of someone interpreting the law to give it the "best" meaning possible is controversial, but a similar attitude is implicit in claims that constitutional interpretation should be representation-reinforcing, or economically efficient, or pragmatic. Such theories often encourage the interpreter to make short shrift of formalist arguments; at the very least, in a situation where formalist arguments are available to support the more theoretically satisfactory interpretation, it would seem perverse not to adopt that alternative. In practice, the justices of the Supreme Court seem to hold the same view: the second Justice Harlan, who is generally seen as fastidiously adherent to traditional legal argument, owes his high reputation in no small part to that.

One response to these observations might be that the difference between Paterson and contemporary lawyers is one of historical context, with Paterson having a more robust view than lawyers today of the Constitution's intrinsic meaning and of the value of formal legal reasoning. But it would be a mistake to exaggerate the difference: as we have already seen, constitutionalists of Paterson's era had a lively sense of the gaps and indeterminacies of constitutional texts. If Paterson had intended his *Calder* opinion to display allegiance to a strict formalism, he would have been staking out what was a contestable position in his own time. In any event, it seems clear that this was not his view, and that he was as willing as most of his contemporaries to decide constitutional issues on nonformalist grounds.[70] In *Calder*, however, Paterson did not do so, apparently because in that case he had come to the conclusion ("[o]n full consideration, I am convinced") that the technical legal argument was the better one—not better for the country, or liberty, or equality, or economic efficiency, or for any of the other good things that can be seen as social and constitutional goals, but better in the sense of being more convincing than the opposite as a matter of legal argument.

While we could dismiss Paterson's action in *Calder* as some sort of primitive legal fetishism, or perhaps the unthinking preference of a lawyer for the folkways and lore of his profession, there are other interpretations. Although nothing in *Calder* directly reflected the fact that by the time of the decision the interpretation of the Constitution was frequently the object of acrimonious political dispute, Paterson and his colleagues certainly knew this. The intellectual chasm evident during the bank bill dispute between Jefferson's and Hamilton's constitutional views had hardened by 1798 into bitter, partisan division. Across a wide range of specific issues (both of constitutional meaning and appropriate public policy), the opinions of most public persons could be predicted with near certainty simply by determining whether the individual was a Federalist (now meaning, roughly, a supporter of Hamiltonian views of federal power) or a Republican (a Jeffersonian). Rather than serving as common ground, the Constitution had become a source of contention between warring factions.

In such a context, technical or professional legal argument remains neutral, not that it fails to reflect deep (if often unexamined) political and moral commitments, but in the sense that the law's argumentative and rhetorical conventions, its conventional uses of precedent and other legal materials, and

51

Part One

so on, are not the creations of the moment and thus can be shared by the factions of the day. Even in the face of unbridgeable political disagreement, the common techniques of law can serve to organize the debate and render the real points of conflict easier to identify. (See the following section.) In less ideologically charged eras, legal formalism, particularly in the form of adherence to precedent, can actually serve to resolve some issues in a manner that prevents them from becoming politically controversial.

PART TWO

Between late October 1787 and late May 1788, Alexander Hamilton and James Madison (with a few contributions by John Jay) wrote *The Federalist*, a series of newspaper essays advocating the adoption of the proposed federal Constitution. Hamilton and Madison had been allies throughout most of the decade, "united in aim. . . by strong national feelings which had little room for fine discriminations. . . . No two men were more energetic in the movement to bring the Constitutional Convention about beforehand, or to have its work ratified afterward."[1] Americans aware at the time of ratification of the true identity of the "Publius" who wrote *The Federalist* expected in all likelihood that this collaboration would continue. Hamilton certainly did: he accepted the position of Treasury Secretary only "under a full persuasion, that from similarity of thinking, conspiring with personal goodwill, I should have the firm support of Mr. Madison."[2]

All such expectations were quickly defeated. By 1792, Hamilton and Madison were perpetrators and victims of a deep and bitter partisan divide in which both similarity of thinking and personal goodwill seemed to have vanished. According to Hamilton, Madison and his close friend Thomas Jefferson were the disingenuous managers of an ambitious faction, possessed by "a disposition to subvert their Competitors even at the expence of the Government."[3] According to Madison, Hamilton and his associates, "having debauched themselves into a persuasion that mankind are incapable of governing themselves," constituted an "anti-republican party" dedicated to "giving such a turn to the administration, [that] the Government itself may by degrees be narrowed into fewer hands."[4] For the next two decades, constitutional discussion was regularly part and parcel of the political struggle between Federalists like Hamilton and Republicans such as Madison. Many of the era's greatest constitutional questions sprang out of partisan strife: the Federalists' Sedition Act of 1798, the furor over the Jonathan Robbins affair, and the Republicans' Judiciary Repeal Act of 1802. (See sections VI–VIII.) Constitutional law and politics were equally entangled on the state level: in Madison's home state of Virginia, for example, social tensions over various issues including religion and slavery unmasked deep constitutional disagreement as well. (See sections IX and X.) It is in this period that one of the most fundamental realities of American constitutional history became clear, that constitutionalism and political conflict are not opposites but siblings.

Political passion can have a distorting effect on one's perceptions: Hamilton was not a monarchist plotter nor did Madison intend to injure the federal government or the Union. At the same time it would be a serious error to minimize the disagreements of the age, which were often severe and deeply rooted in both self-interest and political conviction. It is all the more remarkable therefore that it is in this period that some of American constitutionalism's most enduring threads of coherence and continuity were woven. Federalists and Republicans clashed shrilly over the constitutionality of the Sedition Act, but the Republican attack on the Act was built out of constitutional materials they shared with Federalists; a few years later the Republicans almost universally refused to defend the Judiciary Repeal Act by rejecting the Federalist claim that judicial review is an intrinsic part of our constitutional order. Constitutionalists on both sides of various disputes gave serious and sustained consideration to the intellectual and institutional means of maintaining political community. Figures as different as John Marshall and Aaron Burr suggested that the Congress and the presidency can and should be centers of principled constitutional deliberation even in the midst of party strife, while a remarkable series of judicial opinions in the Virginia state courts wrestled with the question of how judges are to deal with radical constitutional disagreement.

Contrary to the mechanistic view of government sometimes attributed to them, founding-era Americans were painfully aware of the extent to which constitutional stability and, indeed, survival are dependent on individual commitment to the preservation of the constitutional order. In successive, dramatic personal decisions in the years 1808 and 1809, a Republican Supreme Court justice, a Republican president (Madison), and a Federalist district judge left a lasting mark on American constitutional history by protecting the integrity of the constitutional institutions they served even at the cost of forgoing partisan and personal advantage. (See section XI.)

VI. 1798 (2): How to Think about the Sedition Act

A few months after the decision in *Calder v. Bull* we come to a constitutional discussion in another forum characterized by violent disagreement, not (relatively) harmonious concord. The central point of contention in national politics during 1798 involved foreign policy. Revolutionary France's overbearing and erratic behavior had brought Franco–American relations to the breaking point, with the generally Francophile Republicans divided and disheartened, and many of the Federalists convinced that the Republic was in mortal peril of a French invasion or subversion from within. In the spring and summer following *Calder,* the Federalist-controlled Congress took under consideration a battery of laws intended, as Federalists saw it, to put the country in an appropriate state of defense. Among the bills eventually enacted was the famous (or infamous) Sedition Act of July 14, 1798, which prompted the first great debate over the interpretation of what we call the first amendment. (Collectively the statutes were known as the Alien and Sedition Acts and one of the other laws, the Alien Act of June 25, also evoked significant constitutional discussions.)

As enacted, the Sedition Act criminalized conspiracy to impede the execution of federal law as well as defamation of Congress or the president. The conspiracy part of the bill was not controversial constitutionally, and the extensive debates on the bill focused on the provisions regarding defamation. Some of the discussion addressed the details of those provisions: the constitutional debate addressed the provision that made it a crime to "write, print, utter, or publish"

> any false, scandalous, and malicious writing or writings against the government of the United States, or either House of the Congress of the United States, or the President of the United States, with intent to defame the said government, or either House of the said Congress, or the said President, or to bring them, or either of them, into contempt or disrepute; or to excite against them, or either or any of them, the hatred of the good people of the United States.[5]

The Republicans' constitutional attack on the bill had two major prongs. As John Nicholas told the House of Representatives, "[h]e looked in vain amongst the enumerated powers given to Congress in the Constitution, for an authority to pass a law like the present; but he found [instead] what he considered as an express prohibition against passing it."[6] In answer to the first objection, that Congress had no affirmative power to enact such legislation, the initial Federalist response was that the bill was an essential element in the system of national defense and thus authorized by the necessary and proper clause. As the debate continued, and after the bill's enactment, Federalists increasingly relied on the argument that the federal courts already possessed the substantive authority to punish the common-law crime of seditious libel. As a consequence, they contended, the Sedition Act was an exercise of the congressional power to regulate the prosecution of federal crimes. The Republicans' furious denial of both claims provoked an interesting debate, especially on what is meant by "common law," but I want to direct our attention to the first amendment issue.

The first amendment critique of any attempt to punish seditious libel came as no surprise to the Federalists. As Harrison Gray Otis noted during an early debate in the House, "[h]e had expected to have heard the most elaborate harangues in favor of the liberty of the press . . . and such public topics."[7] In answer, the Federalists flatly denied that a sedition bill would abridge freedom of the press. A prohibition on seditious libel is no more a violation of constitutional liberty than is a prohibition on physical assault: in both cases the legal prohibition simply marks the boundary of moral and socially acceptable behavior.

> What, then, is the rational, the honest, the Constitutional idea of freedom of language or of conduct? Can it be anything more than the right of uttering and doing what is not injurious to other? This limitation of doing no injury to the rights of others, undoubtedly belongs to the character of true liberty. Indeed, can it, in the nature of things, be one of the rights of freemen to do injury?[8]

Rational liberty of all sorts is entirely compatible with legal restraints on injurious conduct. "Every man possessed the liberty of action, but if he used this liberty to the detriment of others . . . he became liable to punishment for this licentious misuse of his liberty. The liberty of the press stood on precisely the same footing."[9] Drawing on a distinction found in Blackstone, the Federalists insisted that the punishment of seditious libel places no restraint on liberty of the press, but only on its "licentiousness," the use of expression to harm individuals, government, and society.[10]

The text of the first amendment, the Federalists went on, demonstrated the amendment's compatibility with the distinction they wished to draw between liberty and license. Some noted that the amendment employed different terms in characterizing the limitations it prescribed ("Congress shall make no law *respecting* an establishment of religion, or *prohibiting* the free exercise thereof, or *abridging* the freedom of speech, or of the press"), and concluded that the differences implied that Congress "may make any laws on the subject [of the press] that do not abridge its liberty."[11] The centerpiece of the Federalists' textual argument, however, concerned the words used to describe what the amendment protects, and their reasoning was parallel to that which Justice Paterson accepted in *Calder.* As with the ex post facto clauses, so in the first amendment (they argued) the Constitution has adopted language with a "definite . . . technical meaning."[12] Once again, Blackstone's *Commentaries* played a key role. As Otis explained:

> The terms "freedom of speech and of the press" . . . were a phraseology perfectly familiar in the jurisprudence of every State, and of a certain and technical meaning. It was a mode of expression which we had borrowed from the only country in which it had been tolerated . . . . This freedom, said Mr. O., is nothing more than the liberty of writing, publishing, and speaking, one's thoughts, under the condition of being answerable to the injured party, whether it be the Government or an individual, for false, malicious, and seditious expressions, whether spoken or written; and the liberty of the press is merely exemption from all previous restraints. In support of this doctrine, he quoted Blackstone's *Commentaries.*[13]

The continued existence of the common-law crime of seditious libel in states with constitutional guarantees of press freedom confirmed that Americans understood "liberty or freedom of the press" in its technical Blackstonian sense[14] of "exemption from all [governmental] power over publications unless previously approved by licensors."[15]

It was inconceivable, George Taylor (John Marshall's cousin) informed the Virginia House of Delegates, that the first amendment's use of this language should have any other meaning:

> The persons who framed the amendments to the Constitution of the United States, were certainly men of distinguished abilities and information. Among them was a great proportion of lawyers, whose peculiar study had been the common law. Perhaps every one of them had read and maturely considered Blackstone's Commentaries. . . . Certainly every one of them was acquainted with the laws of his own state, where the terms "freedom of the press," had precisely the same meaning as in England.[16]

The Republicans' arguments to the contrary required them to substitute their own (wild-eyed) notions of freedom for the settled and beneficent legal traditions embodied in the Constitution, and "[t]hose to whom the management of public affairs is now confided, cannot be justified in yielding any established principles of law or government to the suggestion of modern theory."[17]

As we have seen in considering *Calder v. Bull*, arguments based on the Constitution's use of language with a settled meaning at law were far from trivial to founding-era lawyers, and critics of the Sedition Act met the force of the Federalist claims about the first amendment's meaning with a variety of different arguments. Sometimes Republicans put forward a straightforward plain-meaning argument: "[w]hen the words of the Constitution were so express, it seems impossible they could be understood as the gentleman from Massachusetts [Otis] represented them."[18] More often, however, the major Republican spokesmen attempted to show that the Federalist reading of the amendment was unreasonable in light of the amendment's purpose and place in the American constitutional order. Freedom of speech and press is of peculiar importance in a republican government because it is the very medium by which the people are enabled to exercise intelligently their authority over those they choose to govern them. "Indeed, the heart and life of a free Government, is a free press; take this away, and you take away its main support."[19] As James Madison explained:

> [T]he right of electing the members of the government, constitutes more particularly the essence of a free and responsible government. The value and efficacy of this right, depends on the knowledge of the comparative merits and demerits of the candidates for the public trust; and on the equal freedom, consequently, of examining and discussing these merits and demerits of the candidates respectively. . . . [T]he right of freely examining characters and measures, and free communication thereon, is the only effectual guardian of every other right.[20]

For these reasons, "[i]t was striking at the root of free republican Government to restrict the use of speaking and writing."[21]

Once the essential role of free speech and a free press in popular government (we would say "democracy") is recalled, in the Republicans' opinion it was facetious ("a mockery," Madison wrote) to argue that a mere prohibition on prior restraints, when coupled with the danger of subsequent prosecution, was adequate to protect them. "[T]his idea of the freedom of the press can never be admitted to be the American idea of it; since a law inflicting penalties on printed publications would have a similar effect with a law authorizing a previous restraint on them."[22] Contrary to the Federalists' smooth reassurances that the Sedition Act limited only the freedom of those wishing to spread malicious falsehoods, its real effects would reach far beyond the range of those actually prosecuted:

> [I]f printers are to be subject to prosecution for every paragraph which appears in their papers, that the eye of a jealous Government can torture into an offense against this law, and to the heavy penalties here provided, it cannot be expected that they will exercise that freedom and spirit which it is desirable should actuate them; especially when they would have to be tried by judges appointed by the President, and by juries selected by the Marshal, who also receives his appointment from the President, all whose feelings would, of course, be inclined to commit the offender if possible. Under those circumstance, it must be seen that the printers of papers would be deterred from printing anything which should be in the least offensive to a power which so greatly harass them. They would not only refrain from publishing anything of the least questionable nature, but they would be afraid of publishing the truth, as, though true, it might not always be in their power to establish the truth to a court of justice.[23]

The speech and press clauses of the first amendment have a point, a goal that the amendment's purpose must be to secure. "Was it not obvious that the end meditated by the liberty of the press, can as effectually be defeated in one mode as the other, and that if government can by law garble, suppress and advance political opinion, public information, this great end, upon which public liberty depends, will be completely destroyed."[24]

In the light of all these considerations, the Republicans argued, Blackstone could not be taken as an authority on the meaning of the first amendment's language. Applying Blackstone's description of liberty of the press to the speech and press clauses converts the amendment from a prohibition on governmental control of the press into a mere direction of how government should exercise that control: it "so reduces the effect of the amendment, that the power of Congress is left unlimited over the productions of the press, and they are merely deprived of one mode of restraint." The Federalist invocation of Blackstone, furthermore, was "a manifest abuse of Blackstone's authority." His remarks on liberty of the press, John Nicholas said, were not a definition of constitutional limits on government—"England has no Constitution but what may be altered by the Parliament"—but a laudatory description of English law as administered by that government: "after stating the law on this subject, [he] makes a theory to justify the actual state of the law." "Very different are the circumstances in which his doctrine has been applied here" in purporting to construe a written limitation on legislative authority. Blackstone's discussion, to give him his due, rested on the British presupposition that Parliament has unlimited legislative authority; consequently, Madison wrote, "[u]nder such a government as this, an exemption of the press from previous restraint by licensors appointed by the king, is all the freedom that can be secured." But "[i]n the United States, the great and essential rights of the people are secured against legislative, as well as against executive ambition." In the American context, for freedom of the press "to be effectual" it necessarily had to extend to "legislative restraint" through laws as well as executive efforts at censorship.[25] Properly understood, Blackstone provided no support for the Federalists' views.

It is obvious that debate over the Sedition Act before and after its passage was intimately linked to the political struggle over control of the national government. Although the House debates over the bill revealed the existence of a bipartisan expectation that the constitutional question would ultimately be resolved by the federal courts, few if any Republicans acquiesced when the courts consistently upheld the Act.[26] Republican-controlled legislatures in Virginia and Kentucky repeatedly condemned the Act as unconstitutional, while Republicans in Congress attempted unsuccessfully to secure the Act's repeal and later, successfully, to defeat a Federalist attempt to continue it in force after its original expiration date of March 3, 1801. Despite the risk of prosecution, Republican journalists and pamphleteers carried on a lively attack on the Act and on the conduct of the federal courts in the relatively few prosecutions actually brought for seditious libel. Federalists generally defended the Act's validity and wisdom with enthusiasm, although one prominent Federalist, John Marshall, disavowed it.[27] It would be an error, however, not to take seriously the first amendment debate as a constitutional argument, both because private correspondence on both sides strongly suggests that most participants were speaking out of conviction and because of the intrinsic power of the arguments. One of the many unfortunate consequences of the widespread tendency to focus narrowly on constitutional discussion by the Supreme Court is that constitutional law scholars and teachers generally pay little attention to what was by any standards one of the founding era's most sophisticated debates over the meaning of the federal Constitution.

At first glance, the disagreement between Federalists and Republicans over the compatibility of the Sedition Act with the first amendment can appear to be a straightforward conflict between those who were willing to construe the speech and press clauses in accordance with a settled legal understanding, and those who wanted to give the clauses a new, expanded meaning. The Republicans, in short, were offering an innovative reading of the first amendment. Depending on her perspective, a contemporary constitutional lawyer might then conclude that modern first amendment jurisprudence (which, like the Republicans of 1798, rejects the narrow Blackstonian reading) rests on a politically motivated mistake, a fundamental deviation from the original meaning of the provision, or that the unthinkability of limiting the speech and press clauses to a ban on prior restraints demonstrates the necessity of a "living Constitution" that is subject to change through "interpretation." I hope to show, however, that neither conclusion is a necessary one. From a founding-era standpoint, the proper conclusion to be drawn from the debate over the Sedition Act is that it is overly simplistic to distinguish original meaning from subsequent interpretation in this sharp-edged manner. If we wish to do so, that is no doubt our business, but by doing so we depart significantly from the assumptions of the founders.

My first point is that challenges to the applicability of Blackstone and English common-law learning to the interpretation of American constitutional guarantees of free expression did not originate with the Sedition Act crisis, or the Republicans' desire to defeat or overturn the Act. It is now widely recognized that the American press during the colonial era and the Revolution generally exercised a very broad freedom to criticize government measures and officials without significant interference from prosecutions for seditious libel. At the same time, this is often treated as merely showing a divergence between American practice and American legal thought, the latter remaining (it is said) wedded to a narrow Blackstonian understanding of liberty of the press. In fact, however, on a number of occasions prior to the Sedition Act crisis, American lawyers raised questions, implicitly and at least on one occasion explicitly, about the common law's relevance. A prominent example of a document describing the American constitutional liberty in terms arguably inconsistent with Blackstone was the formal reply the U.S. envoys to France made to the French minister Talleyrand during the notorious "XYZ" affair in early 1798. The reply, signed by all three envoys but drafted by John Marshall, discussed among other matters Talleyrand's complaint that the U.S. government had done nothing to "repress[ ]" insulting and defamatory statements about France in the American press.

"The Genius of the Constitution & the opinions of the people of the United States cannot be overruled by those who administer the government," Marshall wrote in response, and continued:

Among those principles deemed sacred in America, among those precious rights considered as forming the bulwark of their liberties, which the Government contemplates with awful reverence; and would approach only with the most cautious circumspection, there is no one, of which the importance is more deeply impressed on the public mind, than the liberty of the press.

Marshall acknowledged that the press's freedom "is often carried to excess [and] has sometimes degenerated into licentiousness," but insisted that even the most severe "calumny and invective" against governments were "a calamity incident to the nature of liberty": "Perhaps it is an evil inseparable from the good to which it is allied, perhaps it is a shoot which cannot be stripped from the stalk, without wounding vitally the plant from which it is torn." In any event, Marshall informed Talleyrand, "the remedy" for the "abuse of a valuable privilege," "which might correct without enslaving the press" has "never yet been devised," and the only check on the press was the individual's right to bring a legal action "in courts, which are alike open to all who consider themselves as injured."[28]

The reply to Talleyrand illustrates, I believe, the ambiguity that accompanied most founding-era comments on freedom of the press before the Sedition Act debate focused attention and galvanized opinion on the issue. The reply described liberty of the press as central to American constitutional freedom, but left unclear what that entailed. Marshall's language strongly intimated that no governmental action that might "wound vitally" the liberty of the press was consistent with American public opinion and "the Genius of the Constitution." The federal government had endured the most "notorious . . . calumnies & invectives" since its inauguration without attempting to suppress or punish their perpetrators, presumably because those administering it thought such "calamit[ies] incident to the nature of liberty" and believed themselves committed to respect for liberty even when abused. Marshall's general reference to the possibility of individual legal actions for libel completed a sentence the main clause of which stressed the federal government's lack of any institutional means for "suppress[ing] whatever calumnies or invectives any individual may choose to offer to the public eye." The language and tone of the reply to Talleyrand seem to me quite inconsistent with Blackstone's view that even true defamations of government should be punishable because they are harmful to government: Marshall clearly treated the prevention of harm to government as a value subordinate, in the American constitutional order, to freedom of the press, and arguably implied that any restriction on the press would have to be judged by the restriction's practical effect on freedom of expression. The reply, in short, said nothing inconsistent with the Republican rejection of Blackstone, and during the later debates over the Sedition Act it was the Republicans, not Federalists, who cited as an authority "that sublime and just construction of the Constitution itself, as to the liberty of the press, to be found in the negotiations of the late envoys to France."[29]

The most explicit surviving discussion of the relationship between the common law and an American constitutional provision protecting press freedom can be found in letters that William Cushing of Massachusetts and John Adams exchanged shortly before Adams left the state to take up his duties as vice president.[30] (Cushing, then chief justice of the Massachusetts high court, was soon to become an associate justice of the U.S. Supreme Court.) Cushing wrote that he "had a difficulty about the construction" of article 16 of the state's declaration of rights, which provided that "[t]he liberty of the press is essential to the security of freedom in a State, and . . . ought not, therefore, to be restrained within this Commonwealth," his difficulty being "whether it is consistent with this article" not to allow truth as a defense in a prosecution for seditious libel. Cushing cited Blackstone for the proposition that the truth of the libel is immaterial in a criminal prosecution, and Lord Coke's Reports for the view that a true seditious libel is in fact more criminal than a lie, and concluded that "as the law of England now stands, truth cannot be pleaded in bar of an indictment." But Cushing did not think that fact the end of the state constitutional inquiry. "The question is—whether it is law now *here*. . . . If therefore that point has never been adjudged here (and I don't know that it has been), perhaps we are at liberty to judge upon it *de novo* upon the reason of the thing and from what may appear most beneficial to society."

Cushing then proceeded to lay out a careful argument for why in his view observance of the constitutional guarantee required "that falsity must be a necessary ingredient in a libel." (1) While Blackstone defined liberty of the press to consist entirely of an absence of prior restraint, "the words of our article understood according to plain English, make no such distinction, and must exclude *subsequent* restraints, as much as *previous restraints*." (2) Cushing then made the same basic argument the Republicans were to formulate in 1798, that in terms of practical effect a subsequent punishment is as much of a restraint as prior censorship and is therefore equally contrary to a constitutional provision protecting press freedom.[31] (3) On the other hand, Cushing reasoned, "one principal object and end . . . of government" is the protection of an individual's character. The "very general and unlimited" words of the Massachusetts provision would need some "guard or limitation" on their scope to enable government to ensure that end without destroying the value of a free press. (4) The purposes of the guarantee of liberty of the press are in general the value to society of "propagating literature and knowledge [which] tends to illuminate men's minds," and in particular the political importance of ensuring "a free scanning of the conduct of administration." (5) In Cushing's opinion, those ends would not be significantly obstructed by permitting prosecutions for libel provided that truth is a defense.[32] Therefore he proposed to reconcile the governmental duty to protect reputation with the guarantee of a free press by construing the state constitutional provision to require the availability of truth as a defense.

In his answer, Adams readily agreed with Cushing that the differences between Britain and the United States rendered simple reliance on English common law questionable: in a republican polity where the governors are elected, "[h]ow are their characters and conduct to be known to their constituents but by the press? If the press is to be stopt and the people kept in Ignorance we had much better have the first magistrate and Senators hereditary." Without further elaboration, Adams endorsed Cushing's view on the import of the Massachusetts liberty of press provision.

Several features of this exchange merit emphasis. Although Cushing conceded that Blackstone's definition of liberty of the press was accurate as to the degree of press freedom "allowed by the law of England," neither he nor Adams thought that the existence of Blackstone's definition gave the expression "liberty of the press" a fixed legal meaning. Instead, both thought that they could and should address the proper construction of the Massachusetts constitutional provision "*de novo* upon the reason of the thing and from what may appear most beneficial to society." In doing so, they took into account the constitutional purposes of liberty of the press in a republican society—which Cushing at least understood broadly to include the value of the dissemination of knowledge in general as well as the communication of political information. Furthermore, both Cushing and Adams assumed without hesitation that the constitutional provision required courts to bring legal practice into accord with the purposes of the provision, in this particular instance by ensuring that libel prosecutions did not subvert those purposes. In this, the underlying logic of their discussion was the same as that of the later Republican critics of the Sedition Act. Cushing, and presumably Adams, endorsed truth as a defense in criminal libel cases because they believed that in fact it would adequately safeguard liberty of the press. Their "disagreement" with the later Republican interpretation of the federal press clause was on the practical question of where the line needs to be drawn in order to secure the goals of the constitutional provisions. Constitutional interpretation, for Cushing and Adams as much as for the Republicans, involves a creative search for the best understanding of the purposes of the text's command, and then for the appropriate means of ensuring that those purposes are fulfilled.

The reply to Talleyrand and the Cushing–Adams correspondence demonstrate that American concern over the common-law understanding of liberty of the press did not begin with the Republicans of 1798: we cannot as an historical matter attribute solely to partisan politics the belief that the American constitutional guarantees of a free press are not simply defined by English precedent or Blackstone.[33] Perhaps more profoundly, the existence of arguments such as these suggests that there is a flaw in the chronological literalism that sometimes afflicts constitutionalists when they discuss the original meaning of a constitutional provision. Founding-era lawyers did not view a constitution as a box the interpretive contents of which were fixed upon its drafting or adoption. Constitutional interpretation wasn't a strictly historical inquiry into what someone thought at some past point in time. However important the understanding of a provision that its makers would have had might be, the constitutionalists of the early Republic shared, universally to my knowledge, the conviction that at times the meaning of a provision required deliberation on what Cushing called "the reason of the thing," what others we have read referred to as fundamental principles and so on. The Republican interpretation of the first amendment had, from their perspective, as good a claim to be the "original" understanding as the Federalist: each was an argument over the text's meaning and significance for a question not hitherto raised. Federalists and Republicans alike claimed that their preferred construction accorded with the common understanding of the words at the time the amendment was adopted, but that was in each case a part of the argument that their interpretation was the correct one, originally and in 1798. There would have been nothing illogical, indeed, in someone noting in 1798 that he would originally have thought the amendment meant X, and only on considering the Sedition Act had realized that X could not be correct.

In *The Federalist*, Madison expressed the common understanding of the founding era when he wrote that "[a]ll new laws, though penned with the greatest technical skill, and passed on the fullest and most mature deliberation, are considered as more or less obscure and equivocal, until their meaning be liquidated and ascertained by a series of particular discussions and adjudications."[34] As Abraham Baldwin told the Senate in 1802:

Governments of written laws, and written constitutions clearly define and settle many things which would otherwise be afloat; but they do not settle everything; questions will arise in administering them, which occasion honest doubt. When a new law is passed, the most upright and enlightened courts require a length of time to settle the practical questions under it, and to give definitive meaning and precision to all its parts.[35]

The founders were not, to be sure, postmodernists or devotees of reader-response theories of meaning. The task of constitutional interpretation was for them no more the wholesale imposition of policy preferences under the guise of interpretation than it was a rigid inquiry into the past. Precisely because the written Constitution is the meaningful (meaning-full) statement of the fundamental law, its proper construction and application at times demand the faithful interpreter to consider issues, and reach conclusions, not anticipated by the Constitution's creators. Chief Justice Marshall made the point in concluding, in *Dartmouth College v. Woodward,* that the contracts clause of Article I, section 10 applies to public as well as private contracts despite the fact that prohibiting interference with the latter was the object originally in view:

> It is more than possible, that the preservation of rights of this description was not particularly in the view of the framers of the constitution, when the clause under consideration was introduced into that instrument. It is probable, that interferences of more frequent occurrence, to which the temptation was stronger, and of which the mischief was more extensive, constituted the great motive for imposing this restriction on the state legislatures. But . . . [i]t is not enough to say, that this particular case was not in the mind of the convention, when the article was framed, nor of the American people, when it was adopted.[36]

If, as sometimes appears to be the case, present-day judges and constitutional scholars can see no difference between an intellectually creative act of constitutional interpretation and a covert exercise in policymaking, the problem may lie with us and not with the founding generation.

VII. 1800: Marshall and the Role of the Political Branches

For less than six months, between December 1799 and May 1800, John Marshall served in the U.S. House of Representatives. Marshall's enduring fame rests, of course, on his much longer tenure as chief justice of the United States, but during his brief time in the House Marshall showed legislative gifts that, in a different career, would have marked him as a great legislator. With consummate political skill, he labored to bridge the gaps separating the moderate Federalists of the southern and middle states from the High Federalists of the northeast, and to ease the severe alienation between many congressional Federalists and President John Adams, whom Marshall strongly supported. At the same time, Marshall was willing to risk evoking personal and even party disapproval in the interests of what he saw as the greater good: he worked with the Republicans on the highly contentious and generally partisan issue of the Sedition Act.

Without any doubt, however, the high point of Marshall's congressional career came on March 7, 1800, during the House's debate on the Jonathan Robbins affair. Robbins was a seaman on an American merchant ship docked in Charleston harbor who was accused of being in fact a Royal Navy petty officer, Thomas Nash, wanted for committing mutiny and murder on the frigate *Hermione* in 1797. When the British consul asked the local federal authorities to turn "Nash" over pursuant to the Jay Treaty between Britain and the United States, U.S. district judge Thomas Bee and the local U.S. district attorney declined to do so without the approval of the president. After President Adams "advize[d] and request[ed]" Bee that extradition was appropriate if the facts warranted the identification of Robbins with Nash, Bee ultimately ordered Robbins delivered to the British in July 1799 despite his last minute claim that he was actually a native-born American citizen illegally impressed into the Royal Navy. Robbins was quickly executed by the British.

Much of the House's time during the early months of 1800 was taken up with repeated Republican attacks on Adams for his handling of the Robbins matter. Some Republicans pilloried Adams for what they portrayed as the heartless betrayal of an innocent American to the British oppressor, while others, led by Edward Livingston, focused on Adams's alleged violation of the Constitution's separation of powers. Livingston laid out the Republican argument in resolutions he introduced on February 20, 1800. In form it was a syllogism. The Constitution "declares that the Judiciary power shall extend to all questions arising under the Constitution, laws, and treaties of the United States, and to all cases of admiralty and maritime jurisdiction." The legal issues raised by the accusations against Robbins all arose "from treaties, laws, Constitutional provisions, and cases of admiralty and maritime jurisdiction." Therefore, Adams's "decision of those [exclusively judicial] questions . . . against the jurisdiction of the courts of the United States," was a violation of

Article III's grant of judicial power to the courts rather than the president, and therefore "a dangerous interference of the Executive with Judicial decisions." For complementary reasons, Judge Bee's compliance was "a sacrifice of the Constitutional independence of the Judicial power."[37]

Livingston's resolutions were couched in what was by now the standard Republican format: the Federalists had once again violated the letter of the Constitution in yet another of their restless attempts to break down the Constitution's salutary limits on centralized power. In reply, Marshall turned Livingston's invocation of the written Constitution against him. The resolutions, Marshall pointed out, rested on a misreading of the text. While Livingston asserted that the Constitution extends "the judicial power . . . to all *questions* arising under the constitution, treaties and laws," in fact Article III vests the judiciary with power over "all *cases* in law and equity arising under the constitution, laws and treaties of the United States." In Marshall's judgment, the difference between Livingston's inaccurate paraphrase and the Constitution's language was "material and apparent." First, Article III's actual language made it clear that federal court jurisdiction extends only to a carefully defined subset of the questions that could arise under the Constitution, the laws, and treaties.

> A case in law or equity was a term well understood, and of limited signification. It was a controversy between parties which had taken a shape for judicial decision. . . . To come within this description, a question must assume a legal form, for forensic litigation, and judicial decision. There must be parties to come into court, who can be reached by its process, and bound by its power; whose rights admit of ultimate decision by a tribunal to which they are bound to submit.

Article III's wording thus implied that constitutional questions that arise in situations or take forms that are not reducible to a case must receive their answers from some other source than the judiciary.

The abstract implications of Article III's language are given specificity by the functions the Constitution demands of the other two branches of government. Execution of the powers the Constitution vests in Congress and the president necessarily and regularly requires each of the political branches to answer questions of law, including questions of constitutional law. The passage of legislation demands judgment about the constitutionality of the legislation proposed; no rule of law can be faithfully executed without decisions as to its meaning and application. Livingston had misunderstood the significance of his own assertion that the federal government is structured by the constitutional "division of powers" and depends on the performance of "the duty of each department to resist the encroachments of the others." In such a constitutional system, Livingston's assumption that the judiciary has exclusive authority to interpret the Constitution, statutes, and treaties was self-refuting:

> If the judicial power extended to every *question* under the constitution it would involve almost every subject proper for legislative discussion and decision; if to every *question* under the laws and treaties of the United States it would involve almost every subject on which the executive could act. The division of power which the gentleman had stated, could exist no longer, and the other departments would be swallowed up by the judiciary.[38]

Marshall's purpose up to this point was to establish his reasons for rejecting as specious Livingston's syllogistic assertion that because the Robbins case must have involved "points of law," those points—and thus the basic question of his extradition—"could only have been decided in court." By itself, of course, the conclusion that the political branches must and therefore can address points of law is compatible with the belief that the courts possess the ultimate power to answer all legal questions. On this view, while the judiciary's practical ability to enforce its interpretations of the law may be limited to those questions that "assume a legal form, for forensic litigation," the authority of its interpretations extends in principle to those decisions that must be decided with de facto finality by the political branches. A demand that other constitutional actors "internalize" the judiciary's interpretations of the law seems implied in statements such as St. George Tucker's assertion in *Kamper v. Hawkins* that "the duty of expounding [the law] is exclusively vested in the judiciary."

In his 1800 speech to the House, however, Marshall flatly rejected any such claim. Indeed, he argued that there are legal issues that the courts cannot answer even in principle: in other words, the American constitutional system gives the *political* branches exclusive, de jure authority to answer some questions of *law*. This latter assertion emerged during the course of Marshall's refutation of the Republicans' overly neat "if legal, then judicial" reasoning. Livingston had cited the Washington administration's dealings with the problems arising out of privateering by the European powers during the 1790s as executive-branch precedent for the assertion that the courts had final authority over questions about the international obligations of the United States. Marshall agreed that the federal courts had rightly resolved disputes over the legal ownership of prize ships when the disputes took the form of private lawsuits, but he denied Livingston's inference that judicial resolution of such cases demonstrated executive subordination to the courts' views on the nation's international rights and duties. In fact, Marshall explained, not only had President Washington maintained his authority to resolve individual cases "brought before the executive as a national demand" rather than "carried before a court as an individual claim," but in adjudicating the private claims brought before them, the courts had governed their decisions on "the fact" of ownership "by the principles established by the executive department." Far from demonstrating executive acquiescence in judicial power to decide legal issues, the prize cases demonstrated the judiciary's agreement that the final answers to some legal questions are for the executive to decide.

For Marshall, therefore, the practical question of which branch applies the law to a particular issue was distinct from the normative question about which branch has the authority to settle the meaning of the law: some "cases in law or equity" that the courts adjudicate are governed by the legal interpretations of the political branches just as some political decisions must conform to the courts' understanding of the law. This obviously raises the question of how one decides whether it is the judiciary or the political branch that has final normative authority. The answer Marshall provided in 1800 was that we should look to the presence or absence, within the question of law, of issues involving political judgment:

> The question whether vessels captured within three miles of the American coast, or by privateers fitted out in the American ports, were legally captured or not, and whether the American government was bound to restore them if in its power, were questions of law, but they were questions of political law, proper to be decided and they were decided by the executive and not by the courts.

As another example of a "question of political law," Marshall cited the question that arose in 1793, when war broke out between Revolutionary France and the European powers, of the United States's obligations to France under the 1778 treaty of alliance. "The casus foederis of the guaranty was a question of law but no man would have hazarded the opinion; that such a question must be carried into court, and can only be there declared." The ultimate legal question posed by the Robbins episode, whether the United States was obliged to honor the British request for extradition, was similar in nature to the prize cases and "the case of the late guarantee in our treaty with France" in that any answer to it would require the exercise of a type of judgment beyond the competence of a court. "The question to be decided is whether the particular case proposed be one, in which the nation has bound itself to act, and this is a question depending on principles never submitted to courts."[39]

Marshall did not expressly define these "principles never submitted to courts" that distinguish the answer to a question of political law from one subject to judicial determination, but his meaning seems clear enough if we consider the examples he gave of "questions of political law." The ultimate determination of issues such as the border between British America and the United States, the duty of the United States to support the French Republic in its war with Britain, and the means by which the United States ought to enforce its neutrality was dependent in part on a judgment about where the nation's interests lay, including its interests in justice to itself and others and in the preservation of national security. The federal courts lack the information to make such judgments wisely, they have no power to enforce such decisions effectively, they lack the political accountability that legitimates a claim to speak for the nation, and unlike the political branches, their decisions are not supposed to be influenced by "consequences" or "policy." Questions of law that involve such factors are necessarily beyond the competence of the judicial branch, to which "the constitution had never been understood, to confer . . . any political power whatever."[40]

Marshall's address to the House left Livingston's argument in tatters and the Republicans in disarray. The greatest constitutionalist among the House Republicans, Albert Gallatin, flatly refused to reply to Marshall. "Gentlemen," he told his colleagues, "answer it yourself. For my part, I think it is unanswerable." Jefferson, who was never much inclined to compliment arguments with which he disagreed, conceded privately to Madison that Marshall had "distinguished" himself "greatly" in the speech.[41] The day after Marshall spoke, the House rejected Livingston's motion by a lopsided majority.

As we have already seen, there was a spectrum of opinion during the founding era on the locus of interpretive authority within the governmental structures created by America's written constitutions. Livingston, to be sure, was almost certainly being opportunistic (as well as inconsistent) in asserting that the interpretation of the laws is the absolute and exclusive prerogative of the courts; during debates in 1799 over the Alien and Sedition Acts he had been active in asserting the House's role as an interpreter of the Constitution.[42] But the view that interpreting the law is peculiarly "the duty and office of the judiciary to make" (in Tucker's words) was widely shared among both Federalists and Republicans. Marshall in 1800, however, staked out a different view, one that suggested both a far more vital role for the political branches in the exposition of the law, and a rather different understanding of the relationship between law and politics. Marshall's reasoning suggested that the resolution of some questions involving the interpretation of rules of law and their application to the circumstances of the world demands the exercise of the type of discretionary judgment that characterizes prudent political action. The process of deciding a question of this sort does not thereby cease to be a matter of applying legal norms (Marshall used the term "principle" in discussing the conclusion the executive reached in the prize cases), but the answer reached includes as well the consideration of issues of prudence and policy, of the public interest in the broadest sense. Political, discretionary decision, Marshall's argument assumed, is not by definition the opposite of legal, rule-governed decision. But in our constitutional order, questions of political law that are simultaneously discretionary and rule-governed are committed to Congress or the president. Judicial determination of such questions is neither necessary nor appropriate.

Marshall's views on this matter, unlike Livingston's, were not opportunistic, and he recurred obliquely to them on several later occasions, including his famous opinion in *M'Culloch v. Maryland*. His most elaborate subsequent discussion came only three years after his speech on the Robbins matter in, of all places, *Marbury v. Madison,* a case often misread to draw a sharp-edged distinction between law and politics, the realm of the courts and the domain of the political branches. In *Marbury,* Marshall wrote that "[b]y the constitution of the United States, the president is invested with certain important political powers, in the exercise of which he is to use his own discretion, and is accountable only to his country in his political character, and to his own conscience." Some of the political powers Marshall had in mind are clearly decisions of pure policy—Marshall himself gave as an example the president's power "of nominating to the senate, and . . . of appointing the person nominated"; but it would be an error to read *Marbury* to imply that every exercise of the president's "political powers" is unreviewable in the sense that the use of those powers never involves the interpretation or implementation of legal rules at all.

The distinction *Marbury* actually drew was not in fact between political acts of will and principled legal decisions, but between questions involving the national interest and questions of individual right—exactly the same distinction Marshall relied on in 1800 in discussing the respective roles of the executive and the courts. The president properly exercises unreviewable political power where "[t]he subjects are political. They respect the nation, not individual rights, and being entrusted to the executive, the decision of the executive is conclusive." The courts are excluded from reviewing the president's exercise of authority when "the executive possesses a constitutional or legal discretion," not because the exercise of such discretion is incompatible with a duty to decide in accordance with legal principle, but because the Constitution assigns differing spheres of responsibility to the two branches. "The province of the court is, solely, to decide on the rights of individuals, not to inquire how the executive, or executive officers, perform duties in which they have a discretion." In contrast, the province of the president is to identify and safeguard the rights of the nation, a task that, as Marshall said in 1800, sometimes requires the president to address issues of legal and constitutional principle. On both occasions Marshall portrayed the sphere of appropriate judicial decision as smaller than, not coextensive with, the sphere of decisions bound by law. "Questions, in their nature political, or which are, by the constitution and laws, submitted to the executive, can never be made in this court."

One of the many ironies in U.S. constitutional history is the identification of John Marshall with that view of constitutional interpretation that locates it almost exclusively in the judicial branch. Another is the common notion that Marshall's great moment of creative insight was his "creation" of judicial review in *Marbury v. Madison*. (As we have seen, there was nothing original, either in form or substance, about Marshall's discussion of that issue in *Marbury*.) These errors have unfortunately obscured what was in fact Marshall's truly creative contribution to American constitutionalism: his vision of a relationship between law and politics that would accord a unique and essential role to political actors in the shaping of American public law, one not duplicable even in principle by the courts. Almost immediately after he espoused this vision, Marshall went on the bench, and thus had little occasion afterward to work out its meaning. That task remains to be done.

VIII. 1802: How Not to Think about the Judiciary Repeal Act

The original Judiciary Act of 1789 established a tripartite federal judicial system staffed by only two ranks of federal judges.[43] The district courts and the Supreme Court, as today, each had distinctive personnel, but in each district an intermediate circuit court (which acted as a trial court in many matters in addition to exercising appellate review over the district court) was constituted by the local district judge sitting together with two justices of the Supreme

Court's six members. The onerous nature of the justices' duty to "ride circuit" was experienced at once, and the surviving correspondence of 1790s justices is replete with complaints about the labor and weariness that accompanied their efforts to hold court in the widely separated locations designated by Congress. The arrangement was questionable in other respects as well, as Justice John Blair noted in a memorandum he wrote for Chief Justice Jay in August 1790: "It is liable, besides, to objection, that men who have decided a cause in one court, [must] determine it again in an appellative capacity. . . . Possibly too, the circuit system may not be perfectly consistent with the spirit of the Constitution, which intended the supreme court as a dernier resort only . . . & it is perhaps rather nice to distinguish between a court & the judges of that court."[44] Despite these problems, and the justices' great unhappiness with the system—it played a role in more than one resignation and may have lead to the premature deaths of Justices Wilson and Iredell—before 1801 Congress's only concession was to permit the circuit courts to operate with only one justice in attendance.

In February of that year, however, Congress enacted and President John Adams signed an "Act to provide for the more convenient organization of the Courts of the United States." The Judiciary Act of 1801 was a thoroughgoing overhaul of the federal court system with many features but its centerpiece was the abolition of the old circuit courts and of the justices' circuit-riding duties, and their replacement with a new set of regional circuit courts with their own distinct body of judges.[45] There can be little doubt that this arrangement was a vast improvement in the structure and efficiency of the federal judiciary—it was virtually identical to that in use today—but despite that fact within little more than a year Congress repealed the 1801 Act, and sent the justices once more on their weary way from district to district. Over a century would pass before Congress again, this time permanently, replaced the anomalous circuit courts with fully separate courts of appeals. The reason for this unfortunate turn of events was the 1801 reform's entanglement with politics.

By February of 1801, the Federalist-controlled Sixth Congress was in its last month of existence, and with its passing all knew that more would change than a few names and faces. The prior fall's elections for members of the House of Representatives were a Republican triumph, and the new Seventh Congress would likely have a Republican majority in the Senate as well. At least as bitter a pill for congressional Federalists, the day before President Adams signed the Judiciary Act into law the House elected the arch-Republican of them all, Thomas Jefferson, as his successor.[46] "[T]he sun of Federalism was about to set," Jonas Platt sadly conceded in a speech in January: "he confessed that he viewed with horror the awful night that would follow." But, notwithstanding that, "whilst he possessed a seat in th[e] House, he thought himself bound to legislate in favor of measures to support the Government."[47] The measure Platt had immediately in mind was the unsuccessful attempt to extend the Sedition Act mentioned in the previous section, but he and his Federalist colleagues were busy indeed during their lame-duck winter session passing a veritable blizzard of measures that in their view would support the government during the awful Republican night.

The Judiciary Act was part of this last minute whirl of activity, and by that fact alone it was suspect in Republican eyes. Whatever its merits in the abstract, furthermore, to many Republicans the Act seemed a brazen attempt to load up the federal judiciary and the federal payroll with partisans of the political faction that the people had determined to oust from power in the national government. Adams quickly filled the sixteen new circuit judgeships— hence the law's subsequent nickname of "Midnight Judges Act." In addition to giving the outgoing Federalist president the opportunity to make these appointments, the Act provided that upon the next vacancy on the Supreme Court the Court's membership was to be reduced to six, neatly denying Jefferson what would otherwise be his first chance to appoint a justice. Take into consideration as well the enactment later in February of a law creating circuit judges and justices of the peace for the District of Columbia, all of whom Adams could appoint if only he could act fast enough, and one can begin to appreciate how Republicans could see the entire enterprise as partisan politics rather than well-intended judicial reform.

Whatever sense of accomplishment the Federalists enjoyed over their judicial handiwork was short-lived. From the beginning of his administration, President Jefferson viewed the federal judiciary as the politicized instrument of the defeated Federalists: "[T]hey have retreated into the judiciary as a stronghold. . . and from that battery all the works of republicanism are to be beaten down and erased."[48] Resentment at the Federalists' behavior and fear of the mischief the federal courts might work thus combined to make an attack on the new judicial system a first priority for the Republican-controlled Seventh Congress, which would convene in December. As Elbridge Gerry reported to Jefferson, "[I]t is generally expected that among the first acts of the next Congress will be a repeal of the extraordinary judicial bill, the design of which was too palpable to elude common observation."[49] In his first annual message, dated December 8 (the day after the new Congress convened), Jefferson pointedly observed that "[t]he Judiciary system of the United States, and especially that portion of it recently erected, will, of course, present itself to the contemplation of Congress," and by early January the Senate was considering a resolution calling for the repeal of the 1801 Act.[50]

The congressional debates over what became the "Act to repeal certain acts respecting the organization of the Courts of the United States" cover hundreds of pages of the *Annals of Congress*. In their course, the senators and representatives touched on many issues: the history of the judicial system, the business present and future of the federal courts, the origins of the partisan division between Federalists and Republicans. At the center of the debate, unsurprisingly, was the question whether the effect of repealing the 1801 Act on the sixteen new circuit judges showed that repeal would be unconstitutional. Article III, section 1 provides that federal judges "shall hold their Offices during good Behaviour, and shall, at stated Times, receive for their services, a Compensation, which shall not be diminished during their Continuance in Office," and the Republicans' intention was not only to terminate the new circuit courts but also to terminate the circuit judges' salaries.[51] Despite the obvious argument, made again and again by the Federalists, that the Republicans' repeal bill would violate this clause twice over, the Republicans insisted that the Constitution fully authorized the bill. They located Congress's affirmative power to abolish the circuit courts in the clause of Article III immediately preceding the one on which the Federalists relied, which vests the judicial power in "one supreme Court, and in such inferior Courts as the Congress may from time to time ordain and establish." Repeal of the 1801 Act would be constitutionally indistinguishable from passage of the Act: in both cases Congress would be exercising the power to create such lower courts, with such powers and jurisdiction, as in its discretion it thought to be for the public good. Doing so, they continued, would in no way violate Article III's protection of the judges' tenure and salaries, for the repeal bill would be an abolition of the office rather than a removal of the officer. Joseph Nicholson argued to the House that the power to abolish offices was indisputable:

> Your supervisors who superintend the collection of your excise duties are appointed by the President and Senate, and hold their offices under the Constitution, not during good behaviour but during the will and pleasure of the President. The tenure by which he holds his office is completely beyond the power of the Legislature, and they cannot remove him. . . . It is as sacred, in relation to the power of Congress, as that of a judge. . . . Yet is there any man on earth [who] can say that we have not a Constitutional right to repeal the laws laying excise duties, by which the office of supervisor is created?[52]

Nicholson thought the notion that the tax collector would continue to draw his salary, the taxes and his own office being abolished, patently ridiculous, but no different in principle than the Federalist argument that Congress could not oust the circuit judges by abolishing their positions:

> Gentlemen say that we cannot do that by indirect means which we cannot do directly; that is, that we cannot remove a judge by repealing this law, inasmuch as we cannot remove him by direct means. But I have proved beyond the possibility of doubt that we may indirectly remove an excise officer by repealing the law under which he was appointed, although we have no authority to remove him in any direct manner. If the principle laid down by gentlemen is not true in the one case, it cannot be true in the other.[53]

This argument, the Federalists responded, was a patent denial of the commands of Article III. Senator Gouverneur Morris conceded that Congress has the discretion to create lower federal courts "in the first instance," but insisted that when those courts are established, "the words are imperative, a part of the judicial power shall vest in them" and the judges appointed to them are secure in their tenure and compensation during good behaviour. There is no analogy on this issue between judges and executive officers, for the judiciary, unlike subordinate executive officials, is intended to be secure against legislative control. Ignoring that constitutional intention, the Republican argument amounted to nothing more than trifling with the solemn words of the Constitution:

> [Y]ou shall not take the man from the office, but you may take the office from the man; you shall not drown him, but you may sink his boat under him; you shall not put him to death, but you may take away his life. . . . [T]he Constitution provides perfectly for the inviolability of his tenure. But yet we may destroy the office which we cannot take away, as if the destruction of the office would not as effectually deprive him of it as the grant to another person.[54]

The argument for the validity of the repeal bill, in the Federalists' view, rested not only on a flagrant disregard for the constitutional text but also on a fundamental misunderstanding of the structure of government ordained by the text: if Congress can deprive federal judges of their offices by the simple expedient of abolishing those offices, Congress can intimidate them out of their vital task of judicial review, and (in Morris's words) "the check established by the Constitution, wished for by the people, and necessary in every contemplation of common sense, is destroyed." "In such a situation of the judges," Nathaniel Chipman seconded Morris, "the Constitutional limitation on the Legislative powers, can be but a dead letter . . . . [I]t will be in vain long to expect from the judges, the firmness and integrity to oppose a Constitutional decision to a law . . . if such a decision is to be made at the risk of office and salary."[55] Judicial review is central to the system of limited and divided powers—John Stanley told the House that "it is the very essence" of American constitutionalism[56]—and the repeal bill thus would undermine the entire system.

The role of judicial review in the repeal debate shifted after February 3. Up to that time, the Federalist argument that repeal was wrong because of its dire implications for judicial review went almost unanswered. The only Republican to take serious note of it, Robert Wright, remarked moderately that he agreed with Morris "that judges ought to be guardians of the Constitution, so far as questions were constitutionally submitted to them," but denied the significance Morris accorded the fact. Judicial review was no more than the courts undertaking, in their sphere, the duty to respect and obey the Constitution common to all federal officers. Wright "held the Legislative, Executive, and Judiciary, each severally the guardians of the Constitution, so far as they were called on in their several departments to act," and saw no reason to think federal judicial interpretation of the Constitution more essential than or superior to constitutional construction by Congress or the president, or for that matter the state courts.[57] On February 3, however, John Breckinridge (the author of the resolution calling for repeal), made a speech that significantly changed the terms of the debate over constitutional structure. "I did not expect," he told the Senate, "to find the power of the courts to annul the laws of Congress as unconstitutional, so seriously insisted upon." The true constitutional doctrine according to Breckinridge is that "the Legislature have the exclusive right to interpret the Constitution, in what regards the law-making power, and the judges are bound to execute the laws they make," and he offered two considerations to support those conclusions: the absence of any provision for judicial review in the constitutional text and the consequence of admitting judicial review, which, in his judgment, would be to empower judges with "the absolute direction of the Government."[58]

The reverberations from Breckinridge's speech echoed throughout the next two months of debate, and from February 3 on the Federalists hammered away at the charge that the Republicans now rejected a constitutional principle that, as James Bayard reminded them, they had invoked during the debate over the Sedition Act: "It was once thought by gentlemen who now deny the principle, that the safety of the citizen and of the States rested upon the power of the judges to declare an unconstitutional law void." In an off-the-cuff, immediate response to Breckinridge, Gouverneur Morris neatly turned the Republicans' traditional rhetoric round on them, declaring that "at length" the Republicans' true goal had become clear—to "establish one consolidated Government over this country" and thus undermine its republican form of government.[59] Henceforth, the hostility to judicial review and thus to limited government allegedly revealed in the Republican quest to repeal the 1801 Act was a major theme in the Federalist assault on repeal.

The Republicans, the Federalists added, were innovators as well as inconsistent: Archibald Henderson denounced "[t]he monstrous and unheard of doctrine which has lately been advanced, that the judges have not the right of declaring unconstitutional laws void," and his colleagues followed suit.[60] In support of their claim that "undisputed practice under the Constitution ha[s] settled the principle," the Federalists mustered an impressively heterogeneous array of authority: decisions of the U.S. Supreme Court, state and lower federal court decisions including *Kamper v. Hawkins,* the debates in the Virginia ratifying convention, a veto message of Republican governor Thomas M'Kean of Pennsylvania (formerly chief justice of the commonwealth's highest court), the law lectures of Republican St. George Tucker (professor at William & Mary as well as state court judge). As Samuel Dana summarized the Federalist position, judicial review "is a doctrine coeval with the existence of our Government, and has been the uniform principle of all the constituted authorities."[61]

Behind their loud protestations about their opponents' misrepresentations and insincerity—so common among both parties as to be meaningless—the Republican response to the Federalists' exploitation of Breckinridge's speech was conflicted and uncertain. The Federalists' reminders of the earlier Republican reliance on judicial review and their (correct) invocation of some of the most distinguished Republican jurists in the country in support of the courts' independence and authority were politically embarrassing; what is more, the Republican speeches on the subject suggested a strong reluctance to tie the repeal proposal to Breckinridge's views on judicial review. Only a few Republicans echoed Breckinridge's ostensibly wholesale attack and none unequivocally endorsed the proposition that courts are obliged to enforce laws they believe to be unconstitutional.[62] More frequently, Republican speakers rejected Federalist assertions that judicial review has a unique or paramount role in the constitutional order while accepting the judges' authority to refuse to enforce laws invalid in their opinion: "This is not only their right, but it is their indispensable duty. Nor is this the exclusive right and indispensable duty of the Judiciary department. It is equally the inherent and the indispensable duty of every officer, and I believe I may add, of every citizen of the United States."[63]

In reading the repeal debates, it is important to bear in mind that most and perhaps all Republican denunciations of a judicial power to "declare a law null and void"[64] assumed a distinction between the power to refuse to enforce a statute on constitutional grounds (a legitimate, or at least unavoidable concomitant of the judicial power), and the power to annul a statute in some absolute sense. "I am willing to admit the Judiciary to be coordinate with the Legislature in this respect," Philip Thompson told the House, "that judges thinking a law unconstitutional are not bound to execute it; but not to declare it null and void."[65] The point of this distinction was unclear,[66] and my sense is that for most of the Republicans who espoused it, the real issue was whether a judicial decision on a constitutional issue required other officers, acting in their spheres of responsibility, to act against their contrary views of the Constitution's meaning. But whatever their exact views, the moderate Republicans had placed themselves, however grudgingly, in agreement with the Federalists that judicial review was a part (even if not the essence) of American constitutionalism. The exact rationale and scope of the power remained in question. the reader will have recognized in the 1802 repeal debate parallels to the conflicting views expressed by the judges in *Kamper v. Hawkins*. The existence of the power in some form, however, was beyond successful question.[67]

Other than on the question of judicial review, there was little public disagreement among Republicans over the constitutional issues raised by the repeal. Privately, some Republicans had other qualms, especially over depriving the circuit judges of their salaries. While the Senate was debating repeal, for example, Vice President Aaron Burr expressed a reservation on this score to a Massachusetts Republican named Barnabus Bidwell:

> The Constitutional right & power of Abolishing one Judiciary system & establishing another, cannot be doubted—The power thus to deprive Judges of their offices and Salaries must also be admitted, but whether it would be constitutionally Moral, if I may use the expression, and if so, whether it would be politic & expedient, are questions on which I could wish to be further advised.[68]

Reassured by Bidwell that "[t]he system was so obviously the offspring of party, that the new Judges had reason to expect its repeal, & have, therefore, less reason to complain," Burr swallowed his concerns.

The Federalists' skills at debate and parliamentary maneuver delayed but could not in the end defeat the Republicans' determination to repeal the 1801 Act, and on March 8, President Jefferson signed into law the initial repeal legislation. A further Act signed by the president on April 29 addressed a mass of details. Despite the Federalists' almost universal conviction that repeal was unconstitutional, there was no significant resistance to its enforcement. The circuit judges protested in a remonstrance to Congress that the Republicans ignored, and after some correspondence about the feasibility of refusing to acquiesce in the repeal, the justices of the Supreme Court resumed riding circuit. At the next term of the Court itself, former Attorney General Charles Lee recapitulated the congressional Federalists' major arguments against the repeal's validity in *Stuart v. Laird*.[69] Writing for the Court, Justice Paterson studiously ignored Lee's attack on the abolition of the new circuit courts and the ouster of the circuit judges. Paterson did respond to Lee's argument that the reimposition of circuit-riding duties was unconstitutional, but only to observe that "that practice, and acquiescence under it, for a period of several years, commencing with the organization of the judicial system, affords an irresistible answer, and has fixed the construction. . . . Of course, the question is at rest, and ought not now to be disturbed."

Already in the 1802 repeal debate one can see—in fully articulated form—a central and difficult question about how we are to understand the Constitution's specifications and limitations of power. One answer is that we should read constitutional limitations much as Holmes said we should understand all of law—as a set of predictions about the circumstances in which some other constitutional actor will interfere with the exercise of power by a given governmental entity or official.[70] A constitutional limitation, on this view, is for all practical purposes defined by the willingness of some other constitutional actor to resist effectively the actions of the entity subject to the limitation. If no other actor is willing or able to resist, it is meaningless and even misleading to speak of a limitation. Looked at from this perspective, Article III's good behavior provision placed no constitutional limitation on Congress's power to oust the circuit judges because the constitutional entities that might have objected (the president, the judiciary, the electorate) lacked either the will or the power (or both) to do so with any effect. In contrast, according to the Republican interpretation of the 1800 elections, the first amendment did prohibit Congress from enacting a seditious libel statute, notwithstanding the courts' approval of the Sedition Act, because a different constitutional entity (the electorate) successfully objected.

Later-day academic lawyers have subjected Holmes's "bad man" theory of law to endless refutations, but a similar attitude toward the law of the Constitution has been at work throughout our history. It appeared most clearly in 1802 in the Federalists' argument that repeal of the 1801 Act was unconstitutional because the opposite conclusion would destroy the basis for judicial review. If the Constitution does not protect the courts against congressional intimidation or retribution, they have in fact no realistic ability to oppose unconstitutional laws, and for that reason no legitimate authority to do so: "if it is once established that the Judiciary is a subordinate and dependent branch of the Government, I acknowledge that they have no right to judge of the constitutionality of a law, or, if they have the power, they will be afraid to exercise it." And the abolition of judicial review would reduce the Constitution's specifications and limitations of congressional power to mere words. As James Bayard put it, "Nothing can be more absurd than to contend that there is a practical restraint upon a political body who are answerable to none but themselves for the violation of the restraint, and who can derive from the very act of violation undeniable justification of their conduct."[71] A parallel tendency to equate the legitimacy of a *power* with its effective exercise can be detected in the common Republican argument that judicial review exists as a (legitimate) matter of governmental practice without having any unique normative role in the constitutional system.[72]

This understanding of the Constitution's specifications and limitations of power has no necessary connection to a general cynicism about human motivations. One can hold it while also assuming that some or even all of the relevant actors exert their power to thwart others' actions out of a conscientious desire to enforce "the Constitution." Where this view is most interesting is in its implication for a constitutional entity's decisions about its own behavior: if constitutional restrictions on, say, the president, are analytically indistinguishable from their enforcement by other constitutional actors, then there seems to be no reason for the president to see his or her obligation to remain within constitutional limitations as any broader than the set of those activities that Congress, the courts, or some other entity will in fact block. The scope and obligation of a limitation, in short, are coextensive with the existence somewhere of the power and will to object to its infringement. Put less abstractly, as long as they remain within the outer limits of conduct that the courts will sustain against constitutional challenge, Congress, the executive, and the states have no need to concern themselves over constitutional questions.

Founding-era constitutionalists were not thoroughgoing Holmesians, however, and they often articulated a quite different understanding of the significance of constitutional limitations on power. In the same speech quoted earlier, Representative Bayard responded at one point to the Republican charge that the Federalists had not identified the line separating Congress's conceded power to modify the jurisdiction of lower federal courts from the allegedly illegitimate abolition of such a court's jurisdiction:

> Do you ask me to draw a line and say, thus far you shall go and no further? I admit no line can be drawn. It is an affair of sound and *bona fide* discretion, because a discretion on the subject is given to the Legislature; to argue upon the abuse of that discretion is adopting a principle subversive of all legitimate power.

"The Constitution is predicated upon the existence of a certain degree of integrity in man," he continued, and so "it has trusted powers liable to enormous abuse, if all political honesty be discarded."[73] Bayard's remarks assumed that there is a distinction between judicially enforced limits on Congress's powers and its own exercise of discretion in lawmaking—his language echoes, probably deliberately, Justice Paterson's well-known description of judicial review as a court's power to assert that "[t]he constitution is the origin and measure of legislative authority. It says to legislators, thus far ye shall go and no further."[74] But he did not mean that there was no constitutional issue in the absence of "a precise line . . . between the discreet exercise and the abuse of" Congress's powers; indeed the point he was making was that it was the House's responsibility to craft its legislation with respect to constitutional principles—to exercise its "discretion" in the common founding-era sense of the responsible, wise application of a legal norm to a specific situation.[75] Legislation that is contrary to the Constitution's norms is an abuse of Congress's powers whether the courts can or will say so, and therefore contrary to Congress's obligations under the Constitution.

Early references to the abuse of power often did not clearly distinguish the foolish or oppressive misuse of power from its exercise in ways that violate constitutional principles (in the speech we have been considering, Bayard discussed the abolition of the circuit courts, which he clearly thought unconstitutional, and a hypothetical confiscatory tax, which he may simply have thought tyrannical), but the idea that the Constitution imposes obligations that require a constitutional actor to police itself was widely shared. A very early example can be found in Secretary Jefferson's 1790 opinion for President Washington that we considered earlier. In the final paragraph of the opinion Jefferson responded to a possible objection to his conclusion that the Senate had no power to control the grade or destination of a diplomatic appointee. As a matter of political reality, the objection went, the Senate could exercise a de facto veto on the president's choice of destination and grade simply by refusing to give its advice and consent to individual nominees. Jefferson dismissed the objection as based on the unacceptable assumption that the Senate would use its constitutional power to do one thing (rule on the fitness of individual nominees) in order to accomplish another (determine the nature of U.S. representation in foreign states). "[T]his would be a breach of trust," Jefferson wrote, "of which that body cannot be supposed capable." Where the Constitution does not directly grant a power, that power cannot legitimately be exercised "thro the abuse of another."

It would be a mistake, I think, to dismiss Jefferson's approach cavalierly, on the assumption that it is either arch or naive to suppose the Senate incapable of abusing its power. To be sure, Jefferson's presumption that the Senate would not abuse its power did not rest on a Pollyanna-like confidence in human virtue (the reader will recall Jefferson's 1791 bank opinion and his equation of the power to do whatever is thought good with the power to do evil). But Jefferson assumed what Bayard was later to say, that out of necessity "the Constitution is predicated upon the existence of a certain degree of integrity in man." For all his fear of congressional aggrandizement, for example, Jefferson himself ended his 1791 opinion with the candid recommendation that if Washington found that the arguments for and against the bank bill were "so even as to balance his judgment, a just respect for the wisdom of the legislature would naturally decide the balance in favor of their opinion." Nationalists less suspicious of the exercise of power were even more willing to admit the necessity of assuming in many circumstances that constitutional institutions and officers will attempt in good faith to observe constitutional norms.

What (if anything) are we to make of the idea that the Constitution places limits on the exercise of political power that go beyond those that are enforced by the courts? As understood in the founding-era this idea subsumes but is broader than the modern political question doctrine, pursuant to which courts occasionally decline to resolve an apparent constitutional question. Burr's question captures this broader notion: when Congress—or the president, or any other actor bound by obligations to the Constitution—wishes to act, it is not a sufficient discharge of the constitutional obligation to determine that the courts are unlikely to invalidate the action. Constitutional actors should go further, to ask (in Burr's words) "whether it would be constitutionally Moral" to act as they propose. To be sure, as the 1802 repeal debate richly illustrates, political-branch constitutional interpretation is likely to be closely intertwined with policy and partisan considerations, and may not produce any generally satisfactory answers. In the latter respect, at least, it is neither different from, nor inferior to, the constitutional interpretations of the courts.

IX. 1804: *Turpin v. Locket* and the Place of Religion

The best-known episode in the history of state constitutions is undoubtedly founding-era Virginia's struggle to define the constitutional relationship between church and state. In the colonial era, the Church of England was Virginia's established church, and as a consequence that body enjoyed legal protection and public support of various kinds, including the provision of glebes, which were farming land intended to provide in part for the upkeep of Anglican clergy. Pursuant to the British government's instruction, a 1661 colonial statute directed that "glebes [be] laid out in every parish," without specifying how the property was to be obtained or in whom title should vest once it was obtained.[76] A 1696 law authorized the parish vestries (lay governing bodies of the local church) "where the same is not already done, to purchase and lay out a tract of land for the glebe . . . at the charge of their respective parishes."[77] Since all residents of the geographic area covered by a parish were subject to parish assessments, this meant that non-Anglicans were in fact required to contribute to the purchase of glebes obtained under the 1696 act and later statutes to the same effect.

Loyalists to the crown to one side, Virginians seem generally to have agreed early in the Revolution that the colonial arrangements should be changed, and section 16 of the declaration of rights adopted in June 1776 provided that "religion, or the duty which we owe to our Creator, and the manner of discharging it, can be directed only by reason and conviction, not by force or violence; and therefore all men are equally entitled to the free exercise of religion, according to the dictates of conscience; and . . . it is the mutual duty of all to practise Christian forbearance, love, and charity towards each other."[78] This provision's implications for church–state relations were far from clear, and both those committed to a complete divorce between religion and government and those who favored some measure of public support for religion saw section 16 as consistent with their views. The history of early state legislation on the subject reflected their struggle. Already in 1776, the state legislature exempted non-Anglicans from liability for parish assessments, but it subsequently declined to act on a more sweeping bill for religious liberty drafted in 1779 by Thomas Jefferson.

By 1784 the tide of sentiment on church and state seemed to be running strongly in the opposite direction. At the petition of Virginia Anglicans, the legislature enacted a statute incorporating the individual parishes of the Protestant Episcopal church. At the same time, a group of legislators led by the popular Patrick Henry proposed a bill to "prov[ide] for Teachers of the Christian Religion" by supporting ministers with public funds without discrimination among Protestant denominations. These developments galvanized the proponents of a complete separation of church and state, among them James Madison (then in the state legislature), who drafted a Memorial and Remonstrance against Religious Assessments that was widely circulated, and endorsed by hundreds of signatures. Through skillful parliamentary maneuvering, Madison managed to delay consideration of Henry's bill long enough for the campaign to arouse public opinion to have its effect, and the election of a new legislature ensured a strong majority against Henry's bill, which died without coming to a vote. Instead, in 1785 the legislature at last enacted Jefferson's 1779 bill "for establishing Religious Freedom," which embodied the complete separation view, stating among other things that "[n]o man shall be compelled to frequent or support any religious worship, place or ministry whatever." The following year, the legislature repealed the incorporation law on the ground that it was inconsistent with the principles of the 1785 Act.[79]

The enactment of the Act for establishing Religious Freedom left one highly contentious issue unresolved: the ownership of the glebe lands the colonial established church had possessed. In the same law of November 1776 that curtailed financial support for the Anglican clergy, the Virginia legislature expressly "saved and reserved" the Anglican church's property claims to hold the glebes, while the 1784 incorporation statute resolved (temporarily) the question of who held title to church property (the minister and vestry as a corporate body).[80] The repeal of the incorporation Act once again left the legal situation in confusion, which subsequent legislation in 1788 (creating trustees for Episcopal church property) and 1799 (declaring the 1784, 1786, and 1788 Acts all "to be void, and of none effect") only served to complicate further.[81] In 1802, the legislature enacted what supporters presumably saw as a permanent solution. The new law permitted parishes with incumbent ministers to retain the income from their glebes while directing the county overseers of the poor to sell a parish glebe as and when there was a vacancy in the parish ministry and apply the proceeds to public support of the poor.[82] The practical effect of this law, particularly in light of the paucity of Episcopal clergy in the early nineteenth century, was to put the glebe system on the road to extinction.

The 1802 statute was quickly challenged. When the overseers of the poor in Chesterfield County announced their intention to sell the glebe of the parish of Manchester, the vestrymen and church wardens of the parish sued the overseers, claiming that the statute was a deprivation of a vested property right, and thus contrary to section 1 of the state Declaration of Rights, which protects the right to acquire and hold property. The plaintiffs also denied the separationist claim that the legislature's pre-1799 recognition of the Episcopal church's right to the glebes had violated the state bill of rights, insisting in particular that the November 1776 statute that recognized the church's claim was a contemporaneous legislative interpretation of article 16's guarantee of religious freedom of conscience. After a hearing, Chancellor George Wythe dismissed the suit, and the plaintiffs appealed to the Virginia Court of Appeals.

Turpin v. Locket was a cause célèbre, perhaps the most important and controversial case that the state court of appeals had as yet encountered.[83] After it was argued in May 1803, the five-member court (with one judge recused) divided three to one in favor of declaring the glebes lawful and the 1802 Act unconstitutional. The court reserved the announcement of the judgment for the fall term, but on the night before the court was to announce its decision, Edmund Pendleton, the court's president and a towering figure on the state and national stages, died. Pendleton's death delayed the decision yet again, and after considerable maneuvering by supporters of the 1802 Act, the legislature elected a distinguished (and to the reader familiar) jurist—St. George Tucker— to replace Pendleton.[84] *Turpin* consequently was reargued in the court's spring 1804 term by a distinguished group of lawyers, including Daniel Call (the court's reporter), Edmund Randolph, the former attorney general of the United States, and George Hay, President Jefferson's son-in-law and the U.S. attorney for Virginia. Unlike Pendleton, who had drafted an opinion striking down the 1802 Act, Tucker was convinced that it was the laws protecting the glebes that were unconstitutional, and together with his old colleague from *Kamper v. Hawkins*, Spencer Roane (who had been elected to the court of appeals shortly after *Kamper*), Tucker voted to affirm Chancellor Wythe and uphold the 1802 legislation. The result was a deadlocked court, with Tucker and Roane balanced by Peter Lyons (who replaced Pendleton as president) and Paul Carrington, who favored reversing Wythe.

Tucker and Roane delivered separate opinions sustaining the 1802 Act, while Carrington and Lyons announced their views in a joint opinion. On the basis of an exhaustive review of the convoluted history of Virginia's Anglican church and its glebes—the reader should be aware that this discussion has greatly oversimplified that history (although Tucker's opinion did not)—

Tucker argued that at the time of the Revolution, legal title to the glebe lands was vested in the individual parish vestries. The intent of the various statutes enacted between 1776 and 1788, he conceded, was to preserve the glebe lands for the Anglican ministry, although the Acts handled (or ignored) the question of legal title in conflicting ways, while the effect of the 1799 and 1802 Acts, if valid, was that glebes in parishes without incumbent ministers would revert to the public.

The ultimate resolution of the issue presented in *Turpin v. Locket* thus rested on a series of constitutional questions governed in Tucker's view by three articles of the Virginia Declaration of Rights: article 1's recognition of the "inherent" and inalienable right of private property, article 16's guarantee of the right of conscience in matters of religion, and article 4's provision that "no man, or set of men, are entitled to exclusive or separate emoluments and privileges from the community, but in consideration of publick services." In Tucker's view, each of the statutes up to 1788 that had purported to acknowledge or vest a legal right to the glebes in the Anglican / Episcopal church was a clear violation of article's 4 prohibition on the public grant of privileges except in consideration of public services. In light of the glebes' origins as a means of providing public support to the colonial established church, "the rents and stipends of the glebes must be considered as an annual stipend paid by the commonwealth to the ministers of the protestant episcopal church," and yet from the time of the dissolution of royal authority, and under article 16, "the promulgation of the religious doctrines of any religious sect ceased to be a common benefit to the community." The various statutory attempts to secure the glebes for a single religious body as well as the 1784 Act's singling out of the Episcopal church for the legal privileges of incorporation, were all transgressions of this principle.

Tucker rejected the plaintiffs' claim that the glebes were private property rights vested continuously in the same bodies politic, Virginia's Anglican parishes, and unaffected as such by Anglicanism's disestablishment. Disposal of the glebes in no way infringed article 1's protection of private property: "The glebes, as such were never private property," and the dissolution of the established church, "which formed a branch or member of the [colonial] constitution," left the glebes (as they had always been in principle) public property to be disposed of in the interests of the entire community. Tucker nonetheless defended the legislature's decision in 1802 not to deprive incumbent Anglican ministers of their income from the glebes; in doing so, the legislature had given appropriate recognition to "the injunctions of moral justice" (by which he meant the clergy's reliance interests) by decreeing a constitutionally tolerable reconciliation of the legal rights the ministers had previously acquired with the prohibition of article 4. "A life, or lives in being, would not long retard the operation of any plan, which might be recommended by the change of the constitution, and of principle, which had taken place." The Act of 1799 was equally valid, for its only effect was to repeal the earlier, unconstitutional laws.

Despite his agreement with Tucker's conclusion, Roane delivered a separate opinion that followed a significantly different line of reasoning. As in his opinion in *Kamper v. Hawkins*, in *Turpin* Roane displayed a predilection for grounding constitutional argument in fundamental principles. The central issue before the court, he explained, was "the effect of the revolution, and the principles of the constitution, upon the subject in question." Roane conceded that the persuasiveness of arguments based on matters of such significance depended in large measure on the predisposition of the hearer:

> I know, also, the danger of different inferences being drawn, from this source, owing to the different *media* through which they pass. I know that some men have more fervour than others; more sensibility in the cause of equal rights. I know that, from this cause, the inferences to be drawn from this source, will, unavoidably, be *tinged* and diversified.[85]

(It is hard to imagine that the colleagues with whom Roane was disagreeing were particularly pleased by this implicit, disparaging description of the sources of their views.) Nonetheless, in *Turpin* as Roane saw it, the implications of the Revolution and the language and logic of articles 4 and 16 of the state bill of rights were mutually reenforcing. It was Virginia's revolutionary adoption of "free and equal government" that deprived the Anglican church of any legal claim on the glebes, for in destroying the previous royal government the Revolution had destroyed "the then *national* church" which had been part of that government. The glebes, which came into existence either by grant to the now-extinct church or by purchase with public funds, thus reverted to public ownership. All that the 1802 Act did was "to put in train for a just appropriation, the contemplated portion of the public property."[86]

The codification of the Revolution's constitutional meaning in the state bill of rights made the implications of the Revolution for the glebes clear. Together articles 4 and 16 had rendered the legislature powerless to vest any private religious group with exclusive privileges, and thus the various Acts purporting to confirm or vest title to the glebes in the Anglican church were unconstitutional and incapable of creating vested rights:

> If it be said that the acts of 1776 and 1784 have forestalled the act of 1802, by investing the glebes in the protestant episcopal church, I answer that the

bill of rights had previously forestalled them, by interdicting grants of public property to individuals or societies, except in consideration of public service; and by inhibiting the legislature from favouring or endowing one religious society in preference to others.[87]

Roane dismissed the argument that the 1776 Act was itself a contemporaneous interpretation of the bill of rights, insisting that the Act was internally inconsistent and "marked with a want of knowledge of our constitution, [and] of respect for its clearest principles." Most fundamentally, the Act was at most "a legislative construction of the law and constitution on this subject, which, however respectable, . . . must yield to that of the judiciary."

Judge Carrington and President Lyons took a very different view of the question. The defendants (and their colleagues) held a deeply erroneous understanding of the major principles at stake. In colonial times, the established church held title and enjoyed a vested right to the glebes as a distinct religious society. The Revolution, furthermore, was a fundamentally conservative event: "revolutions are intended to preserve, not to take away rights: Nor was it ever pretended, that an alteration, in the form of a government, affected private property." Nothing about the revolutionary change in government prevented Anglican parishes from carrying out their primary "functions," and thus there was no reason to suppose that the Revolution of its own force dissolved the church. (Carrington and Lyons pointed out that no law had ever declared the king to be "an integral part of the established church." By "the doctrines of the common law," therefore, the ouster of royal authority did not impair the church's continued existence.) Unless some specific constitutional provision produced a different conclusion, therefore, the 1802 Act was an invalid deprivation of vested property rights.

Neither article 4 nor article 16 of the state bill of rights, furthermore, provided any support for the legislature's attempt to expropriate the Episcopal church's property. Article 4, they pointed out, does not forbid all grants of special emoluments and privileges, but only those that are not in consideration of public services. But the very language of the bill of rights shows that "the grant of a small piece of land to any religious society, to support a minister to teach the principles of christianity, would be a grant for a public purpose" within the meaning of article 4. Carrington and Lyons read article 15 ("no free Government, or the blessings of liberty, can be preserved to any people but by a firm adherence to justice, moderation, temperance, frugality, and virtue") and article 16 ("it is the mutual duty of all to practice Christian forbearance, love, and charity, towards each other") together and concluded that the bill of rights thereby identified the principles of "the *christian religion*" as the basis for the free government and society it defined. Teaching those principles was therefore unquestionably a public purpose. Article 16's preceding clause ("all men are equally entitled to the free exercise of religion, according to the dictates of conscience") was not to the contrary, for "the whole relates to the rights of conscience" and did not "forbid[ ] the continuation of the establishment, or the incorporation of religious societies."

Perhaps the strongest element in the plaintiffs' case against the constitutionality of the 1802 Act was their argument that the legality of the church's claim to the glebes was settled by the uniform opinion and practice of the legislature (at least up to the adoption of the 1799 statute), beginning with the first postrevolutionary statute addressing the matter in November 1776. The reader will recall Justice Paterson's comments for the federal Supreme Court in *Stuart v. Laird*, decided only two months before *Turpin*, that "a contemporary interpretation" followed by "practice, and acquiescence under it, for a period of several years, commencing with the organization of [a legal] system [can] fix[ ] the construction" of the constitutional text.[88] The argument from practice in *Turpin* was even stronger: the rationale underlying the 1802 Act's attempt to expropriate the glebes, as Daniel Call told the court, was "repugnant to the contemporaneous exposition of the act of 1776, and the practice under it for six and twenty years." Indeed, since the legislature that enacted the 1776 law was in fact the same body that, acting as a convention, had adopted the state constitution and bill of rights, its apparent acceptance of the constitutionality of permitting the church to retain the glebes rested, one would assume, on the members' understanding of their own handiwork.

The strength of this argument was involuntarily acknowledged by the conflicting answers that the lawyers for the defendants and Judges Tucker and Roane gave it. Attorney General Nicholas flatly denied the argument's legitimacy: "Nor will the contemporary exposition, derived from the act of 1776, aid the appellants; for such an argument is inadmissible in a constitutional question; which should be decided by the letter of the instrument; and not by any practice under it." In addition to being contrary to well-established common-law wisdom about the interpretation of written instruments, this position contradicted the mainstream of American constitutional discussion. In *Stuart v. Laird*, for example, the distinguished lawyer Charles Lee, arguing against the constitutionality of the 1802 repeal, conceded that "[a] degree of respect is always due to precedents and past practice," but tried unsuccessfully to persuade the Court that in that particular case, the practice need not control its decision.[89] Tucker's approach was different: implicitly conceding the authority of legislative constructions through practice, he insisted that on this subject the legislature had endorsed no interpretation of the bill of rights. The various statutes recognizing or vesting rights to the glebes in the Episcopal church had been enacted "without their validity, or the power of the legislature to pass" such laws "being questioned, even by the legislature." This lack of legislative commitment to a particular understanding of the state bill of rights was evidenced by "the conflicting, and even opposite, acts of the legislative body. If they cannot be reconciled to each other, it will be our duty to pronounce those to be valid, which are most easily reconcilable to the dictates of moral justice, and the principles of the constitution."

Roane gave the most elaborate response to the argument from practice, making three major points. The first, which in varying terms he repeated several times, was that the 1776 Act was too incompetent an interpretation of the bill of rights to lend validity to subsequent legislation that assumed it to be correct. The Act's glebe provision was inconsistent not only with the bill of rights but with the Act's own preamble; still more egregious, its exemption of non-Anglicans from further contributions to parish assessments expressly referred to the legislature's power to maintain or even designate anew an established church—a view of the constitution's meaning that according to Roane not even "the least liberal of our fellow citizens" would assert.[90] The legislature's errors, to be sure, were pardonable. Caught between "contending parties" on the degree to which church and state should be separated, and conscious of "the necessity of *union* in our struggle against the common enemy," the legislators had done the best they could, preserving in the Act's preamble the principle of religious liberty "which, as members of the convention, they had so nobly and recently established," while ordaining a temporary compromise on the practical issues. Roane's second argument was that giving precedential force to the 1776 Act would contradict the principle of separation of powers since the same body adopted the bill of rights and then supposedly interpreted it in the Act; for Roane this was equivalent to uniting "the powers of *passing* and executing laws in the same persons, [which] forms no contemptible definition of despotism." Finally, and probably most fundamentally for Roane, he relied on the understanding of constitutional structure he had set forth in *Kamper v. Hawkins* ten years before: "a legislative exposition of the law and constitution . . . however respectable . . . must yield to that of the judiciary." Constitutional interpretation is ultimately an exercise of the judicial function that a system of separation of powers assigns to the courts, not the legislature, and the constitutional views of the latter have only such weight as they are persuasive to the judges. It is judicial precedent, not legislative exposition, that settles constitutional meaning.[91]

Carrington and Lyons took special pains to defend the argument from practice. They relied in part on the peculiar circumstance that the same body had adopted the Virginia bill of rights and enacted the 1776 statute. Rather than lessening the authority of the latter for separation of powers reasons, as Roane claimed, this enhanced the statute's significance. "For both depend upon the acquiescence of the people, as the convention was not deputed to make the constitution; or to pass laws under it; and, therefore, if the people acquiesced under the constitution, they acquiesced in the interpretation also." As a more general matter, they laid claim to the high ground of a commonly accepted rule of construction:

> That written constitutions are, like other instruments, subject to construction; and, when expounded, the exposition, after long acquiescence, becomes, as it were part of the instrument; and can no more, be departed from, than that. . . . [The legislature's] contemporaneous and subsequent decisions amount to so many recognitions of the first interpretation by the convention . . . [w]hich . . . makes, in effect, the construction, as to those subjects, part of the instrument.[92]

For the very reason that constitutional construction is a form of legal interpretation, a court ought to respect long-standing practice under the instrument, as it would with respect to a written grant or contract. Judicial review is not the exclusive means of establishing constitutional meaning, and a proper respect for their duty to decide constitutional cases according to law (including the law of interpreting legal documents) requires judges to defer to legislative interpretations in appropriate circumstances.

Pendleton's death had left the court of appeals evenly divided and after delivering their joint opinion Judge Carrington and President Lyons announced that "the decree of the chancellor stands, and is to be affirmed, as upon a division of the court." This left the validity of the 1802 Act without a definitive resolution for the moment; Tucker tactfully commented that Pendleton's presence "would probably have reconciled the doubts of all who doubted; and would have produced acquiescence, at least, in those who were not convinced," but in fact it was Tucker's views, not those that Pendleton would have espoused, that (with one exception to be noted) were treated as authoritative. The state courts uniformly respected sales of vacant glebes by county overseers, and the Episcopal church itself made no further protest, so that "under th[e] authority of [the 1798 and 1892 Acts] almost all the glebe lands in the state were disposed of before the year 1830."[93] In 1815, however, the constitutionality of the glebes and the validity of the 1802 Act came before a different tribunal, the Supreme Court of the United States.

Terrett v. Taylor was an action brought by the vestry of the Episcopal church in Alexandria against the overseers of the poor in Fairfax County. The plaintiffs wanted to sell the parish's glebe lands and apply the proceeds to the needs of the church, but apparently found the property unmarketable because of the overseers' claim to it under the law. Under the peculiar legal regime then governing Alexandria (at that time a part of the District of Columbia), they had to bring their action to quiet their title to the glebe and enjoin the overseers from laying claim to it in the federal circuit court for the District, even though the decision was to be governed generally by Virginia law. Writing for a unanimous Court, Justice Joseph Story studiously ignored *Turpin v. Locket,* and roundly endorsed the argument that the 1776 Act was "a contemporaneous exposition of the [Virginia] constitution" entitled to special consideration because "it was promulgated or acquiesced in by a great majority, if not the whole, of the very framers of the constitution" ("men," he noted, "of the very first rank for talents and learning"). On the basis of practice as well as principle, therefore, Story concluded that the legislation confirming the Episcopal church's claim to the glebes was "not inconsistent with the constitution or bill of rights of Virginia."[94] The logic of that conclusion would seem to be that the 1802 Act was invalid under the state constitution, but Story declined to rest the Court's judgment on an interpretation of Virginia's fundamental law. Instead he pronounced the 1802 statute "inoperative" to divest the church of the glebes "upon the principles of natural justice, upon the fundamental laws of every free government, upon the spirit and letter of the constitution of the United States, and upon the decisions of most respectable judicial tribunals." The 1802 Act was, as it were, cosmically unconstitutional.[95]

Long after *Turpin* and *Terrett,* Virginia's highest court revisited the issue of the glebe lands for a final time. In 1827, the overseers of the poor in Loudoun County sold the glebe lands of Shelburne parish pursuant to the 1802 Act. The plaintiffs in *Selden v. Overseers of the Poor of Loudoun* were the parish's vestry, church wardens, and minister, and according to the decision's reporter they attempted to fit their case within Justice Story's federal-law holding by basing their claim against the overseers on the federal Constitution. The state supreme court affirmed the chancery court's dismissal of the plaintiff's case with a two-word per curiam opinion ("Decree affirmed."), but the only judge to write an opinion, Robert Stanard, explained why in his judgment the court had to reject the plaintiffs' (apparently nonexistent) state constitutional claim. (He did not expressly mention their federal constitutional claim, or *Terrett v. Taylor*, at all.) Stanard noted that his consideration of the proper decision in *Selden* "strongly inclines me to assent to" the position taken by Wythe, Tucker, and Roane in *Turpin* and that if he had been on the *Turpin* court, "my impression is that I should have concurred in the[ir] opinions." But he reasoned that in light of the long-standing and universal practical acceptance of their position, he could not treat the decision as an open one. "In such a case the injunction stare decisis is of most commanding authority, and challenges obedience from every judge who is not supported in his dissent by an unhesitating conviction that the decision from which he dissents is clearly erroneous." With that exquisite irony history sometimes displays, the conclusion Tucker and Roane had labored to maintain in the teeth of the argument from practice found its final legal justification in the logic of that very argument.

The opinions in *Turpin v. Locket* revealed the existence of a fundamental divide, on Virginia's highest court and among prominent members of its bar, about the correct interpretation of the state bill of rights. The fissure between the views of Tucker, Roane, Nicholas, Hay (let's call them the radicals), and the position of Pendleton, Lyons, Carrington, William Fleming, Call, Randolph (let's call them the conservatives),[96] was profound, and went far deeper than the constitutionality of the 1802 Act, complicated as that issue was in itself. As the radicals interpreted it, Virginia's bill of rights had established as a constitutional command the complete disjuncture between church and state that was implicit in a Revolution "founded on principles utterly subversive of ecclesiastical coercion and monopoly." In a sense, indeed, for the radicals the constitutional law of religious liberty in Virginia was a continuation of the Revolution, involving the progressive application of a commitment to "free and equal government," the implications of which may have been unclear at first, or unrealizable due to circumstances. Whatever their individual views of the argument from practice, the radicals agreed that early practice under such a novel constitutional mandate could stem from a failure to recognize the existence of a constitutional issue, or error as to its correct resolution, as easily as from a sound understanding of the constitution's practical import. Rather than providing an interpretive advantage, proximity to a constitutional document's creation may mean that the early interpreter lacks the insight that reflection and experience can provide. That being the case, contemporaneous exposition and early practice ought to yield to a later, sounder understanding of "the principles of the constitution." "I am sure there is nothing in the temper of this court," Judge Roane concluded hopefully, "which will repudiate the dearest rights of the people, because, in the first moments of their acquirement, they were ignorant of their existence."

The conservatives read the bill of rights in a very different manner. For them, articles 4 and 16 were discreet texts addressing specific, undesirable governmental practices rather than markers within the constitutional document of some broad and revolutionary constitutional purposes. Both of them had clear core meanings—the prohibition of sinecures and religious persecution, respectively—and in light of what they saw as the goal of constitutional interpretation, the elimination of ambiguity in favor of clear legal rules, the early and consistent constructions of the articles were authoritative, as beyond the legitimate authority of judges to dispute as the constitutional text itself.

Fundamental disagreement over the basic meaning of a constitutional provision or principle is unsettling. Where it exists, it invites bitter and unresolvable conflict, and for this reason it is tempting to deny its possibility—de jure, as it were. Unfortunately (perhaps) that denial cannot be honestly maintained in the face of history. The Virginia court's division over religious liberty in 1804 is only one of many instances in which the law of an American constitution has displayed a fault line of meaning that goes all the way down to the bedrock of the interpreters' beliefs and commitments. The 1791 debate over the national bank bill is a good, and extremely early, example of that phenomenon with respect to the law of the U.S. Constitution. Jefferson and Hamilton were not at odds over a technical or isolated question of interpretation, but over the very nature and rationale of the Constitution's detailed grants of power to Congress. (More subtly, they were united on the unavoidability of bringing one's basic political worldview to bear on the interpretation of the Constitution, and thereby in sharp and perhaps fundamental disagreement with Randolph's desire to keep constitutional discussion on the plane of technical professional argument.) The reader will easily supply more recent examples.

Of the two conflicting schools of thought in the 1804 controversy, it was the conservatives, I think, who had a plausible overall solution to the problem—namely, long-standing practice. The advantages of adherence to practice are obvious: doing so reduces ambiguity and its costs, respects settled expectations, and places some of the responsibility for a decision that is going to be unpopular no matter which direction it goes on someone other than the decisionmaker. The last consideration, by the way, should not be seen as sheerly self-protective; there is considerable social value in those interested in a dispute, and particularly those disappointed in its outcome, being able to attribute the outcome to something other than the happenstance of one side having one more vote than the other.

Practical considerations of this sort were as obvious to the founding generation as they are to us, and were sometimes invoked as a basis for adherence to long-standing practice. In explaining his decision as president to sign into law a national bank bill despite his constitutional objections in 1791, Madison pointed out the consequences of disregarding settled practice; doing so "introduce[s] uncertainty and instability in the Constitution, [and] in the laws themselves; inasmuch as all laws preceding the new construction and inconsistent with it are not only annulled for the future, but virtually pronounced nullities from the beginning," and "disturb[s] the established course of practice in the business of the community." In his opinion for the Court in *M'Culloch v. Maryland*, Chief Justice Marshall echoed Madison, adding that "an immense property has been advanced" in reliance on the political branches' conclusion that the bank is constitutional. But for some constitutionalists in the early Republic, adherence to settled practice was not only prudent but also a duty. Carrington and Lyons made this point, perhaps cryptically, in their opinion in *Turpin:* "when expounded, the exposition, after long acquiescence, becomes, as it were, part of the instrument; and can no more, be departed from, than that." But what could they mean by such a remark?

One answer may be quickly dismissed; Carrington and Lyons were not ignoring the fact that American constitutions are written documents rather than courses of governmental practice like the English constitution. Indeed, the passage just quoted was part of their response to Attorney General Nicholas's attack on the authority of practice, an attack they summarized as the argument that the legislature can not "alter the constitution; or give it a meaning which the words would not bear." The authority of practice, as they saw it, stemmed directly from the fact that the Virginia constitution and bill of rights are legal instruments and thus, "like other [such] instruments, subject to construction." As they correctly intimated, the common-law tradition of textual interpretation gave great weight to a text's past interpretations, and Carrington and Lyons (like many of their contemporaries) believe that doing so was part of the obligation of a constitutional interpreter to treat a constitution as law. Perhaps the most thoughtful of these was Madison. In various discussions of his reasons for signing the second bank bill in 1816, Madison repeatedly described adherence to "authoritative, deliberate, and continued decisions" as the duty of a conscientious constitutional interpreter. Madison's "abstract opinion of the text" did not change between 1791 and 1816: reading Article

1, section 8 on its own, he remained convinced that it did not empower Congress to incorporate a national bank. But as a responsible constitutional interpreter, Madison did not believe himself authorized to follow his own "abstract and individual opinions" in the teeth of "a construction reduced to practice during a reasonable period of time." Deference to such a construction as "fix[ing] the interpretation" of the text ought to be "consider[ed] . . . a constitutional rule of interpreting a Constitution."

Madison gave several complementary reasons for viewing adherence to settled practice in this light. The Constitution, he believed, was created against a background assumption that decisions applying it to particular issues would resolve ("liquidate") its ambiguities and its meaning with respect to unanticipated questions:

> It could not but happen, and was foreseen at the birth of the constitution, that difficulties and differences of opinion might occasionally arise in expounding terms and phrases necessarily used in such a charter . . . and that it might require a regular course of practice to liquidate and settle the meaning of some of them.[97]

Respect for practice thus is as much a part of the enterprise of living by the written Constitution the founders had adopted as is respect for the text itself. (Indeed, on one occasion Madison chided a correspondent for placing too much weight on the difference between the "literal and constructive meaning" of the document.) In Madison's view, someone who rejects wholesale the authority of constitutional practice (as Attorney General Nicholas apparently did in *Turpin*) is refusing to engage in constitutional interpretation at all, even if he or she does so in the name of the text.

Madison also thought that long-standing practice could become probative evidence of the interpretation of the Constitution held by the people themselves; if he had vetoed the 1816 bank bill, he would have acted in "defiance of all the obligations derived from a course of precedents amounting to the requisite evidence of the national judgment and intention." Today we are doubtful about claims that political and legal processes are controlled by some abstract public will, but I do not think that Madison (if he shared our perspective) would have regarded his point as therefore moot. On issues where radical disagreement is possible on the basis of the text, the existence of sustained adherence "by the public [and] its agents" to one of the interpretations proposed is the only possible means short of a constitutional amendment for resolving the dispute that does not leave the issue permanently open to a potentially endless series of interpretive reversals. The individual interpreter, therefore, ought to view an interpretation that has achieved consistent success in the forums of official public opinion as "a construction put on the Constitution by the nation, which, having made it, had the supreme right to declare its meaning."

There was, I think, in Madison's mind a third justification for the "constitutional rule" of adhering to practice. Madison had a lively sense of the limitations and biases that shape the judgments of any interpreter of the Constitution, and equally of the unavoidable ambiguity of human language. The ambiguity makes principled disagreement on constitutional issues possible; the prejudiced nature of all constitutional arguments makes principled disagreement inevitable, but also suggests the need for a degree of humility on the part of any interpreter. Republican opponents and Federalist enforcers of the Sedition Act were alike convinced that their interpretation of the first amendment was the correct one, and yet both could not be right. Respect for settled practice acknowledges the possibility of error on one's own part as well as the interpreter's commitment to constitutional interpretation as a shared, public enterprise, rather than the preserve of a professional caste or a temporary partisan majority. In its presence, Madison once wrote, "I d[o] not feel myself, as a public man, at liberty to sacrifice all these public considerations to my private opinion."

Neither Madison nor any of those who agreed with him were arguing that adherence to practice was an absolutely inexorable command. A very significant limitation on the authority of practice was the insistence that it be sustained over some significant period of time. Even when that condition is met, Madison conceded that "there may be extraordinary and peculiar circumstances controlling the rule [of adherence]," although he characterized such a situation in terms showing that he thought it would be a rare occurrence. Marshall's views were the same: while "a bold and daring usurpation might be resisted" even after long acquiescence, the practice of government with respect to "a doubtful question, one on which human reason may pause, and the human judgment be suspended," could be labeled such a usurpation only with great difficulty. (Interestingly, Marshall intimated that practice might be of less weight in a decision in "which the great principles of liberty" are involved.) For these early constitutionalists, the threshold the interpreter must meet to displace settled meaning with personal opinion is high indeed; the reader will recall Judge Stanard's comment in *Leigh v. Overseers* that a departure from long-standing practice must rest on "an unhesitating conviction that the decision from which he dissents is clearly erroneous."

In many ways, modern constitutional lawyers proceed on very different premises than those of Madison, Marshall, Carrington, and Lyons. The denial of significance to political-branch practice as opposed to judicial precedent—already found in a fully blown form in Roane's *Turpin* opinion—is as a practical matter dogma on the Supreme Court, and many constitutional scholars would reject as naive or nonsensical the claim that political decisions, even long-standing and sustained ones, can "fix the interpretation" of the Constitution. While the opinions of the justices discuss the Court's precedents interminably, most or all of the justices apparently understand respect for past decisions as a counsel of prudence or convenience rather than a duty of conscience. At the same time, the justices often treat a single decision—by the Court—as dispositive, in direct contradiction to the common founding-era assumption that it is a course of precedents over time, not the first (or most recent) decision that happens to be made, that deserves the most weight. In fact, few observers believe that stare decisis is determinative in many cases where constitutional disagreement runs deep, which are precisely those situations in which Madison thought practice and precedent have their most important role to play. Indeed, given our heightened sensitivity to the game theory aspects of judicial and political decisionmaking, the notion of adhering to a practice or precedent that one thinks deeply wrong can appear foolish and self-defeating, a kind of legal fetishism that adult, postmodern lawyers clearly should reject.

There are many problems, conceptual and practical, with any suggestion that we address the issue of fundamental constitutional disagreement along the lines that Madison and others proposed. But the issue cannot be avoided, only ignored, and when we pretend ignorance we leave the nation's fundamental law subject, as Madison feared, to "the spirit of party . . . the pursuit of some favourite object," or the "solitary opinions" of the ninth justice in an otherwise evenly divided Court.

X. 1806: *Hudgins v. Wright* and the Place of Slavery

Two years after *Turpin v. Locket,* Chancellor Wythe tossed another constitutional bombshell, styled *Hudgins v. Wright,* into the lap of the Virginia court of appeals.[98] Hudgins—we do not know the given names of any of the parties—claimed to be the lawful master of the Wrights (a woman, her daughter, and her granddaughter) and as a factual matter had kept them as slaves. The suit began when the Wrights discovered that Hudgins intended to send them out of Virginia. It is possible that Hudgins, like many Virginia slaveowners in this period, believed that the days of slavery in the commonwealth were numbered and wanted to convert his chattels into cash while he could, or he may simply have been trying to capitalize on the high prices entrepreneurs in the rapidly expanding frontier slave country of Georgia, Alabama, and Mississippi were willing to pay. The lot of slaves in the deep south and what was then the southwest was notoriously harsher even than in Virginia, and this as well as a simple reluctance to leave their home and friends may have had something to do with the Wrights' decision to challenge their enslavement after (apparently) living as slaves all their lives. Whatever their reasons for acting, the Wrights resolved to seek their freedom through legal means.

In some way now lost to us, the Wrights enlisted the aid of George K. Taylor, whom we have already met as the leading Federalist spokesman in the Virginia House of Delegates during that body's debate over the Sedition Act. (The reader will recall that Taylor was Chief Justice Marshall's brother-in-law, but Taylor was a formidable lawyer in his own right.)[99] In order to prevent the case being mooted by the involuntary departure of his clients from the state, Taylor sought and obtained from Chancellor Wythe a writ of *ne exeat*. The purpose of a *ne exeat* was to prevent disputed property from being removed from the jurisdiction of the court pending resolution of the dispute, and it was sometimes employed in Virginia in cases involving the ownership of slaves. Despite the obvious incongruity of invoking the writ on the Wrights' behalf when their claim was that there was in fact no *property* in dispute, Taylor's choice was wise; there would have been complications attendant on seeking an injunction while the related writ of *ne exeat regno*, by which a person could be ordered not to leave the state until the resolution of a legal controversy, would have been directed to the wrong party.[100] At the same time, or perhaps shortly afterward, Taylor filed a bill seeking a judgment that the Wrights were free as a matter of law and in due course Wythe held a hearing.

Taylor's main argument, and as far as we know his only one, was that the Wrights were descended from "a free Indian woman." Virginia law had permitted the enslavement of Native Americans only briefly, from 1679 to 1691, or perhaps 1705; if the Wrights were descendants of a Native American woman brought into bondage at any period other than that, they were in principle free. (Status passed through the female line.) In making their case, however, Taylor faced several difficulties. First, as he apologetically told the court of appeals in the subsequent appeal, "[t]he peculiar circumstances under which the bill was drawn" (we can only imagine them, although as reported Taylor's argument assumed that the judges would understand the excuse) had led to "inaccuracies . . . in stating the genealogy" of the Wrights. Moreover, the evidence he was able to present Chancellor Wythe was unclear as to the sex of the Wrights' Native American ancestor, and vague as to when the ancestor was enslaved. The Wrights' skin color was light—Taylor told the appellate court that they were "perfectly white" although the reporters indicated that "there were gradual shades of difference in color" between them and only the youngest satisfied Taylor's description, but earlier decisions indicated that the plaintiff in a suit for freedom had the burden of proving his or her descent in "the maternal line" regardless of skin color.[101]

Despite the legal weaknesses in their case, the Wrights found a sympathetic ear in Chancellor Wythe. He shared the general belief of his era that slavery was, at least as a theoretical matter, a moral evil, and acted on his belief to the limited extent of emancipating three household servants. But Wythe had made no prior public act bearing on the continued existence of slavery as an institution before the case of the Wrights came before him. In deciding *Hudgins v. Wright*, therefore, Wythe's decision marked a startling break in his career as a statesman and judge, for Wythe decided in favor of the Wrights on two distinct and alternative grounds, one novel and the other revolutionary. At the hearing, "perceiving from his own view" that the Wrights' skin color was light and the youngest plaintiff's appearance entirely that of a white person, Wythe shifted the burden of proving the identity of their ancestor to Hudgins. The evidence, while it did not clearly establish the Wrights' assertion that their maternal ancestor was a Native American, unquestionably did not show that the ancestor was of African descent, or an Indian enslaved between 1679 and 1691 / 1705. The defendant having failed to satisfy his burden of overcoming the presumption of freedom Wythe had created from the Wrights' appearance, the chancellor held the plaintiffs entitled to freedom.

If Wythe had stopped at that point, *Hudgins v. Wright* would have been of present-day interest solely for its evidence of the tendency for American slavery law to become ever more deeply racial in its structure and procedures; after the court of appeals affirmed his judgment it was the law in Virginia that the location of the burden of proof in a suit for freedom depended on the trier of fact's perception of the plaintiff's racial category. But Wythe went on to articulate a second basis for his judgment, one that employed race neither in the articulation of the rule nor in its application. Wythe's opinion unfortunately is lost, and we are dependent on the reporters for the following, tantalizingly brief summary of his reasoning:

> [T]he late chancellor . . . determined that the appellees were entitled to
> their freedom . . . moreover, on the ground that freedom is the birth right
> of every human being, which sentiment is strongly inculcated by the first
> article of our "political catechism," the bill of rights,—he laid it down as a
> general position that whenever one person claims to hold another in slav-
> ery, the *onus probandi* lies on the claimant.[102]

Hudgins, we should recall, was not the moving party in *Hudgins v. Wright;* he
was not in a procedural sense "the claimant." Nonetheless, Chancellor Wythe
appears to have concluded that just as he believed in *Turpin v. Locket* that articles 4 and 16 of the Virginia state bill of rights limit the state's power to aid
the Episcopal church, so article 1 of the bill of rights limits the power of the
state (through the agency of its courts) to aid anyone claiming the right to hold
another human being in bondage. With respect to slavery as well as religion,
for Wythe the bill of rights committed the Commonwealth of Virginia to the
perhaps painful task of learning how to fulfill the principles it had placed in its
fundamental law.

Modern scholars having expressed differing views on exactly how large a
practical change Wythe's constitutional holding called for; after all, Wythe did
not rule slavery unconstitutional. Given the reaction of virtually everyone else
in Virginia's legal system to the holding, Wythe's contemporaries appear to
have thought the change Wythe ordained was a large one indeed. St. George
Tucker's opinion suggested a reason; Tucker pointed out that in Virginia
"there is no . . . Register of births for any but white persons, and those Regis-
ters are either lost, or of all records probably the most imperfect." If the appearance of an alleged slave made no difference to his or her prima facie case
for freedom, and the would-be owner had to prove the fact of descent from a
female ancestor legally reduced to slavery, an indeterminate but doubtlessly
large number of Virginian slaves were potential victors in suits for freedom.
Furthermore, once one accepts Wythe's premise that article 1 applies, at least
in part, to persons held in bondage, and that there is not a priori reason why
that or other articles of the bill of rights might not require further adjustments
in the law of slavery, Wythe's reasoning threatened the theoretical as well as
the practical structure of slavery in Virginia.

Much or all of this seems to have been clear enough in 1806. As Tucker remarked, "the principles laid down in the [chancellor's] decree, have been
loudly complained of."[103] Taylor himself did not rely on Wythe's constitutional holding in presenting the Wrights' case to the court of appeals; he argued instead that the evidence that the Wrights had some Native American

ancestry was sufficient to shift the burden of proving them slaves to the defendant, a burden that Hudgins had failed to carry. Randolph, in response, rejected Wythe's constitutionally based reversal of the usual burden of proof with an implicitly constitutional argument of his own: "In deciding upon the rights of *property*, those rules which have been established, are not to be departed from, because *freedom* is in question." The text of article 1, as Randolph did not need to remind the court that decided *Turpin v. Locket*, is concerned with property as much as with liberty; both are "inherent rights" that no social "compact" can alienate.

With no one defending the chancellor's constitutional holding, the court of appeals could have followed Taylor's lead and decided *Hudgins v. Wright* without addressing that issue, but the judges were unwilling to take that way out. The five judges concurred unanimously in a brief judgment, delivered by President Lyons, that emphatically rejected Wythe's argument and, almost as an aside, affirmed his decision that the Wrights were entitled to freedom:

> This court, not approving of the chancellor's principles and reasoning in his decree made in this cause, except so far as the same relates to white persons and native American Indians, but entirely disapproving thereof, so far as the same relates to native Africans and their descendants, who have been and are now held as slaves by the citizens of this state, and discovering no other error in the said decree, affirms the same.[104]

Thus the court agreed with Wythe that the defendant should bear the burden of proof in a suit for freedom where the person claimed as a slave appeared to the trial judge to be white or Native American in appearance. The rule in *Turpin v. Locket* seems to have been a change, in a more libertarian direction, from preexisting law, albeit one that rested on assumptions about the heritability of physical characteristics rather than article 1 of the bill of rights. Unlike Wythe's reasoning, this rule caused little public concern, for it left unaffected the great majority of those held in bondage in 1806 Virginia.

Two members of the court—*Turpin's* radical judges St. George Tucker and Spencer Roane—delivered lengthy opinions explaining their agreement with the court's decision. Roane focused his attention on the questions of evidence that Randolph had raised, his one oblique reference to Wythe's constitutional argument coming in a telling paraphrase of article 1 ("all men are by nature equally free and independent, and have certain inherent rights . . . namely, the enjoyment of life and liberty")—it was of "white people" that Roane spoke, he said, when he invoked "the blessings of liberty to which all such persons are entitled." Roane did not see himself as illiberal in issues of equality (recall his emphasis on equal rights in his *Turpin* opinion) and he was proud of the fact, as he saw it, that his era was more "just and liberal on the subject of slavery" than the past; but none of that changed for him the social fact that "in this country" a person who looks African is presumptively a slave. The legal presumption requiring such a person "to make out his right to freedom" simply followed from that fact about the world.

If anyone on the court of appeals could have been expected to approve of Wythe's constitutional reasoning, it was Tucker. Unlike Wythe, Tucker had been "an active political fighter for emancipation . . . personally involved in the struggle on the legislative front and on the general educational level."[105] Only three years before *Hudgins v. Wright,* Tucker had republished an anti-slavery pamphlet he had written in the 1790s as an appendix to his American edition of Blackstone's *Commentaries,* which was a runaway bestseller by the standards of the early Republic. In it he quoted article 1 of the Virginia bill of rights—accurately, without Roane's racial gloss—and described it as

> no more than a recognition of the first principles of the law of nature, which teaches us this equality. . . . It would be hard to reconcile reducing the negroes to a state of slavery to these principles, unless we first degrade them below the rank of human beings, not only politically, but also physically and morally . . . but surely it is time we should admit the evidence of moral truth, and learn to regard them as our fellow men, and equals.[106]

Under Virginia's slave laws, Tucker went on, "the right of property, and the right of personal liberty, [and] even the right of personal security"—in short, each of the three "inherent rights" guaranteed to "all men" by article 1—"ha[ve] been, at times either wholly annihilated, or reduced to a shadow." Tucker, in short, seemed publicly and prominently committed to the proposition that Virginia's bill of rights showed the moral illegitimacy not just of requiring people to prove their claim to freedom but of the entire institution by which they were held in bondage.

In addition, as Tucker was aware, Wythe was not the only American judge to have found a "free and equal" bill of rights provision legally inconsistent with the preexisting law of slavery. While he was his state's chief justice, William Cushing gave article 1 of the Massachusetts bill of rights (which differed from Virginia's article 1 only in insignificant detail) a reading even more daring than Wythe's. The defendant in the 1783 case of *Commonwealth v. Jennison* was white, and was prosecuted for beating a black man. His defense was that the victim was his slave and the beating legitimate corporate punishment. In his charge to the jury, Cushing invoked the Massachusetts article 1 in stating that "slavery is in my judgment as effectively abolished as it can be by the granting of rights and privileges wholly incompatible and repugnant to its existence." This language was not precisely the same as a flat declaration that article 1 had rendered slavery unlawful, but it clearly invited the *Jennison* jury to reject the defendant's argument on the ground that his victim's right to liberty and personal security was guaranteed by article 1 notwithstanding the defendant's alleged claim on the victim's services. The jury convicted Jennison, and several years later a Jeremy Belknap wrote a letter describing the decision as "a mortal wound to slavery in Massachusetts." The recipient of Belknap's 1795 letter was Tucker.[107] It was not unthinkable then, in legal or professional terms, to give article 1 a construction that at least circumscribed the institution of slavery. And that is what Wythe had done.

All of this said, Tucker agreed with his colleagues that Wythe had misapprehended the legal significance (Tucker referred to "the operation") of article 1. Perhaps because of his well-known support for abolition, Tucker thought it appropriate to explain "this difference of opinion from the chancellor." Wythe had failed to read that provision in its historical context, and doing so revealed the error in his reasoning:

> [T]he first clause of the Bill of Rights . . . was notoriously framed with a cautious eye to this subject, and was meant to embrace the case of free citizens, or aliens only; and not by a side wind to overturn the rights of property, and give freedom to those very people whom we have been compelled from imperious circumstances to retain, generally, in the same state of bondage that they were in at the revolution, in which they had no *concern, agency,* or *interest.*[108]

Just as he and Roane had looked beyond the bare letter of the bill of rights in concluding that it required an absolute separation between church and state, so here Tucker looked beyond the letter of article 1 to determine its implications for the law of slavery. Despite its reference to "all men," the scope of article 1 was determined by the historical circumstances of its birth: "we" (white Virginians), locked in the "imperious circumstances" of a desperate revolution in which "they" (African Americans) were nonparticipants and, worse, a potential threat to our cause, could hardly be thought to have intended to create a fatal maelstrom of disagreement among ourselves by depriving many of us of one of the very rights for which we were fighting. The bill of rights states high constitutional ideals but, as a later jurist was to say of the U.S. Constitution, it is not a suicide pact.

Furthermore, Wythe's argument depended on an improperly narrow focus on only part of article 1. Read as a whole, that article accords the right to "the means of acquiring and possessing property" as high a dignity as the right of personal liberty. It is a "fundamental principle of our constitution," Tucker had written in *Turpin v. Locket,* "that private property shall be sacred and inviolable." This principle, "to be found in our bill of rights," "neither . . . can or ought to be, shaken by this court, or by any authority in the state." The principle is broad and applies even to property rights that an individual acquires under a statutory scheme that is itself unconstitutional: the legislature was free to repeal the statute incorporating the Episcopal church if (as Tucker thought) the statute was "unconstitutional . . . provided it does not annul, or avoid any private right, which may have been legally acquired by any individual in his natural capacity, under such act." Despite the fact that a law conflicts with the bill of rights, private property rights obtained in conformity to the law's requirements then come within the protection of the same bill of rights. No matter how politically illegitimate, then, the institution of slavery might be under article 1, that same article safeguarded the legal rights of the slaveowner. And this result, Tucker asserted (no doubt correctly), was as the makers of article 1 intended. Slavery would not end in Virginia through judicial decision.

Chancellor Wythe did not live to see his work in the Wrights' case undone. Over eighty at the time of his decision, he had made a will dividing his estate between a nephew and Michael Brown, one of the household servants whom he had emancipated. Shortly after Wythe decreed the Wrights' freedom, his nephew poisoned both Wythe and Brown in an effort to secure the entire estate to himself. The state's attempt to prosecute the nephew failed because the crucial witness was Lydia Broadnax, another former slave freed by Wythe: under Virginia law an African American could not testify against a white person.

Hudgins v. Wright is a profoundly interesting case from several perspectives. In terms of judicial psychology, the actions of both Wythe and Tucker are curious. Did Wythe really think he might get away with throwing a judicial time bomb into the legal substructure of Virginia slavery, or was his constitutional holding merely a gesture? And why did Tucker gratuitously note his disagreement with Wythe's reasoning? Was his decision to agree with his colleagues a failure of nerve or of vision, and if so, why not simply concur silently in the court's decision?

Whatever Wythe's motives, Tucker well may have taken practical considerations into account in disagreeing with him. In the same letter describing

Commonwealth v. Jennison as a "mortal wound" to slavery in Massachusetts (where slaves had been few and the institution of almost immeasurably less economic significance than in Virginia), Belknap had told Tucker that "the general answer" to the question how Massachusetts ended slavery was "by publick opinion," and that the process had not taken place over night: the public consensus that abolished slavery "began to be established about thirty years ago," in other words about twenty years *before Jennison*. Cushing announced his antislavery construction of the bill of rights in a radically different setting than the one in which Tucker found himself; and even if his colleagues had been willing to agree, it is difficult to imagine that (white) Virginian public opinion would long have tolerated a judicial decision that precipitously threw the state into a process of dismantling slavery. To be the lone dissenter on a court otherwise committed to "entirely disapproving" Wythe's constitutional argument may well have seemed to Tucker likely to destroy his own ability to contribute to the antislavery cause in the future.

My immediate interest in *Hudgins v. Wright* lies in a different direction, in what the case says about race in American constitutional reasoning. It is a common (if not undisputed) observation that slavery and its racist aftermath have cast a long shadow over American constitutionalism, not only in the obvious moral sense that American fundamental law for so long a time validated and protected racial caste and oppression, but more subtly through its impact on how we think about constitutional matters. *Hudgins*, I believe, illustrates—in a somewhat ironic fashion—this latter point. What was "wrong" with Wythe's opinion, as Tucker saw it, was that Wythe's approach was too abstract. He took the words "all men are by nature free and independent" and read them without any regard for who wrote them or when they were written. The 1776 Virginia bill of rights was an instrument framed and adopted as fundamental law by a society of slaveholders, no doubt of differing views on the morality and expediency of the institution, but united in their desire to maintain their personal rights—and particularly their property rights—against interference. (In their opinion in *Turpin*, President Lyons and Judge Carrington wrote that "revolutions are intended to preserve, not to take away rights: Nor was it ever pretended, that an alteration, in the form of a government, affected private property.") From this perspective, Virginia's slaves were no more a part of the political body that fought *this* revolution and sanctioned *this* article 1 than were Virginia's Loyalists. The constitution created by this society of slaveholders thus was marked—and marred—by its origins.

Wythe's abstraction sought to cover over this history, but the resulting portrayal of Virginia's constitution as a presumptively antislavery document was •

a mirage, a flattering untruth that could not provide the basis for a legitimate judicial decision. The judge's duty, Tucker wrote in *Kamper v. Hawkins,* is "to expound what the law *is,* "and although that principle is an empowering one, authorizing the judge to follow the law of the constitution rather than conflicting lesser laws, by the same token it is a limitation: the judge is not authorized to say what the law of the constitution *should be* but is not. Brought out of the realm of abstraction into the historical world of a slaveowning society, article 1's legal "operation" was to protect the slaveowners' property rights, however much its words might suggest that this was at the expense of the moral rights of those they had "retain[ed] . . . in bondage."

Chancellor Wythe turned to the abstract in an attempt to escape the unpalatable historical truth that the Virginia constitution reflected a fundamental decision not to dismantle the preexisting institution of slavery. In parallel fashion, the post–Civil War uses of abstraction have often served, whether intentionally or not, to obscure the historical truth that the Civil War amendments to the federal Constitution reflected a fundamental decision to do just that, dismantle slavery.[109] The classic example, of course, is the Supreme Court's notorious decision upholding de jure racial segregation in *Plessy v. Ferguson.* The *Plessy* Court's analysis of the railway segregation statute under review treated the constitutional issue of equality as an abstract exercise in logic: a law that requires X to sit only with other Xs and Y to sit only with other Ys imposes exactly the same restraint on X and Y. As Justice John Marshall Harlan said in dissent, this was to miss (or pretend to miss) the point of state-ordained segregation altogether, "which, *in fact,* proceed[s] on the ground that colored citizens are so inferior and degraded that they cannot be allowed to sit in public coaches occupied by white citizens." In the real world in which African Americans were enslaved and remain the objects of prejudice and oppression, racial segregation is a means of carrying on that oppression, and its abstract evenhandedness a mere "pretense of recognizing equality of rights" that is "cunningly devised to defeat legitimate results of the war."[110]

It is difficult to characterize the *Plessy* majority's resort to abstraction as anything other than a deliberate evasion of social reality—Justice Harlan wrote, with bitter irony, that "[n]o one would be so wanting in candor as to assert" that the segregation statute's purpose was nonracist—but the underlying problem with abstraction in this area exists even when those invoking it do so in good faith. Constitutional interpreters err when they construe the command of the fourteenth amendment that no state should deny to any person "the equal protection of the laws" without remembering the amendment's historical context: the nation's resolve that one particular racial group should be included within the political community as equals. As Tucker recognized in *Hudgins,* a judge who employs an abstraction labeled "equality" is at risk of saying not what the law of the Constitution is, but rather what the judge wishes it to be.

XI. 1808–1809: A Forgotten Crossroads in Constitutional History

May 1808

The twelve-month period beginning in May 1808 was one of the most important in the entire history of American constitutional law. Three men made decisions, in each case a personally difficult decision, that signaled a crucial and beneficial turning point in the administration of the system of fundamental law that the U.S. Constitution ordains. The legitimacy of subsequent constitutional decisionmaking rests, I believe, on the extent to which the decisionmakers follow the precedents set in that fateful year.

The first of these men was William Johnson, associate justice of the U.S. Supreme Court. Johnson was a South Carolinian of working-class origins who managed to attend Princeton and then rise to prominence in his home state's politics at an early age. He became speaker of the state house when twenty-six, and a year later was elected to the state's constitutional court. When Justice Alfred Moore's resignation in 1804 gave President Jefferson his first opportunity to make an appointment to the Supreme Court, the president concluded that Moore's successor should be from South Carolina. Albert Gallatin, by now Jefferson's secretary of the treasury, no doubt reflected Jefferson's own views when he wrote that "[t]he importance of filling this vacancy with a Republican and a man of sufficient talent to be useful, is obvious," and Jefferson gave deliberate consideration to several well-known Republicans before selecting Johnson. Jefferson's choice thus was an endorsement both of Johnson's professional accomplishments at the age of thirty-two and of his political opinions. A memorandum prepared for Jefferson described Johnson as "an excellent lawyer . . . of irreproachable character, republican connections, and of good nerves in his political principles," a characterization echoed by Federalist William Plumer's comment that Johnson was "a zealous Democrat but said to be honest and capable."[111] Johnson's most notable action in his first three years on the bench was consistent with these evaluations: in early 1807 he entered a lone dissent against Chief Justice Marshall's ruling for the Court in a politically charged case involving the administration's efforts to prosecute former Vice President Burr and his associates for treason.[112]

In the spring of 1808, a case involving issues of both law and politics came before Johnson, presiding over the federal circuit court in Charleston. The case arose under a statute, enacted by Congress in December 1807, that imposed a total embargo on American trade with the warring European powers and their dependencies. The Embargo Act of 1807 was the culmination of several frustrating years in which the Jefferson administration had struggled to persuade the British and the French to respect American neutrality on the high seas. When it became known in late 1807 that the superpowers had adopted reciprocal policies prohibiting neutral trade with the other and intended to seize American ships violating their policies, Jefferson successfully proposed that the United States respond with an embargo, which Congress enacted in party-line voting. As originally conceived the purpose of the Embargo Act was the purely defensive one of avoiding the loss of American ships, cargo, and seamen, but over time it came to assume a second role as a means of exerting economic pressure on the Europeans. Under either rationale, the Embargo Act immediately became the centerpiece of American foreign policy (an important Republican newspaper with close connections to Virginia's Republican leadership called the embargo "the leading policy of the U.S.")[113], and the Jefferson administration was committed from the beginning to its vigorous enforcement. Over the course of the first few months of the year, Congress enacted a series of laws extending the embargo and strengthening the executive's powers to enforce it, culminating in an Act of April 25 that contained, among other provisions, the following section 12:

> That the collectors of the customs be, and they are hereby, respectively authorized to detain any vessel ostensibly bound with a cargo to some other port of the United States, whenever in their opinions the intention is to violate or evade any of the provisions of the acts laying an embargo, until the decision of the President of the United States be had thereupon.[114]

Acting on the president's instructions, Secretary Gallatin issued a circular to the collectors informing them that they should regard "excessive shipments of certain commodities" as prima facie ground for suspicion and that the president desired all vessels with such cargoes detained.

In May 1808, a Charleston shipowner named Adam Gilchrist sought clearance papers for his freighter the *Resource*, loaded with rice and cotton and ostensibly bound for Baltimore. The Charleston collector of customs, Simeon Theus, entertained no personal suspicion that the *Resource*'s real destination was anywhere else, but its cargo fell within the Gallatin circular's description of vessels to be detained automatically, and Theus therefore declined to issue the papers. Gilchrist then sought a writ of mandamus from Justice Johnson, sitting on circuit, to compel the collector to release the *Resource*, and in his answer to the motion, Theus conceded that but for the circular he would not detain Gilchrist's ship. Given the essentially friendly nature of the dispute, Theus made no objection to the circuit court's jurisdiction and authority to issue the mandamus if warranted on the merits.

Johnson read Gallatin's circular in the light of what appeared to be its rationale, and concluded that the collector was being overly cautious because the *Resource* did not "come within the spirit and meaning of [Gallatin's] instructions," and in any event the circular was only a "recommendation, not [a] command." From the private correspondence of Jefferson and Gallatin, to which of course Johnson had no access, it seems clear that Johnson was misreading the intent of the circular, but if he had confined his discussion to the question of interpreting Gallatin's words, his decision to order Theus to clear the *Resource* would almost certainly have attracted little or no attention from anyone other than the grateful Gilchrist. (Indeed, Gallatin had already written another circular revoking the instructions at issue before Johnson.) But Johnson did not rest his decision on this argument alone. He found that there was "no ambiguity" in the language of section 12, which left "the granting of clearances . . . absolutely to the discretion of the collector; the right of detaining in cases which excite suspicion is given him." The statute gave the collector no authority to detain a vessel in the absence of misgivings about its real destination, and neither Gallatin nor the president himself had any statutory authority to direct the collector to act otherwise:

> On the latter question there can be no doubt. The officers of our government, from the highest to the lowest, are equally subjected to legal restraint; and it is confidently believed that all of them feel themselves equally incapable, as well from law as from inclination, to attempt an unsanctioned encroachment upon individual liberty. . . . We are of opinion that . . . without the sanction of law, the collector is not justified by the instructions of the executive, in increasing restraints upon commerce.[115]

It is impossible now to know whether Johnson understood that he was provoking a maelstrom by these words. Rather than being a perhaps mistaken interpretation of an already superseded directive, his decision was a political bombshell: Charles Warren wrote that "[n]o decision in a Federal court ever rendered up to that time (except that in the *Burr Case*) received so full publication or so widespread notice in the newspapers."[116] The Federalist press universally approved Johnson's opinion as confirmation from a Republican judge that the Republican administration was fundamentally lawless; the initial Republican response was mixed, with some pro-administration journalists downplaying the decision and others denouncing it as "another memorable example of the profligacy of the Judiciary."[117] Any doubt about the administration's view of Johnson's action vanished when Attorney General Caesar Rodney, acting at the behest of a furious Jefferson, made public an elaborate opinion presenting a series of increasingly severe criticisms of Johnson's decision.[118] The circuit court had no jurisdiction over Gilchrist's motion for a mandamus, Rodney argued, and he ostentatiously noted that it was "scarcely necessary to remark" that the collector's "tacit acquiescence" could not confer it. Assuming arguendo that the court had possessed jurisdiction to hear the motion, there were four distinct reasons at common law why it was improper for Johnson to grant the writ.

Rodney reserved the bulk of his opinion for a strongly worded attack on Johnson's decision as a violation of the constitutional separation of powers. He readily conceded that the judiciary is "the source of legal redress for wrongs committed by ministerial officers; none of whom is above the law"; Gilchrist was entitled to seek damages from the collector. But, Rodney continued,

> there appears to be a material and obvious distinction, between a course of proceeding which redresses a wrong committed by an executive officer, and an interposition of a mandatory writ, taking the executive authority out of the hands of the president, and prescribing the course, which he and the agents of any department must pursue. . . . [I]t would seem that under the name of a judicial power, an executive function is necessarily assumed, and that part of the constitution perhaps defeated, which makes it the duty of the president to take care that the laws be faithfully executed.

The issue was no longer whether the *Resource* was lawfully detained—Rodney in fact made no effort to defend the conformity of Gallatin's circular to the statute—but the constitutional distribution of authority.

The publication of Rodney's opinion provoked a second storm of commentary in the press, with Republican papers praising the attorney general's "clear and lucid" reasoning and Federalists denouncing the opinion as an outrageous and unconstitutional attempt to intimidate the judiciary. About a month later, Johnson responded to Rodney in a signed public statement, being unwilling, as he explained, to suggest by silence that he had been "borne down by reasoning or awed by power."[119] While he systematically rebutted each of Rodney's arguments, Johnson admitted that it was "very possible that the court may have erred in their decision" to issue the mandamus. He also noted wryly that Rodney had "completely put aside" the substantive question of whether Gallatin's instructions were lawful: "The argument is not that the executive have done right, but that the judiciary had no power to prevent their doing wrong." Despite his admission of fallibility, however, Johnson flatly rejected Rodney's charge that the decision involved any usurpation of power. Rodney's critique stemmed from a fundamental misunderstanding of the role of the courts in the constitutional order:

> The courts do not pretend to impose any restraint upon any officer of government, but what results from a just construction of the laws of the United States. Of these laws the courts are the constitutional expositors; and every department of government must submit to their exposition; for laws have no legal meaning but what is given them by the courts to whose exposition they are submitted. It is against the law, therefore, and not the courts, that the executive should urge the charge of usurpation and restraint: a restraint . . . which it is very possible the president may have deserved the plaudits of his country for having transcended, in ordering detentions not within the embargo acts, but which notwithstanding it is the duty of our courts to encounter the odium of imposing.

The reasoning in this tightly written but ambiguous passage will repay close attention.

Johnson's premise is a familiar one to the reader: that it is the particular task of the courts to say what the law is. Just as other judges in the founding era invoked it as the basis for judicial review of legislation, so here Johnson relied on it in explaining why Rodney's separation of powers accusation was erroneous. Each of the three branches necessarily "restrains" the others in the exercise of its functions—Congress, for example, by legislation places duties and limitations on both the executive and the courts—and Adam Gilchrist's case did nothing more than illustrate this constitutional commonplace. The various embargo statutes placed a duty on the collector ("to grant a clearance whenever the forms of the law have been complied with") that Theus had (reluctantly) not performed; once Gilchrist brought this violation of the duty imposed by the laws within the cognizance of the judiciary, it became the duty of the court to announce the fact and supply a remedy. Rodney's attempt to distinguish damages and mandamus as, respectively, legitimate and illegitimate remedies against executive officers was a red herring: by vesting in the courts "the judicial Power," Article III authorized and obliged them to exercise "both . . . the faculty of judging and of applying physical force to give effect to a decision." The power to provide a remedy "adapted to the exigency of each case" thus is "a mere incident to the judicial power," and in the absence of congressional direction it would have been the court's duty to devise a form of proceeding that would accomplish that result in a case within its jurisdiction. (In fact, Johnson believed that the Judiciary Act of 1789 had provided clear congressional authorization for the use of the writ of mandamus.) When the circuit court issued the mandamus to collector Theus, it was exercising a core function of the judiciary. The "restraint" of which the attorney general was complaining stemmed from the system of law that the Constitution, and Congress acting under the Constitution, had created. By implicitly waiving the question of whether Johnson had been correct on the merits, Rodney had thus abandoned the proper ground for criticizing the court, that its action was not based on a "just construction of the laws of the United States."

It is one thing to assert that a court must follow its own view of the law in making decisions; it is quite another to assert that the other branches of government must adopt the judicial view in preference to their own where these interpretations are in conflict. When, for example, Tucker remarked in *Kamper v. Hawkins* that "the duty of expounding the law must be exclusively vested in the judiciary," the most obvious way to interpret his comment is that an authoritative judicial construction of a law fixes its meaning and henceforth other constitutional actors must as it were "internalize" that construction, even if they disagree with it, and apply it within their own spheres as well.[120] Johnson may have been making the same point in his 1808 remark that because the courts are "the constitutional expositors" of the laws, "every department of government must submit to their exposition; for laws have no legal meaning but what is given them by the courts to whose exposition they are submitted." In the context of the *Gilchrist* case, on the other hand, he perhaps may have intended to make a more specifically relevant assertion, that when a legal question is "submitted" to the courts, other governmental actors must submit to their ruling on its "legal meaning" in that case.

The unspoken but unmistakable subtext of the harsh Republican criticisms of Johnson was that he had betrayed the president who appointed him and the party to which he owed his prominence by making a decision and (still more) characterizing it in a manner that played into the hands of the Federalists. (Attorney General Rodney even suggested in private correspondence that Johnson's action was motivated by personal political ambition.) In his public statement, Johnson took oblique note of these accusations by contrasting the president's role with that of the courts. The president has a broad responsibility to safeguard the public good, and therefore "may have deserved the plaudits of his country for having transcended" the "legal meaning" of the laws; if Johnson is not being wholly sarcastic he is glancing at a view that Jefferson himself sometimes expressed, that urgent public necessity may call on high executive officers to act beyond the laws for the good of the people and "trust[ ] to their justice for the transgression of the law."[121] The beginning and end of a court's responsibilities, on the other hand, lie in allegiance to the law. Whatever may be appropriate for the president to do when the law ordains a result contrary to the public good, a court is obliged to follow its view of the law no matter what the odium of doing so may be.

The uproar over Johnson's decision and his public dispute with the attorney general took months to die down (as late as December 1808 Johnson was being rebuked by a Georgia grand jury for his "daring precipitancy"), and introduced considerable uncertainty about whether the president could exercise any centralized control over the enforcement of the embargo laws. Privately, Secretary Gallatin conceded that on the merits Johnson had been correct, and that under the April 25 Act as written all that he or the president could do was make recommendations to the collectors. Furthermore, Gallatin admitted that "the Court, supposing that they had jurisdiction, could not, from the manner in which the question was brought before them, have decided otherwise than they did."[122] Acting at Gallatin's urging, Congress enacted an enforcement bill in January 1809 expressly giving the president the authority to issue "instructions" to the collectors, and the particular legal issue Adam Gilchrist had stirred up was at rest.

October 1808

The second man faced with a difficult decision in this fateful twelve-month period was John Davis, U.S. district judge for Massachusetts. Davis was older than Johnson, about forty-seven, and had enjoyed a longer and more varied career than the South Carolinian, serving at the state level both in the state house and as a member of the 1788 convention that ratified the Constitution. Through his education at Harvard, his social position, his legal practice, and his political convictions, Davis was a thoroughly embedded member of the Federalist elite that dominated Massachusetts in the 1790s: in 1811 John Quincy Adams referred to Davis's "political opinions and more especially . . . his social connections" as well-known and distasteful to (Republican) "public Sentiment." Indeed it may have been through his Federalist political connections that Davis came to the attention of President Washington, who appointed him in succession comptroller of the currency and U.S. attorney in Massachusetts. Davis served in the latter position for almost the entire administration of John Adams, and in February 1801 Adams appointed him district judge. At least prior to going on the bench, Davis was not shy about displaying his political affiliations: he was, for example, one of the featured guests at an 1800 Boston banquet given to honor Alexander Hamilton, mentioned alongside such Federalist stalwarts as former congressman Fisher Ames and Governor Caleb Strong.[123]

The federal district court, in which Davis sat alone, was the court of original jurisdiction in admiralty cases, and as a consequence it was before Davis that the executive branch had to bring enforcement actions under the Embargo Act that originated in Massachusetts. The embargo bore heavily on Massachusetts, with its commerce-based economy; and public opinion, aroused in part by a skillful campaign of public petitions and remonstrances, was running strongly against it. Early in the summer of 1808, the state's independent-minded U.S. senator John Quincy Adams was driven to resign his seat and was effectively drummed out of the Federalist party for his support of the embargo. Perhaps more important for someone like Davis, a prominent member of his professional and social circle, state chief justice Theophilus Parsons, had "made no secret" of his belief that the Embargo Act was unconstitutional. Davis himself might have been expected to be equally hostile toward enforcement of the embargo. It was in this context that the case of the brigantine *William* came before Davis's court.[124]

The U.S. attorney took action against the *William*, claiming that the vessel had served as the middle carrier in a complicated scheme intended to evade the embargo and export "sundry . . . goods, wares and merchandize . . . to some foreign port or place" in violation of the embargo Acts. If true, the *William* would be forfeited to the government. The vessel's owners were represented by two friends and former professional associates of Davis, William Prescott and Samuel Dexter. (Dexter was the judge's college classmate to boot.) The Federalist press treated the news that Prescott and Dexter intended to challenge the constitutionality of the embargo with great satisfaction, one remarking that "[f]rom the weight of talents engaged the arguments will attract a high degree of public interest," and Davis's courtroom was crowded with spectators during the several days in which the lawyers argued the constitutional question.[125]

A week later, on October 3, Davis upheld the embargo Acts in a remarkable, extraordinarily interesting opinion. He began by taking note of "the solemn weight and magnitude of the inquiry" and his personal wish that the question had been "reserved for the higher tribunals of the nation." But that wish could not be fulfilled, Davis conceded, because the function of judicial review is central to an American constitutional system. Davis was in agreement thus far with those of his contemporaries (among them, Roane and Tucker in 1794 and the congressional Federalists of 1802) who saw the judiciary as having a special role in safeguarding the Constitution. "A comparison of the law with the constitution is the right of the citizen. Those who deny this right, and the duty of the court resulting from it, must regard with strange indifference, a precious security to the individual, and have studied, to little profit, the peculiar genius and structure of our limited government."[126] Unlike others who held this general perspective, however, Davis did not think that a court should treat all constitutional questions in the same manner. A court's proper approach to a claim that Congress has violated the Constitution depends on the way in which Congress is supposed to have erred.

Davis classified "[o]bjections to an act of congress, on the ground of constitutionality," into three groups:

> (1) A repugnancy to some of the exceptions or restrictions to the legislative authority expressed in the constitution of the United States. (2) A repugnancy to some of the affirmative provisions, in the constitution. (3) A want of conformity to the powers vested in the legislature, by the constitution; or that the act in question is not authorized by any of those powers.[127]

Davis gave as examples of categories (1) and (2) laws violating, respectively, the Article I prohibition on bills of attainders and ex post facto laws, and the Article III requirement that all criminal prosecutions except impeachments be tried before a jury. Provisions of this sort, as Davis saw it, ordain specific legal rules, no different from statutory mandates except in their dignity, and equally susceptible to judicial construction and application:

> Affirmative provisions and express restrictions . . . are sufficiently definite to render decisions, probably in all cases, satisfactory; and the interferences of the judiciary with the legislature, to use the language of the constitution, would be reduced to "cases," easily to be understood, and, in which the superior, commanding will of the people, who established the instrument, would be clearly and peremptorily expressed.[128]

Faced with a law containing a "clearly described and determined" violation of such a provision, Davis concluded, "it would appear to be the duty of the national courts . . . to regard" such a law "to be so far void."

The main constitutional argument in the case of the *William*, however, fell within Davis's third category: Davis's friends Prescott and Dexter were claiming that the embargo laws were nullities because "congress have not power or authority, by the constitution of the United States thus to interdict commercial intercourse with foreign nations." And that, for Davis, raised the preliminary but important question whether "a mere exceeding of the powers of congress, in legislation, without a repugnancy to express provisions of the constitution, [is] among the proper objects of cognizance in the federal judiciary." Davis reviewed at length what he may have believed to be an exhaustive list of federal court exercises of judicial review up to 1808 (the list did not, ironically, include *Marbury v. Madison*),[129] none of which, he pointed out, expressed "an opinion, as to the power of the court, where the objection to a statute is grounded . . . on a supposed undue extension of a given power." (*Marbury*, had he discussed it, clearly would have fallen in his second category and thus would not have changed his conclusion.) Davis then turned to the *Federalist*'s references to judicial review, and concluded that according to "this excellent commentary" on the Constitution, the judicial "power to declare [acts of Congress] void exists, only, in cases of contravention, opposition, or repugnancy, to some express restrictions."[130]

Neither judicial precedent nor the Constitution's most notable commentary established, in Davis's judgment, the court's power to act on claims belonging in category (3). Furthermore, Davis saw a fundamental objection to doing so: in order to determine that a law goes beyond any of the Constitution's affirmative grants of power, and can be treated as void on that ground alone, a court would have to exercise a sort of judgment perilously close to that constitutionally entrusted to the legislature:

> To determine where the legitimate exercise of discretion ends, and usurpation begins, would be a task most delicate and arduous. It would, in many instances, be extremely difficult to settle it, even in a single body. It would be much more so, if to be adjusted by two independent bodies, especially if those bodies, from the nature of their constitution, must proceed by different rules. Before a court can determine, whether a given act of congress, bearing relation to a power with which it is vested, be a legitimate exercise of that power, or transcend it, the degree of legislative discretion, admissible in the case, must first be determined. Legal discretion is limited. . . . Political discretion has a far wider range. It embraces, combines, and considers, all circumstances, events and projects, foreign and domestic, that can affect the national interests. Legal discretion has not the means of ascertaining the grounds, on which political discretion may have proceeded.[131]

In other words, in enacting legislation pursuant to the Constitution, Congress makes judgments about the ways in which the bill would execute, safeguard, or fulfill the purposes of one or more express powers. These judgments necessarily involve predictions about the empirical effects of the legislation and its likely impact on the overall activities of the federal government that cannot be brought within the scope of traditional judicial decisionmaking.

In contrast to cases in categories (1) and (2), Davis feared that entertaining category (3) claims would require the judiciary to address questions—the degree of necessity of a given law and the extent to which it in fact serves some goal entrusted to Congress—that courts are ill equipped to handle and about which judicial decisions are likely to seem to Congress and the public more as disagreements over policy than applications of a legal rule.[132] To be sure, he admitted, "[cases] might be put, of acts, so manifestly without the sphere of objects, committed to the national government, that the judiciary branch might be competent to pronounce them invalid, not as repugnant to any particular clause of the constitution, but to its whole expressed design and tenour," but Davis thought this a theoretical possibility at most.[133]

"Considerations of this nature have induced a doubt of the competency, or constitutional authority of the court" to invalidate federal statutes in category (3) cases, but Davis declined to give a final opinion on the question, since in his judgment the embargo Acts were plainly constitutional under the commerce and declaration of war clauses of Article I, section 8. That conclusion was no means an inevitable one. Justice Joseph Story, no foe of broad federal power, later wrote that the Embargo Act unquestionably "went to the utmost verge of constitutional power,"[134] and Davis would have been well within President Jefferson's own well-known general views on constitutional interpretation if he had concluded that the embargo could not be sanctioned under any of the enumerated grants of power except by the sort of broad construction of congressional authority that Jefferson had deprecated in the 1790s. An argument against the embargo couched in such terms would have been embarrassing, at the least, to the administration and the president personally, but Davis declined to make it. Instead, relying on "views of the national powers . . . coeval, in my mind, with the constitution," Davis thought himself "bound to overrule the objections to the acts in question . . . believing them to be constitutional laws."

In the course of laying out his reasons for thinking so, Davis made several comments that amplify his preliminary discussion of judicial review. Responding to the argument that the commerce clause's grant of power to "regulate" foreign commerce did not include the power to "annihilate" it, Davis pointed out that even if one thought that argument persuasive as a construction of the text (he did not) the embargo Acts were not, literally, a total ban on foreign commerce. "[A]nd how shall the degree, or extent, of the prohibition be adjusted, but by the discretion of the national government?" On what legal basis could a court determine that the Constitution forbade Congress from "considering the present prohibitory system, as necessary and proper to an eventual beneficial regulation," or from seeing it as a measure taken "for purposes of safety, of preparation [for war], or counteraction" to foreign aggression under Congress's powers relating to war. Confined as he thought a judge ought to be to "the abstract question of constitutional power," Davis saw "nothing to prohibit or restrain" the embargo.

The Republican press lauded Judge Davis's judicial independence in language reminiscent of the praises Federalist journalists had extended to Justice Johnson earlier in the year, while the Federalist papers suddenly lost interest in the case of the *William,* in many instances literally ignoring it. John Quincy Adams, an informed if hardly unbiased observer, wrote a Virginian correspondent that the latter would not easily guess "what means were used and by whom to bias [Davis's] decision, nor how much disappointment has followed from [his] honest firmness and incorruptible integrity." A few years later, Adams urged President Madison to appoint Davis to a vacant seat on the Supreme Court despite the latter's politics: "you will . . . permit me the recollection that Mr. Davis on one signal, and not untrying occasion, manifested at once the steadiness of his mind, his inflexible adherence to the Law, his independence of party prejudices and controul, and his determination to support at the Post allotted to him the Administration of Government in all Constitutional Measures."[135]

Davis's decision was, as it happened, important to "the Administration of Government." Widespread popular resistance to the embargo continued, but even its most virulent critics acknowledged that Davis had rendered resistance, at least in Massachusetts, contrary to law. As Josiah Quincy told the federal House of Representatives in a speech bitterly attacking the validity of the embargo, he could not deny that Davis had "declared in this instance the constitutionality of the law" and that as a consequence "this law [is] obligatory upon the citizen, while it has all these sanctions. . . . The embargo laws have unquestioned sanction—they are laws of the land."[136] When the embargo was lifted, in early 1809, it was through Congress's action, not judicial command.

April 1809

The final critical decision in the twelve months under consideration was reached by James Madison, president of the United States. Madison turned fifty-seven in the spring of 1809 and could look with satisfaction at a spectacular career of public service that was by no means over. Madison was a national figure in a sense to which neither Judge Davis nor even Justice Johnson could aspire. But with such stature came a visibility that exceeded even theirs, and a month after becoming president Madison encountered a good example of the difficulties that fame can bring.

This particular difficulty—President Madison would face many during his two terms in office—had its origins in an episode of the Revolutionary War, and like the problems Johnson and Davis had wrestled with earlier, it involved a ship. In the late summer of 1778, a group of American sailors who had been impressed into the Royal Navy seized the British sloop *Active* and set sail for a New Jersey port. While the *Active* was en route, the *Convention,* a warship sailing under the authority of the Commonwealth of Pennsylvania, sighted the *Active* and compelled it to make port at Philadelphia. In a proceeding before a state court to determine to whom the proceeds of the capture belonged, four parties laid claim to the *Active:* the impressed sailors led by Gideon Olmstead, the master of the *Convention,* the commonwealth as owner of the *Convention,* and the master of *Le Gerard,* an American privateer that (its master claimed) had been sailing with the *Convention* and was entitled by prior agreement to a share in the prize. In the face of this confusion, and a jury verdict that the Olmstead party had not in fact been in complete control of the *Active* when the *Convention* overtook her, the court reached the Solomonic decision to divide the prize money into four equal parts.

Olmstead and his fellows appealed this ruling to the commission for appeals in prize cases that the Continental Congress had established and obtained a determination that they were entitled to the entire proceeds, but the state court refused to comply with the commission's decision because state law forbade appeals in such cases based on questions of fact. Eventually the commonwealth's share of the prize money ended up in the hands of the state treasurer David Rittenhouse and, after his death, of his daughters. Years later, after the ratification of the federal Constitution, Olmstead and three colleagues sought to enforce the appeals commission's judgment in federal district court and obtained a decision by Judge Richard Peters that they were entitled to the proceeds. Rittenhouse's daughters, Elizabeth Sergeant and Esther Waters, refused to obey Peters, and also ignored a resolution by the state legislature calling on them to deliver the money to the commonwealth; but when Olmstead requested that Peters enforce his judgment, the federal judge refused. As he explained in a submission to the U.S. Supreme Court, Peters did not wish to risk "embroiling" the federal and state governments by initiating a coercive process that the state authorities might resist (the state resolution instructed the governor to protect the Rittenhouses against any federal action), and declined to grant Olmstead's motion in order to bring the issue before "the superior tribunal of the United States." If the Court believed Olmstead was entitled to have Peters's judgment enforced—as Peters himself did—the Court would have the power to issue a mandamus compelling Peters to order the money seized.

In February 1809, a few weeks before Madison's inauguration, the Supreme Court unanimously ruled in Olmstead's favor.[137] Chief Justice Marshall rejected any suggestion that a state legislature could determine authoritatively that a federal district court lacked jurisdiction or interfere with the processes of federal justice, and dismissed the argument that the eleventh amendment barred Olmstead's claim.[138] It being settled law that the old appeals commission had enjoyed final authority to review state court prize decisions, Pennsylvania had no lawful claim to any of the prize money, and Olmstead was entitled to a mandamus. Any hope that the state would accept without further ado the decision of the federal "superior tribunal" quickly came to an end. On March 6, two days after Madison became president, the state legislature began consideration of ways and means to resist the Supreme Court's judgment and, more generally, to shield the state against federal interference. On April 3, the legislators adopted a resolution asserting that "as *guardians of the State rights,* they cannot permit an infringement of those rights, by an unconstitutional exercise of power in the United States' courts," and Governor Simon Snyder ordered the militia to prevent the execution of Peters's decree by force. The state militiamen repeatedly stopped the U.S. marshal from serving papers on Sergeant and Waters; the marshal in turn summoned a federal *posse comitatus* "to suppress the force and arms embodied, in opposition to the constitution," and on April 12 a federal grand jury indicted several of the militiamen. What had begun as a relatively mundane dispute over the money remaining from the sale of the *Active* three decades earlier had now escalated into a crisis threatening an armed confrontation between state and federal authorities.

Both Governor Snyder and the majority of Pennsylvania's legislators were Republicans, and the irony of being on the verge of conflict with subordinate officers of a Republican administration in Washington did not escape Snyder. Furthermore, President Madison was not just any Republican, but (as was well known) the actual author of the resolutions the Virginia legislature had adopted in 1798 denouncing the Alien and Sedition Acts as unconstitutional. Madison had then written that "the powers of the federal government . . . result[ ] from the compact to which the states are parties . . . and . . . in the case of a deliberate, palpable, and dangerous exercise of other powers, not granted by the said compact, the states who are parties thereto have the right, and are in duty bound, to interpose, for arresting the progress of the evil, and for maintaining, within their respective limits, the authorities, rights and liberties appertaining to them."[139] Pennsylvania's resolution of April 3 was modeled on Madison's handiwork, and both the resolution and the governor's subsequent deployment of the militia could be seen as the commonwealth's attempt to exercise the right and fulfill the duty Madison had identified of interposing state authority against the unconstitutional usurpation of power by the federal government, in this case by the Federalist Judge Peters and the Federalist Chief Justice Marshall at the immediate expense of Republican Pennsylvania. And Snyder could be sure that Madison was aware of the enormous importance of Pennsylvania's loyalty to a Republican administration still wrestling with widespread anger and resentment in largely Federalist New England.

On April 6, while tensions were still mounting, Snyder wrote Madison, tactfully but clearly reminding the president of the latter's association with Republican principles and Republican politics:

> I am consoled with the pleasing idea, that the chief magistracy of the Union is confided to a man who merits, and who possesses so great a portion of the esteem and the confidence of a vast majority of the citizens of the United States; who is *so* intimately acquainted with the principles of the Federal constitution, and who is no less disposed to protect the sovereignty and independence of the several states, as guaranteed to them, than to defend the rights and legitimate powers of the General Government; who will justly discriminate between opposition to the constitution and laws of the United States, and that of resisting the decree of a Judge, founded, as it is conceived, in a usurpation of power and jurisdiction, not delegated to him by either.[140]

Snyder concluded by "assur[ing]" Madison of his "fixed determination, in my public, as well as in my private capacity, to support" Madison's administration "in all the *constitutional* measures it may adopt." The threat implicit in this "assurance," written when a representative of Madison's administration was attempting to aid the federal courts in what Snyder viewed as a usurpation of power, was clear.

Snyder's letter did not specify how the governor hoped that Madison would act in order "to adjust the present unhappy collision of the two governments in such a manner as will be equally honorable to them both," but Snyder may have thought the answer was obvious. Attorney General Rodney's attack on Justice Johnson the year before had hotly denied the validity of a federal court's "taking the executive authority out of the hands of the president, and prescribing the course, which he and the agents of any department must pursue." To all appearances Rodney's views were the official position of the administration in which Madison had been secretary of state (the doubts of Gallatin and perhaps others were not publicly known), and they implied that Judge Peters could not compel the marshal to execute his decree, whatever the Supreme Court might say. If on President Madison's view of the underlying constitutional issues the courts were in error, either because the old appeals commission had exceeded its authority or because Olmstead's case ought to be barred under the eleventh amendment, he then should insist that the marshal pursue the course of action he, not Peters, prescribed. The marshal would be in jeopardy of contempt proceedings by the court, of course, but if this theory of the constitutional relationship of the executive and judiciary were correct, in principle the marshal would not be in contempt. Less extreme means of acting on Madison's independent constitutional judgment (for instance, by ordering the marshal to dismiss the *posse comitatus* and the U.S. attorney to avoid any further legal action against officers) might also be pursued.

Madison's April 13 response came by return post and was an abrupt and complete refusal to intervene on the state's behalf:

> Considering our respective relations to the subject of [Snyder's letter and the legislative resolutions that accompanied it], it would be unnecessary, if not improper, to enter into any examination of some of the questions connected with it. It is sufficient, in the actual posture of the case, to remark that the Executive of the U. States, is not only unauthorized to prevent the execution of a Decree sanctioned by the Supreme Court of the U. States, but is expressly enjoined by Statute, to carry into effect any such decree, where opposition may be made to it.[141]

Observing that the state legislature had nervously left some latitude for the governor to stand down from direct conflict with the federal government, Madison concluded that "[i]t is a propitious circumstance therefore, that whilst no legal discretion lies with the Executive of the U. States to decline steps which might lead to a very painful issue, a provision has been made by the Legislative Act transmitted by you, adequate to a removal of the existing difficulty." Madison too could veil a threat in a compliment: "And I feel great pleasure in assuring myself, that the authority which it gives will be exercised in a spirit corresponding with the patriotic character of the State over which you preside."

Snyder, then, had entirely misread Madison's position on the relationship between the judicial power of the United States and the authority of the states. Neither the theoretical origins of federal power in a compact among the states, nor the president's independent responsibility to interpret the Constitution and laws (both ideas that Madison indeed accepted) gives the president any discretion with respect to executing the judiciary's decisions. The president's only task in that regard is to ensure that final decisions of the judicial branch are effectively enforced, a duty endorsed and supported by Congress.[142] Madison therefore flatly refused to address Pennsylvania's various constitutional arguments that the federal courts were acting unconstitutionally. Whether they were was not a question within the ambit of Madison's—or Snyder's—responsibilities.

Division among leading Pennsylvania Republicans, Madison's refusal to intervene, and the federal marshal's intrepid performance of his duty (he succeeded in arresting Sergeant despite the state militiamen surrounding her house by climbing several backyard fences and sneaking in through a window) caused the state's resistance to collapse rapidly. The militia dispersed and the state's chief justice denied Sergeant's petition for habeas corpus, holding that she was lawfully in federal custody. Without the support of his own judiciary, Governor Snyder submitted and Olmstead was paid. The U.S. attorney proceeded to prosecute the militiamen and, after Madison once again refused to intervene,[143] they were convicted and sentenced to short prison terms and moderately light fines. After being assured that the militiamen were in essence the honest dupes of Snyder and his cronies, Madison pardoned them on May 6, and what the president described as "the affair of Olmstead" was over. Despite the firm stand he had taken publicly, Madison was deeply relieved that the crisis had passed "without the threatened collisions of force. It is bad eno' as it is; but a blessing compared with such a result."[144]

One question, raised publicly by the Federalist press but perhaps pondered by others including the humiliated Snyder, was whether Madison's predecessor would have given the federal courts, or rather the Federalist judges, such uncompromising support. "Had this rebellion broken out in the Presidency of Mr. Jefferson, we could not have hoped for the interference of the Executive," one paper asserted. In the first days of his retirement to Monticello, Jefferson noted this speculation anxiously and wrote Madison, perhaps in part to reas-

sure him, that he hoped no one would be troubled by such scurrilous speculation. "I trust that no section of republicans will countenance the suggestions of
the Federalists that there has ever been any difference at all in our political
principles, or any sensible one in our views of the public interests."[145] Despite
his deep suspicion of the federal judiciary, a hostility not shared by Madison,
Jefferson apparently did not disagree with Madison's (and the Federalist) understanding of the executive branch's role in enforcing the courts' administration of the rule of law. Here, as on the question of judicial review, it is
important to note the existence of widespread agreement, transcending partisan animosities, over a fundamental mechanism in the constitutional structure. With exceptions as rare in practice as they are favorite topics of
theoretical discussion, the Olmstead affair began an unbroken tradition of executive branch implementation of judicial decisions.

The year that began in May 1808 confronted Justice Johnson, Judge Davis,
and President Madison each with a conflict between conflicting interests.
Each was asked to make a decision that was likely to cause him serious personal difficulty, alienate friends and political allies, and give aid and comfort to
political forces that he believed to be deeply inimical to the welfare of the
country. Furthermore, in each case there was a perfectly plausible legal argument for taking the less difficult route. With no apparent hesitation, however,
each took the harder road of making an unpopular decision out of a sense that
it was the right one in principle.

Somewhat remarkably, these three decisions were alike not only in the integrity they demanded of Johnson, Davis, and Madison, but also in their long-
term implications for the American constitutional order. As we have seen
repeatedly, both on the federal and the state levels, the adoption of written
constitutions by no means eliminated the possibility and reality of deep political conflict. Instead, the result was often to reshape the forms of political debate into questions of constitutional interpretation without thereby preventing
that debate from incorporating the ideological and even partisan concerns of
the opposing sides. Despite the perseverance of conflict, however, in 1808 and
1809 as in 1802, we can see important indications of agreement on the structure within which constitutional argument takes place. The Republicans of
1802, however grudgingly, refused overwhelmingly to join in Senator Breckinridge's attack on judicial review. In *Gilchrist v. Collector of Charleston,* Justice
Johnson refused to permit his partisan affiliations to mute his insistence that
executive officers are generally subject to the process of the courts. In *United*

States v. The William, Judge Davis refused to permit his partisan affiliations to affect his willingness to uphold legislative and executive action. And by insisting that the Supreme Court's decision in *United States v. Peters* would be enforced, not because he thought it correct but because it is the president's duty, President Madison refused to permit his partisan affiliations to deter him from ensuring that the Court's judgment was executed.[146] American constitutional law rests on the principles embodied by these decisions and on the examples given by Johnson, Davis, and Madison of steadfast adherence to convictions about the constitutional structure.

At the beginning of this section I characterized the results of the three decisions we were to consider as both crucial and beneficial, and so I believe them to be. It cannot be denied, however, that the events of 1808 and 1809 left an unresolved ambiguity in American constitutional law. Recall Justice Johnson's words in his 1808 public statement: "every department of government must submit to [the courts'] exposition [of the laws]; for laws have no legal meaning but what is given them by the courts to whose exposition they are submitted." When we first considered this passage, I noted that its language was ambiguous—Johnson may have meant only that the other departments must submit to judicial exposition with respect to those cases that have come before the courts, in which case his point was very close to President Madison's assertion that the executive's duty is to enforce judicial decrees, not argue about them. Or did Johnson mean more broadly that a judicial exposition of the law has the same authority that people like Madison, Carrington, and Lyons accorded to settled governmental practice, that it becomes, as it were, part of the law itself, and binds everyone without regard to any particular case? The latter, presumably, cannot be so in an unrestricted sense, for in that event not even the Supreme Court itself could overrule a decision by the Court, regardless of how erroneous the decision was in principle. But even if we nuance this broader view, for example by recognizing the legitimacy of overruling precedent when it is recent, isolated, or patently wrong, a difficulty remains. If executive officers, including the president, are bound to obey and enforce judicial decisions, what institutional mechanism other than judicial self-policing is there for guarding against judicial error? Perhaps there need be none; but I cannot help but recall the urgent insistence of the Federalists of 1802, that without some external and effective means of keeping Congress within constitutional boundaries, Congress would be for all practical purposes boundless in its power. The rationale for confidence that the federal judiciary, in contrast, can be self-policing in observing the limits on its power is unclear.

PART THREE

When a vacancy on the U.S. Supreme Court occurred in 1823, Attorney General William Wirt wrote President James Monroe a letter that would have been unimaginable at an earlier time. If Monroe's first choice declined, Wirt advised, the Republican Monroe ought to appoint James Kent despite Kent's decidedly Federalist politics. "The Constitution is the public property of the United States," and not the preserve of a political party. "The people have a right to expect that the best means will be adopted to preserve it entire," including when appropriate the exercise of a deliberate disregard for partisan sentiments.[1] Monroe did not, in the end, have to decide whether to accept Wirt's counsel (his preferred nominee, Smith Thompson, belatedly agreed), but Wirt's advice was a sign of the times. The years immediately following the War of 1812 were characterized by relative constitutional harmony. The Federalists disappeared as an organized political force and constitutional discussion did not as yet ordinarily reflect the growing divergence in sectional interests between the slaveholding southern states and the free states of the north and west. (The debate in 1819 and 1820 over admission of Missouri as a slave state temporarily unmasked the constitutional aspects of sectional disagreement. This was so alarming that much of the next fifteen years' debate over constitutional matters can be seen as a successful effort to deny the fact.) Political and constitutional disagreement by no means disappeared, but they were largely uncoupled, on the national level, from partisan alignments.

A recurrent source of friction over the meaning of the federal Constitution arose out of the desire of a powerful faction to employ federal legislative power in support of commercial development. Republican nationalists such as Henry Clay and (through the mid-1820s) John C. Calhoun advocated federal "internal improvements" and other programs with this aim in mind and were opposed in turn on grounds both of policy and of constitutional legitimacy. The constitutional dimensions of the dispute were heightened by Presidents Madison and Monroe, who generally favored nationalist policies while questioning their compatibility with republican (and Republican) orthodoxy. Madison set the stage by vetoing an internal improvements bill on his last day in office; among the issues he raised was concern over how to reconcile a nationalist view of Congress's powers with the existence of judicial review of congressional legislation. (See section XII.) During Monroe's administration, opponents and advocates of internal improvements debated not only the constitutional merits of individual proposals but also the forms of argument that are necessary and appropriate in order to ensure fidelity to the Constitution. (See section XIII.) The U.S. Supreme Court's famous opinion in *M'Culloch v. Maryland* derived its original significance from this context.

Underlying this period's constitutional and political clashes was a shared vision of the states and of the United States as republican polities, domains in which the rule of law prevails. The seriousness with which presidents and congressmen debated federal internal improvements was only one of many manifestations of this vision. Beyond the structural implications of the rule of law, constitutionalists of the day were also aware of its significance for individuals. That the rule of law to which the American constitutional order is committed has as a central goal the protection of personal liberty was a commonplace, but one that Attorney General Wirt like many others took seriously. (See section XIV.) For the most part, however, participants in legal and political debate preferred to ignore the glaring contradiction between their republican orthodoxy and the continued existence of human chattel slavery. North Carolina judge Thomas Ruffin's opinion in *State v. Mann* was a notable exception: Ruffin went out of his way to underline the incompatibility of slavery with republicanism even as he protected the southern states' "peculiar institution." (See section XV.)

XII. 1817: President Madison Vetoes His Own Bill

The editors of Madison's papers term the Olmstead affair the "first public crisis" of his presidency. Madison himself provoked the last when, on the final day of his second term, he vetoed the Bonus Bill, a favorite measure of the Republican leadership in Congress. The veto dumbfounded Madison's congressional allies, who had seen the bill's passage and (as they expected) approval by Madison as a crowning achievement of his administration. Several months later Speaker of the House Henry Clay described their feelings: "no circumstance, not even an earthquake that should swallow up one half of this city, could have excited more surprise than when it was first communicated to this House, that Mr. Madison had rejected his own bill—I say his own bill."[2] Madison departed public office trailing confusion in his wake.

The roots of the Bonus Bill lay in the aftermath of the War of 1812. The story of that war lies beyond the scope of this work, but the reader should recall that it was a touch and go affair, with its nadir coming as President Madison fled Washington before British troops torched the President's House and much of the rest of the capital besides. Despite the war's many reverses, however, Americans came out of it with a surprising degree of national good will and optimism. Buoyed by the Republic's success in fighting the British Empire to what one could see as a draw, and by Andrew Jackson's great final victory outside New Orleans, the electorate sent to Washington a postwar Congress dominated by politicians whose Republican roots lay more in the unifying and democratic strands in Jeffersonian thought than in its pessimism and solicitude for state autonomy. And presiding over this wave of Republican nationalism was James Madison. Madison's first annual message of the postwar period, sent to Congress in December 1815, laid out a program of nationalist legislation that would have done credit to an early 1790s Hamiltonian. Madison called for consideration of a national bank, the creation of additional federal military academies, revision of the laws governing the militia so as to bring it more firmly under central federal control, strengthening of the navy, enactment of a protective tariff to foster American manufacturing, establishment of a national university, and the creation of a great system of roads and canals (collectively, "internal improvements") "under the national authority." In the enthusiasm of the times, few members of Congress worried much about the implications of Madison's brief reference, in proposing this last item, to the "happy reflection that any defect of constitutional authority" could be remedied through the amendment process. Speaking in March 1818, Henry St. George Tucker, the son of the famous jurist, told the House of Representatives that Madison's remarks had been "conceived to admit that Congress possessed certain powers in relation to the subject," even if Madison's language suggested that those powers were "not as extensive perhaps as the interests of the nation might require."[3]

Despite widespread participation in what Madison had lauded as "those national feelings [and] liberal sentiments. . . which contribute cement to our Union and strength to the great political fabric of which that is the foundation," the adoption of Madison's ambitious program could not be the work of a day, or even of a single congressional session. The signal legislative accomplishment of 1816, Madison's last full year in office, was the enactment in March of a statute creating the second Bank of the United States. (Congress allowed the charter of the first national bank to expire in 1811, and many people including Madison believed that the Republic's subsequent war efforts had been materially hampered by the lack of a central, nationally oriented financial institution.) A tariff act was passed the following month, but as time ran out on Madison's presidency and the Fifteenth Congress, leading Republicans in Congress focused on fulfilling his call for a system of federal internal improvements. The National Bank Act provided an answer to the crucial question of funding: the Act had required the bank's incorporators to pay a $1.5 million "bonus" to the United States as consideration for its charter, and in December 1816 Representative John C. Calhoun proposed legislation that would create from the bonus a fund for financing roads and canals in accordance with Madison's vision. Calhoun argued that the Bonus Bill was not subject to constitutional objections. The bill would be an exercise of the enumerated power to spend money and would require the consent of the states involved, thus obviating the objection that federal internal improvements would be an invasion of the states' territorial integrity. The bill was fiercely opposed by a coalition of Federalists and dissident Republicans, and it was only by small (and in the House, razor-thin) minorities that Congress passed the Bonus Bill and sent it to Madison.

The message in which Madison informed the House of Representatives of his veto presented a thoroughly Republican constitutional case against the Bonus Bill, albeit one that seemed to date from 1791 or 1798 rather than the Republican nationalism of 1817. Madison briefly ran through arguments that were almost identical to those he had mounted against the original national bank, the most basic being that "a view of the Constitution" that would find in it authorization for the Bonus Bill would, in Madison's opinion, "have the effect of giving to Congress a general power of legislation instead of the defined and limited one hitherto understood to belong to them." Since 1791, Madison had consistently adhered to the principle that an interpretation of the Constitution that left no substance to the principle that it creates a government of limited powers cannot be right. On its face, therefore, the Bonus Bill had to rest on a misinterpretation of the Constitution. To be sure, Madison had conceded with respect to the national bank that settled constitutional practice could establish the legitimacy of a particular exercise of federal power that might in the abstract seem to violate the limited-government principle. In his judgment, however, approval of the Bonus Bill on this ground would require "a reliance on insufficient precedents." For Madison, then, the bill was a test of whether postwar Republicans would remain anchored to their fundamental constitutional moorings. As Jefferson wrote approvingly of the veto a few months later, "our tenet ever was, and indeed it is almost the only landmark which now divides the federalists from the republicans, that Congress had not unlimited powers to provide for the general welfare."[4]

Madison raised an additional objection to the Bonus Bill, one that rested on the role of judicial review in the constitutional structure. His brief argument in 1817 hearkened back to a much earlier discussion in the Report of 1800 that he wrote in defense of Virginia's 1798 resolutions attacking the Alien and Sedition Acts. There Madison had criticized the Federalists' broad interpretation of Congress's powers under the necessary and proper clause as having, among its other baleful consequences, the result of necessarily excluding issues of the scope of congressional power from judicial review: if Congress "may employ all such means as . . . may have a tendency only to promote an object for which they are authorized to provide . . . everyone must perceive that questions relating to means of this sort must be questions for mere policy and expediency; on which legislative discretion alone can decide, and from which the judicial interposition and control are completely excluded." In 1817, Madison applied the same reasoning to the argument that Congress's proper objects of legislation extend to whatever will serve the common defense and general welfare.

> Such a view of the Constitution, finally, would have the effect of excluding the judicial authority of the United States from its participation in guarding the boundary between the legislative powers of the General and the State Governments, inasmuch as questions relating to the general welfare, being questions of policy and expediency, are unsusceptible of judicial cognizance and decision.

Put another way, if the constitutional measure of Congress's powers is whether an act serves the common good, there is no distinction, in cases where the constitutional issue is whether Congress has exceeded the scope of its delegated powers, between the constitutional issue and considerations that everyone would view as matters of "policy and expediency."

Two years after Madison's veto, Chief Justice John Marshall addressed the same question of the distinction between legislative and judicial judgment in

M'Culloch v. Maryland. Marshall argued that earlier doubts about the value of a national bank had disappeared: "That it is a convenient, a useful, and essential instrument in the prosecution of [the federal government's] fiscal operations, is not now a subject of controversy." Given Marshall's rejection of the old Jeffersonian argument that only absolute necessity can justify Congress's exertion of an implied power, the chief justice concluded that the universal admission of the bank's practical value in the conduct of activities clearly authorized by the Constitution left no room for judicial disagreement:

> The time has passed away, when it can be necessary to enter into any discussion, in order to prove the importance of this instrument, as a means to effect the legitimate objects of the government.
>
> But were its necessity less apparent, none can deny its being an appropriate measure; and if it is, the decree of its necessity, as has been very justly observed, is to be discussed in another place. . . . [W]here the law is not prohibited, and is really calculated to effect any of the objects intrusted to the government, to undertake here to inquire into the decree of its necessity, would be to pass the line which circumscribes the judicial department, and to tread on legislative ground. This court disclaims all pretensions to such a power.[5]

Like Judge Davis in *The William* ("I say nothing of the policy . . . . It is not within my province."), Marshall and Madison assumed that no one would assert that a court could strike down a statute out of disagreement with its policies. By triangulating *M'Culloch* with *The William* and Madison's 1817 veto message, we therefore can easily see the various conclusions they reached on the basis of this shared assumption.

(1) Marshall agreed with both Madison and Davis that courts must exercise the power of judicial review with a careful eye to questions of "place," of the locus of legitimate authority to address a given constitutional issue. All three agreed that no court can legitimately lay claim to the legislative power of determining how important or useful a law would be, or, in Marshall's language, "the degree of its necessity." (Madison noted approvingly that the Court had "justly disclaim[ed] all pretension" to "stepping on Legislative ground.") (2) Marshall and Madison agreed that claims that Congress had exceeded the scope of its powers ought to be, in our terminology, justiciable. Davis strongly suggested, without finally concluding, that they are not. (3) Marshall and Davis agreed that the Constitution authorizes Congress to enact any measures that in its judgment serve the broad purposes it entrusts to Congress (Davis: "general policy and interest"; Marshall: "[t]he sword and the purse, all the ex-

ternal relations, and no inconsiderable portion of the industry of the nation"). Madison, on the other hand, thought Congress's purposes were limited by Article I, section 8's enumeration of specific powers, because otherwise Congress would be, in effect, omnicompetent.[6]

In a letter to Spencer Roane commenting on Marshall's attempt in *M'Culloch* to combine judicial review with a broad understanding of Congress's powers, Madison returned to the separation of powers problem he thought the attempt created. The Court, he worried, had written itself out of any role in avoiding the emergence of congressional omnicompetence:

> Does not the Court also relinquish by their doctrine, all controul on the Legislative exercise of unconstitutional powers? According to that doctrine, the expediency & constitutionality of means for carrying into effect a specified Power are convertible terms; and Congress are admitted to be Judges of the expediency. The Court certainly cannot be so; a question, the moment it assumes the character of mere expediency or policy, being evidently beyond the reach of Judicial cognizance.[7]

M'Culloch, Madison acknowledged, had announced that the Court would invalidate statutes the real object of which was not within its scope, but he dismissed this as an empty reassurance. Given Marshall's "broad and pliant" understanding of Congress's legitimate purposes, "by what handle could the Court take hold of the case?" "In the great system of Political Economy having for its general object the national welfare, everything is related immediately or remotely to every other thing," and Congress would assuredly regard any law it wished to enact as a measure serving the common good. How could the Court disagree "without stepping on Legislative ground, to do which they justly disclaim all pretension."

Madison's question remains as salient as when he first wrote it—indeed, more so, for the Supreme Court has generally sided with Marshall and Davis on the scope of Congress's constitutional purposes since the beginning of the twentieth century. In *Champion v. Ames*, for example, the Court held in 1903 that the Constitution permitted Congress to ban the shipment of lottery tickets in interstate commerce despite the (entirely correct) argument of the dissenters that Congress's real interest was not in interstate commerce itself but in enforcing as far as possible its views on the morality of lotteries. While the Court subsequently undercut *Champion* in the two Child Labor cases, it did so without overruling it, and in 1941, in *United States v. Darby*, the Court returned decisively and, at least to date, finally to the nationalist position it adopted in *Champion*. Similarly, in cases involving the taxing power such as *United States v. Kahriger*, the Court has refused to invalidate federal taxes despite strong showings that Congress's actual purpose was not to raise revenue but to penalize or suppress the taxed activity. The modern Court's major spending power decisions, *United States v. Butler* and *South Dakota v. Dole*, have expressly rejected Madison's view that congressional ends are limited by the Constitution's enumeration of powers, despite the fact that both were decided by majorities rather un-nationalist by modern standards. While Madison might applaud the modern Court's insistence that it will review congressional legislation for its conformity with the limits implicit in Article I's grant of powers, he would surely worry that in doing so the Court was at serious risk of exercising a sort of judgment properly to be reserved to Congress.[8]

The problem, however, is more fundamental still: modern constitutional law is permeated by doctrines under which courts undertake to reach their own judgments about the necessity and expediency of legislation. Consider, for example, one of the most familiar modes of judicial review, strict scrutiny, employed in the context of the first amendment, the equal protection clause, and (in modified form) elsewhere. In the standard formulation, a court employing strict scrutiny demands that a law under review serve a governmental interest that—in the court's view—is "compelling" and that does so through means that—in the court's view—are "narrowly tailored" to accomplish that interest. Particularly with respect to the first, compelling interest, part of the test, it is difficult to imagine a more direct repudiation of Marshall's assertion in *M'Culloch* that "to inquire into the decree of [a law's] necessity, would be to pass the line which circumscribes the judicial department, and to tread on legislative ground."

One might respond that strict scrutiny is a judicial device employed to enforce certain express prohibitions on Congress (Davis's first category) and that the Marshall–Madison–Davis agreement concerned arguments that Congress has exceeded its powers' affirmative reach (Davis's third category). Here too, however, the modern Court does not hesitate to do what early constitutionalists would have thought it ought not. Both in the commerce clause and the fourteenth amendment areas, the Court has evolved doctrines that permit it to hold invalid congressional statutes not because they do not pursue and even, to some extent, achieve the goals of those grants of power, but because—in the Court's view—the particular activity regulated does not "affect interstate commerce sufficiently" or lacks a judicially acceptable "congruence and proportionality between the injury to be prevented or remedied and the means adopted to that end." Modern constitutional law is one long violation of the point on which President Madison, Chief Justice Marshall, and Judge Davis (author of one of the most thoughtful founding-era discussions of the issue) agreed: that questions about whether in fact a statute will actually be of service, and of enough value to warrant its enactment, to Congress's goals are entirely beyond judicial consideration.

Constitutional law, as we have already seen, is not a set of static legal propositions, and it does not follow from its variance from Madison, Marshall, and Davis that there is anything wrong with the modern Court's penchant for imposing its own judgments in what a founding-era constitutionalist might have seen as questions of expedience and necessity. At the very least, however, their views are a reminder of the connections between the Court's views on substantive constitutional matters and its understanding of the forms of argument that are permissible or not in the exercise of judicial review. An observer might well fear that in their eagerness to reach the right constitutional result, as they see it, the courts can become forgetful of "the line which circumscribes the judicial department," wherever that line is to be located.

XIII. 1818: The Congress Thinks about Internal Improvements

President Madison's veto presented the Republicans' congressional leadership, still committed to the creation of a system of federally funded internal improvements, with a difficult task. They would have to sell the program in the new Congress that would convene in December 1817, with all the political uncertainties that involved, and they would have to do so in the teeth of constitutional objections now endorsed by one of the nation's premier constitutionalists. Madison's successor, James Monroe, further complicated the problems when, in his first annual message to Congress (delivered in written form on December 2), he announced his adherence to Madison's views:

> Disregarding early impressions, I have bestowed on the subject all the deliberation which its great importance, and a just sense of my duty required, and the result is, a settled conviction in my mind, that Congress do not possess the right. It is not contained in any of the specified powers granted to Congress; nor can I consider it incidental to, or a necessary mean, viewed on the most liberal scale, for carrying into effect any of the powers which are specifically granted.[9]

Monroe acknowledged that the issue was one on which "our most enlightened and virtuous citizens" could and did disagree, and he firmly endorsed the policy of federal internal improvements, but he insisted that in "cases of doubtful construction" the proper course of action was to seek a constitutional amendment providing Congress with "an explicit grant of power."

One could hardly blame the nationalists in Congress if they had given up in despair at this point, but in the House the leadership was bold, energetic, and convinced that they were in the right on the constitutional issue. Undeterred by the political difficulties, the day after Monroe's message Speaker of the House Henry Clay stacked a select committee on the topic with nationalists and appointed as its chair Henry St. George Tucker, a lawyer (and future judge) whose abilities rivaled those of his distinguished father but whose constitutional views, at this point, were close to Clay's. Twelve days later, Tucker submitted on behalf of the committee an elaborate report, presumably his handiwork in essence, vindicating at length a measured claim for congressional authority over internal improvements. Unlike the Bonus Bill, which had authorized expenditures for roads, canals, and the improvement of natural waterways in rather general terms, the report called for federal funding of military and post roads, and canals where justified on national security grounds. In short, Tucker's committee had proposed a system more obviously and tightly related to congressional powers expressly granted in Article I, section 8.

The House was occupied with other matters for the next couple of months, including a debate over a federal bankruptcy bill that was another project of the nationalists, and it was not until March 6, 1818 that it took up the subject of Tucker's report. The debate that ensued was in many respects a recapitulation of the same arguments for and against broad construction of its authority that Congress had considered periodically since 1791. Indeed, Lemuel Sawyer (an opponent of federal internal improvements) immediately moved to avoid what he predicted would be "a tedious and useless debate":

> Does this House, said Mr. S., wish to hear long speeches? Have we not already had so many, that wearied patience had cried out, enough, enough! Every gentleman's mind had long been made up . . . on this subject. . . . [H]e did not think it necessary to prove, by argument, that the proposition was unconstitutional. To him it was a matter of faith and feeling, and in matters of faith, we may lay reason aside.[10]

Sawyer's motion was defeated, but his religious analogy proved to be prophetic: much of the 1818 debate revolved around the question of whether support for federal internal improvements involved apostasy from the true (Republican) constitutional faith.

Madison's veto message, both by its source and by its reasoning, was an implicit reminder that the Republican party's constitutional origins were rooted in opposition to the Federalist nationalism of the 1790s. The Republicans' political triumph over Federalism as a political force in Congress had been so complete that the battles of the 1790s seemed to many in 1818 rather ancient history, and the old language of opposition an unfamiliar idiom. (Speaker Clay remarked at one point that he had not even seen a copy of Madison's Virginia Report for years and had not remembered its language until an opponent of internal improvements had showed him a copy.)[11] Nonetheless, the Republican nationalists were aware of the tension between the constitutional vision underpinning their legislative program and the older Republican perspective Madison's veto reflected. Indeed, one important vehicle through which the original Republican skepticism over federal power remained alive was the work of Representative Tucker's venerable father, Judge St. George Tucker. The elder Tucker's greatest labor as professor of law at William & Mary was the preparation of an American edition of Blackstone's *Commentaries,* published in 1803. In addition to footnotes providing information about federal and Virginia law, Tucker prepared a series of appendices on various topics. One of these appendices substantially reproduced his 1795 pamphlet on slavery; among the several discussing issues of federal constitutional law was a veritable treatise of almost two hundred-fifty pages on the proper construction of the Constitution. This "American Blackstone" was widely known, both because of the practical value of its Americanizing features and because of Tucker's stature as a jurist; the reader will recall the prominent invocations in Congress of his views during the 1802 debate over repeal of the Midnight Judges Act.

Judge, or rather Professor Tucker framed his discussion of federal constitutional interpretation by analyzing the nature of the Constitution as a compact. The language of compact was common in 1790s Republican arguments: in the resolutions they anonymously drafted for the Kentucky and Virginia Resolutions, for example, Jefferson and Madison grounded a strict reading of congressional power in the Constitution's status as a compact among the states as political bodies. Tucker's 1803 publication picked up on this language and attempted to give it a more nuanced and legally precise significance. Inasmuch as it is a *federal* compact among the states, Tucker wrote, the Constitution is in essence an "alliance [or] treaty" among "sovereign and independent states," and its interpretation is to be governed by the "maxim of political law, that sovereign states cannot be deprived of any of their rights by implication."

The Constitution is also, "to a certain extent," what Tucker labeled a *social* compact imposing obligations directly on the individual citizen. But it is a *written* social compact among the citizens of "sovereign democratic sta[t]es" whose union finds its entire purpose in the protection of freedom. The legal implication of these considerations, in Tucker's judgment, could be summarized in a twofold rule of construction: "the powers delegated to the federal government, are, in all cases, to receive the most strict construction that the instrument will bear, where the rights of a state or of the people, either collectively, or individually, may be drawn in question."[12]

Republican nationalists such as Clay and the younger Tucker had no disposition to question the fundamentally libertarian cast that the latter's father ascribed to the Constitution, and they were determined, no doubt for reasons of expediency as well as principle, not to permit their opponents to seize the high ground of republicanism. On the second day of the debate, Clay tried to preempt the issue. Responding to Philip Barbour's invocation of the compact theory of the Constitution, Clay claimed that he "had imbibed his political principles from the same source as the gentleman who had last addressed the Committee [of the Whole,] the celebrated production of Mr. Madison, when a member of the Virginia Legislature, of the period of 1700 . . . from that paper, and from others of analogous principles, he had imbibed those Constitutional opinions which had influenced his political course." The disagreement over internal improvements, Clay insisted, was "not as to principles, but as to the application of them." The bedrock of the Republican constitutional stand of 1798–1800 was a commitment to constitutional freedom, both in its negative and positive forms. The threat to that freedom in 1798 was posed by "the career of a mad administration" determined "to destroy the Constitution by a plethora" (which in Clay's English was a medical term referring to an excess of fluid in the body's vessels and organs), but he "begged the gentleman . . . to reflect, that that was not the only malady by which the Constitution could be afflicted; another complaint, equally dangerous . . . was an atrophy." Precisely because the Constitution's purpose is to safeguard the people's freedom, it would be wrong to "deny to the Constitution . . . that vigor which is necessary, in the exercise of its powers, to fulfil the purposes of its institution."

Clay therefore proposed a twofold rule of construction that implicitly amended Judge Tucker's 1803 version:

> In expounding the instrument, he said, constructions unfavorable to personal freedom, or those which might lead to great abuse, ought to be carefully avoided. But if, on the contrary, the construction insisted upon was, in

140

all its effects and consequences, beneficent; if it were free from the danger
of abuse; if it promoted and advanced all the great objects which led to the
confederacy; if it materially tended to effect the greatest of all those objects—the cementing of the Union, the construction was recommended
by the most favorable considerations.[13]

Federal power, in short, can be the servant of constitutional freedom as well as
its enemy, and the Constitution ought to be interpreted with that Republican
truth in mind. "[I]ngenuity in frittering away the Constitution is not consistent," Clay said, "with my idea of the great principles of 1798, in which I profess implicitly to confide."[14]

Clay's attempt to appropriate the legacy of the Republican struggle
against the Alien and Sedition Acts did not go unnoticed by the Republican
opponents of federal internal improvements. To judge by the nationalists' reactions, the most vigorous attack on their Republican bona fides came from
Hugh Nelson of Virginia. Because Nelson's speech was not recorded for some
reason,[15] we are dependent on nationalist paraphrases of his remarks, but we
can sketch an outline of his claims. Nelson apparently directly attacked Clay's
purported faithfulness to "the republican doctrines of 1798" as a sham. In the
name of those principles, he "sound[ed] the alarm, and invite[d]" all true Republicans "to the last battle for State rights." As other Virginian representatives put it, Nelson "proclaim[ed] the sovereignty of the States to be in danger
of invasion; nay, more, of actual subversion." "It is in the last of their fields
that the liberties of the States are to be cloven down, and the Federal Government is to triumph over them." Only a narrow or strict construction of congressional power could save the Constitution.[16] Disapproval of the internal
improvements bill recommended by Representative Tucker's committee, in
short, was to be the litmus test for Republican orthodoxy.

Tucker himself was stung by Nelson's charge of apostasy into responding,
which he did on several levels. Tucker amplified Clay's earlier denial that Republican (or republican) principles required a consistent opposition to congressional power. "In the construction of this Constitution, there is not, there
cannot be a system of orthodoxy" defined by a predisposition for or against
the legitimacy of federal legislation. "Agreeing, as we do, in principle, there
must always be a variety in the application." Even more fundamentally, Nelson's elevation of "strict construction" into an algorithm for the solution of
constitutional problems mistook the very nature of constitutional argument:

> Will gentlemen attempt to bring into the discussion of a question like this,
> the principles of mathematical science, or the attenuated logic of meta-

physics? The subject does not admit of it. You cannot lay down the principles of Government with mathematical exactness. . . . No, sir, it is not a mathematical, it is a moral certainty, that we are to expect on these great questions of political right.[17]

Nelson's attempt to define Republican orthodoxy thus was a vain and arrogant effort to avoid the difficult questions of judgment that can sometimes attend the interpretation and application of a written Constitution—vain in that the disagreements among opponents of internal improvements proved that their vaunted strict constructionism yielded no certainty ("Sir," Tucker sardonically asked, "with these [disagreements] before your eyes, who shall pretend to say what is orthodoxy—what is heterodoxy?"); arrogant in that his refusal to accord any weight to the long history of giving liberal readings to Congress's powers when exercised in a benign fashion amounted to a rejection of the legislative "buoys which the wisdom of the nation has fixed."

The day after Tucker spoke, James Pindall (like Tucker one of the minority of Virginia's representatives who favored federal internal improvements) invoked the elder Tucker's reasoning, though not his name, in defense of Congress's power. Both sides in the debate, Pindall noted, tended in their arguments to simplify a Constitution that Tucker's analysis showed to be complex in its nature:

> Whilst those who affirm our power to construct roads consider the Constitution as a modification of social compact, defining and conferring legislative powers; gentlemen on the other side, who deny the power in question, seem to be out of humor whenever the instrument is viewed in any other than its federative character, or as an international convention, to be construed as a Treaty between independent Powers.

In fact, as Judge Tucker's treatise noted, the Constitution "is a compact both social and federal in its character," and by the same logic that derived a strict rule of construction from its federal aspects Pindall argued that "provisions [that are] clauses of a social compact" ought to receive a different and more lenient interpretation. (The implication, of course, was that internal improvements could be based on such provisions.) However, Pindall waived that point and conceded for the sake of argument that the question should be tested by rules of construction premised on a view of the Constitution "as a mere federative instrument, or treaty."[18]

Treaty provisions providing for "the equal and common advantage of all the parties," Pindall correctly asserted, are to be interpreted broadly according to the leading international law authority Emerich de Vattel:[19] "conceiving that national improvements tend to the benefit of all, I yield my assent to those who liberally expound our great charter" on that subject. In addition, contrary to Barbour's and Nelson's claims that earlier Congresses' broad interpretations of Article I, section 8 had no precedential authority, according to Pindall international law clearly ordained the contrary view. Because a treaty's language is to be construed in accordance with the common meaning of its terms at the time the treaty was concluded, "the contemporaneous acts of those concerned, and . . . early acts and interpretations by those who lived and acted in times less remote than ourselves from the origin of the treaty" are of great interpretive value. Because a treaty is contractual in nature, later "acts of construction acquiesced in by the parties" are probative evidence of the high contracting powers' understanding of their compact. The extensive list of "legislative precedents and official executive opinions" that Representative Tucker's committee report had cited were therefore in themselves proof that Congress possesses the power in question. Even approached from the opposition's favored perspective, therefore, the Constitution plainly authorized Congress to enact a system of internal improvements, and their attack on the validity of such a system rested not on Judge Tucker's neutral standards of interpretation but on the raked-over coals of a long-dead dispute found in "the annals of contending factions."[20]

Late in the debate, the House agreed to replace Tucker's limited committee resolution with a series of four resolutions that would permit it to gauge more precisely the members' constitutional views. Three of the four referred to a congressional power "to construct," respectively, post and military roads, canals for interstate commerce, and canals for military purposes, in each case with a proviso that just compensation be paid for any private property taken for these purposes. The first resolution, however, resolved "That Congress has power, under the Constitution, to appropriate money for the construction of post roads, military, and other roads, and of canals, and for the improvement of water-courses."[21] This wording was (no doubt deliberately) ambiguous. On the one hand the insertion of the reference to appropriating money could be seen as limiting Congress in some fashion to funding projects that it might not be able to undertake directly. As an interpretation of the scope of Congress's power, that position was later to prove attractive to President Monroe among others, although as we have seen Madison had rejected it as a meaningless limitation on Congress in his 1817 veto message. On the other hand, the resolution approved federal expenditures on roads, canals, and waterways without limiting them to improvements serving military, post, or interstate commerce purposes. When Joseph Desha, a moderate supporter of federal internal improvements, suggested that the resolution be amended to strike the reference to *other* roads, William Lowndes successfully opposed him, arguing that the House ought to be allowed "to vote on the broad proposition,"[22] and an 1819 debate in the House suggests that the resolution's supporters did not see confining Congress to appropriating money as especially limiting.[23]

Perhaps because the first resolution meant different things to different members, the House approved it by a considerable margin, while the other three resolutions failed to win a majority.[24] The Republican nationalists had triumphed, but the meaning of their victory was equivocal at best. The Fifteenth Congress passed no legislation clearly resting on a broad construction of Congress's power, and the subsequent history of the issue saw the nationalists in Congress and in Monroe's cabinet repeatedly fumble their intermittent political opportunities to enact their vision. In 1822, Congress and the president replicated the political snarl-up of 1817, with the legislature passing and Monroe vetoing on constitutional grounds a modest proposal to keep up an existing national road even though Monroe in the meantime had come to agree that Congress could use its spending power to fund internal improvements. Thereafter most arguments over particular internal improvements proposals concerned their national value—and their economic impact on the localities concerned—rather than the constitutional issues. It was political and social change, not constitutional scruples, that ultimately derailed the nationalist vision of Clay, Tucker, and Calhoun, a process symbolized by Calhoun's conversion to an extreme states rights view of the Constitution irreconcilable with his earlier convictions but politically expedient in an era of increasing sectional discord.

The impulse to structure constitutional discussion in some more or less algorithmic form—canons of construction, standards of interpretation, doctrines—is, I think, both unavoidable and problematic. As we have seen repeatedly, not even the most fervent commitment to close textual analysis in constitutional debate can overcome the text's ambiguities and silences. The accumulation of a history of political practice and judicial precedent is accompanied by the felt need to discern patterns in the materials relevant to the debate. The twofold canon of interpretation that the elder Tucker proposed in 1803 was his attempt to encapsulate, in a form useful in future interpretive debates, over a decade of Republican constitutional thought: the suspicion of power evident in Jefferson's 1791 bank opinion, the image of the Constitution as a compact among sovereign states, the strongly libertarian cast of the Re-

publican attack on the Alien and Sedition Acts of 1798. The Republican nationalists of 1818 were equally intent on making sense of the constitutional
authorities of their day, which included Tucker himself and the old Republican wisdom he summarized but encompassed as well almost two decades of
Republican rule. Their response was to seek the continuity in principle between their expansive nationalism and Tucker's defensive Jeffersonianism,
and they located that continuity in two places—a shared commitment to the
Constitution as oriented toward "freedom," and a history of constitutional ex-
perimentation in which uses of federal power that Tucker would have feared
inimical to liberty had proven benign.

To serve "the genuine principles of DEMOCRACY" that Tucker identified in
1803 as the Constitution's animating purpose,[25] the nationalists of 1818
thought it necessary to revise the specific structure of interpretation that he
had formulated, incorporating the lesson of history that democratic liberty
can be served as well as threatened by the exercise of national power. "If there
should ever be a construction of the Constitution dangerous to liberty," a
nationalist House committee reported in 1822, "there will be an apology for
repeated resistance," but "when there has been a series of legislation in pur-
suance of a construction of the Constitution which is calculated to promote
the best interests of the country, it is not consistent with wisdom, or the peace
and welfare of society, to disturb it."[26] The doctrines or canons of interpretation that shape constitutional discussion must evolve if they are to make sense
of the ongoing history of constitutional government. At one point during the
1818 debate, the younger Tucker asked in exasperation if the opponents of internal improvements thought constitutional discussion must always start with
a interpretive clean slate:

> Do gentlemen suppose that if, which Heaven permit! this confederation of
> States shall last for a century, we shall, throughout that period, be continu-
> ally mooting Constitutional points; holding nothing as decided; admitting
> no construction to have been agreed upon; and, instead of going on with
> the business of the nation, continually occupied with fighting, over and
> over again, battles a thousand times won?[27]

Representative Tucker's lament is understandable, but in one sense the
answer to his question cannot be other than yes, we do continually moot constitutional points, even at times ones that seemed settled. Doctrine and precedent, no matter how long established, are not text; in a system resting on a
written Constitution there is no principled way to reject out of hand an argument that settled interpretive points have been settled in error. The Republi-

can nationalists' concession that constructions "dangerous to liberty" ought to be challenged was an implicit acknowledgment that even a strong commitment to stare decisis, whether with respect to practice or judicial precedent or both, must be balanced against the possibility that allegiance to practice and precedent can threaten the fundamental nature of the Constitution. Constitutional debate as the founding generation and its successors have practiced it would be unworkable without the creation of canons and doctrines and other conceptual tools for shaping the issues, but it would lose its mooring in the written Constitution if the distinction between doctrine and precedent (however venerable) and the Constitution "itself" were entirely elided.

XIV. 1821: The Attorney General and the Rule of Law

William Wirt was one of the greatest public lawyers of the early Republic. As a young Republican lawyer he was a member of the defense team representing the defendant in a notorious Sedition Act prosecution, *United States v. Callender,* and later sat at the opposite table as one of the prosecutors in *United States v. Burr.*[28] In later years he served briefly as U.S. attorney in Virginia and then for almost twelve years (1817–1829) as attorney general of the United States, the longest period anyone has held that office. Wirt did as much to shape the position of attorney general as anyone before or since, and long enjoyed a reputation, as an early-twentieth-century court put it, as a "learned . . . great and able lawyer."[29] One of Wirt's central accomplishments was his regularization of the attorney general's role as the executive branch's chief interpreter of the law. Under the Judiciary Act of 1789, which created the office, the attorney general had only two duties: "to prosecute and conduct all suits in the Supreme Court, in which the United States shall be concerned, and to give his advice and opinion upon questions of law when required by the President of the United States, or when requested by the heads of any of the departments, touching any matters that may concern their departments." Upon his appointment, Wirt discovered that his predecessors had been in the habit of responding, apparently in their official capacity, to requests for legal advice from the houses of Congress and even private individuals. Perhaps out of the same sense of informality that led them to ignore the Judiciary Act's description of their duties in that regard, they had kept no records of the advice they had given, rendering impossible any continuity in the legal views of the office of attorney general across changes in that officer's identity.

Wirt quickly set about to change all this. In very early opinions he declined requests for advice from private citizens and federal government employees "simply on the ground that I have no legal authority to answer [them] officially," and in 1820 he informed the House of Representatives that the same lack of authority exempted him from responding to the House's request for a legal opinion. Wirt did not believe himself bound by the contrary practice ascribed to earlier attorneys general: "my predecessors in office have left nothing for my guidance; and I am constrained, therefore, to act on my own construction of the law as it stands."[30] Determined not to repeat their mistake, and by avoiding it to give dignity and consistency to the legal views of the attorney general, Wirt kept careful records of all his official acts. The extraordinary length of his tenure meant that by the time he left office, Wirt had created a significant body of executive-branch precedent in many areas of public law, including the law of the Constitution. The underlying perspective from which Wirt wrote his opinions was that of a moderately nationalist Republican. By temperament and personal associations Wirt was opposed to divisive invocations of "the principles of 1798," but at the same time he was committed to a "republican orthodoxy" requiring scrupulous observance of legal norms—a sort of Jeffersonian textualism without Jefferson's paranoia over public power: "in a government purely of laws, no officer should be permitted to stretch his authority and carry the influence of his office beyond the circle which the positive law has drawn around him."[31] The result was a body of opinions that sketched out a remarkably apt portrait of the mindset of public lawyers in his generation.

What Wirt called "republican orthodoxy" depends on the will of legal actors to act in ways faithful to the text(s) of the law. Early in his time as attorney general, Wirt encountered what he found a disturbing example of the difficulties attendant on acting in that manner. The issue arose from a request by the House of Representatives that, pursuant to his duties under the Judiciary Act, Wirt argue the case of *Anderson v. Dunn* in the Supreme Court.[32] Thomas Dunn was the sergeant-at-arms of the House and at the House's direction had arrested John Anderson for allegedly acting in contempt of the House. (Anderson's offense was that he attempted to bribe a member of the House to help him obtain congressional approval of financial claims against the United States.) The House found Anderson guilty of the contempt, sentenced him to a verbal reprimand by Speaker Clay (perhaps a weightier punishment than it might appear at first, given Clay's verbal skills), and ordered Dunn to release him. Anderson then brought a tort action against Dunn in the federal circuit court in the District of Columbia, claiming that the House had no lawful authority to order Dunn to assault and detain him. In anticipation that the case would be heard eventually by the high Court, Clay asked Wirt to be prepared to argue it in that forum.

In his letter in response, Wirt asked Clay if the latter had considered the question whether representing Dunn would fall within the terms of the Judiciary Act, which required the attorney general to argue cases "in which the United States shall be concerned." But was "the United States . . . concerned" in *Anderson v. Dunn?* The government of the United States, Wirt pointed out, is not a unitary, hierarchical entity, but rather a set of institutions with interests and concerns that can and sometimes do conflict:

> Suppose a collision of authority between the Senate and House of Representatives, in the persons of their officers; which of them must I regard as the United States, so as to be bound officially to appear for them? Suppose such a collision between any other two departments of the General Government: could either of them be considered as more the United States than the other?[33]

Wirt did not question that *the House* had a stake in the outcome of Anderson's legal action, or that it was in any way improper for the House to seek to vindicate its authority, theoretically and practically, by successfully defending its officer against legal liability. Wirt was completely willing to represent Dunn for the House; the question was whether he could do so *as the attorney general,* speaking for the interests of the United States.

The correct answer to that question was complicated still further for Wirt by Anderson's claim that the House's actions had transcended its authority under the Constitution. Anderson, in other words, was invoking the citizen's right to challenge the constitutionality of governmental action that Republicans such as Wirt had trumpeted during the Sedition Act crisis. As Judge Roane had said long before in *Kamper v. Hawkins,* when a court hears such a claim the people and their government are, at least potentially, arrayed on opposite sides. The same logic, Wirt noted, applied in *Anderson v. Dunn* as well: "I confess that, in a question which is made one of unconstitutional oppression between an individual and the House of Representatives singly, I cannot discern very distinctly how the United States at large can be said to be more concerned on the one side than on the other." The "United States at large"—and, one might almost say, the constitutional system of government—is as much concerned with the liberties of the individual as the powers of its institutions.

We do not know, unfortunately, whether Clay was persuaded by Wirt or for some other reason declined to press the issue, but in the end Wirt represented

Dunn in his private capacity. (In the early Republic the attorney general was not the head of an executive department and was expected to supplement his salary with an outside private practice. The House paid Wirt a fee for arguing *Anderson v. Dunn* in the Supreme Court.) Like his letter to Clay, Wirt's argument to the Court relied heavily on the duty of governmental actors to remain within their legally ordained spheres. The only question before the Supreme Court was whether the House had the lawful authority to punish contempts, a power he believed it clearly possessed for several reasons, including its constitutional responsibility for impeachment. Once it had answered that question in the affirmative, Wirt and his co-counsel Walter Jones informed the Court, its powers ceased: the legislative power of contempt was exclusive of any other and thus placed a legal limit on the judicial power to adjudicate cases of assault and battery. The Court accepted their definition of the issue presented and reversed the circuit court.[34]

Wirt's brief letter to Clay raised many important questions that he had no need to resolve. Perhaps most obvious are the separation of powers issues lurking underneath the surface of statutory construction. Nothing in Wirt's letter intimates that Congress lacked the power to require the attorney general to represent the House (or Senate) in similar litigation with a private party. His point was that Congress had not done so, at least not with sufficient clarity to make him comfortable assuming the role. But what about conflict between Congress, or a house of Congress, and the executive branch? The implications of Wirt's reasoning, which differentiated the interests of federal governmental institutions from those of the government or the United States at large, but accepted the legitimacy of the individual institutions seeking to vindicate those interests, are unclear. Wirt had a genuine and far-reaching respect for congressional authority. In 1823, for example, he advised the president that the latter could not himself exercise powers vested by statute in a subordinate officer even when the latter fails to carry out an affirmative duty. The president's only recourse is to replace the malfeasant subordinate with a different individual who will carry out his duties.[35] At the same time Wirt's insistence that an executive officer limit his or her official actions to the area within "the circle which the positive law has drawn around him" commands obedience to the law, not Congress. In modern times the executive branch has repeatedly asserted the authority to disregard or to decline to defend in court congressional acts that it deems unconstitutional, and in turn scholars and members of Congress have denounced this as a dereliction of the president's duty to take care that the laws are faithfully executed. Which is the course of duty—obedience to the clear statutory command of Congress, or to the executive's independent and contrary understanding of what will often be the ambiguous command of the Constitution?

Perhaps more fundamental in its implications is Wirt's intimation that one ought to consider individual liberty one of the interests of the United States that can be at stake in litigation. Many modern constitutional doctrines, strict scrutiny in first amendment and equal protection cases being a good example, ask courts to consider the nature and weightiness of the governmental interest in undertaking actions that are on their face constitutionally problematic. Wirt's letter suggests that the usual understanding of that inquiry is too narrow and institutionally focused. The concerns of the United States, according to Wirt, do not lie solely with the wishes or even the well-being of its governmental structures, but are directly involved in an individual's claim of unconstitutional oppression.[36]

XV. 1829: Writing *State v. Mann*

Next to the infamous Dred Scott case, *State v. Mann* is probably the best known American judicial decision involving the institution of slavery. The decision's prominence during the antebellum period was due in part to the fact that the author of the North Carolina Supreme Court's opinion, Thomas Ruffin, was a judge with a national reputation. Beginning at an early point, however, Ruffin's opinion in *Mann* began to attract attention for its language and what that language revealed about slavery as well as the author. In 1853, for example, the great abolitionist Harriet Beecher Stowe wrote that "[n]o one can read this decision, so fine and clear in expression, so dignified and solemn in its earnestness, and so dreadful in its results, without feeling at once deep respect for the man and horror for the system."[37] Ruffin did not achieve these effects without effort. By chance three drafts of his opinion survive, and a comparison of them sheds important light on the final product and on Ruffin's thinking about the place of slavery in an American constitutional order.[38]

State v. Mann was a criminal prosecution for assault and battery allegedly committed on a slave woman named Lydia. John Mann hired Lydia and her services from Elizabeth Jones for a period of one year, during which time Lydia angered him through what the state supreme court reporter called "some small offense." When Mann attempted to "chastise" her (presumably by some type of physical punishment), Lydia "ran off, whereupon the defendant called upon her to stop, which being refused, he shot at and wounded her."[39] The state then prosecuted Mann for a cruel and unreasonable battery. In North Carolina, it was settled law in 1829 that a criminal indictment would lie for an unjustified assault upon a slave by a white person other than the slave's owner. In an 1823 case, *State v. Hale,* Chief Justice John Louis Taylor had observed that this rule was strongly supported by "usage. . . the repeated conviction and punishment of persons charged with this offence" and was an appropriate reflection of "the humanity of our laws."[40] Joseph J. Daniel, the judge who presided at Mann's trial, relied on *Hale* in instructing the jury that if Mann's conduct "was cruel and unwarrantable, and disproportionate to the offense committed by" Lydia, he was guilty because "he had only a special property in her." The jury convicted Mann and the latter appealed. Before the state supreme court, North Carolina attorney general Romulus M. Saunders insisted that the case was governed by *State v. Hale* and that the evidence of Mann's use of a weapon "calculated to produce death" clearly warranted the jury's verdict.

Ruffin seems to have had little trouble reaching the conclusion that the judgment below had to be reversed. From his first draft on he acknowledged the authority of *Hale* while insisting that *Hale* was not controlling under the facts. Mann was not a legal stranger to Lydia—the situation covered by *Hale*—but entitled to "possession and command" of her during the period of his lease, and "in reference to all other persons but the general owner, the hirer and possessor of a slave, in relation to both rights and duties, is, for the time being, the owner." Judge Daniel had erred therefore in relying on *Hale,* and Mann's liability to criminal prosecution could not rest on the fact that his property interest in Lydia was a limited one. However, Attorney General Saunders, perhaps anticipating that the supreme court would distinguish *Hale,* had presented a distinct basis on which the court could affirm Mann's conviction: the master–slave relationship, he argued, was analogous to other asymmetrical legal relationships—parent–child, master–apprentice, teacher–student—and under the legal principles governing such relationships the superior is criminally liable for the infliction of disproportionate and unjustifiably harsh punishment. Slavery does not lie outside the world of law, but like all social relationships recognized by the law, it is subject to legal definition and to limitations on the discretion of the parties involved in the interests of society, including its interest in protecting persons who are vulnerable because they occupy positions of legal inferiority.

Most of Ruffin's final opinion, and most of the energy he expended in writing and revising the opinion, were directed toward the fundamental issue the attorney general's argument had raised: What is the relationship between the institution of slavery and a constitutional order ordaining the rule of law? The heart of Ruffin's answer was that slavery and the rule of law are fundamentally irreconcilable, that slavery requires for its maintenance and economic value a relationship between master and slave that cannot be shaped in any meaningful way by legal principles. Law can provide an external definition to the situations in which that relationship will be deemed to exist (affirmatively with respect to a hirer like Mann, negatively with respect to a legal stranger as in *Hale*) but, in the absence of an act of political will by the legislature, the internal shape of that relationship is beyond legal control. The North Carolina rule that a master could not take the life of his or her slave, which Ruffin did not purport to change, was only an apparent exception, being more in the nature of another external limitation to the sphere of that which is legally ungovernable.

Ruffin's successive drafts reveal the care with which he prepared an opinion that would present his conclusion in the starkest possible light. The first draft reads much like the slavery opinions of other judges of the period, Chief Justice Taylor's in *State v. Hale* being a good example, in that it labored to excuse and explain North Carolina law and society and, of course, the court and its members. A decision on such an issue, Ruffin began the draft, left a judge regretful that the decision had to be made at all, and torn between "principles of policy [and] the feelings of the man." However strong those feelings, however, in his official capacity a judge must act according to principles and policy, and so Ruffin concluded the paragraph with a thumbnail sketch of the considerations the court had to take into account, all of them sensible, even honorable bases for a decision that on first appearances he knew to be harsh and inhuman:

> Courts are obliged, however reluctantly, to recognize the rights of the owner to full dominion over the Slave, as essential to their value as property, to the public peace as dependent upon their subordination, and, indeed, while slavery in its present form shall continue to exist, as most effectually securing the general protection and comfort of the slave himself.

A fair-minded reader, the first draft suggested, would sympathize with the court's emotional discomfort with the decision while recognizing the importance of the decision's objectives, which were, in a rising crescendo of importance, the protection of economic values (stated abstractly and thus without

152

emphasizing the slaveholder's personal, selfish interests), social peace, and (above all) the slave herself.

Over the next two drafts, Ruffin completely reworked the opinion's first paragraph, transforming its tone and, in the process, the emotional impact of the opinion as a whole. He retained versions of what were originally the first two sentences (about regretting the need to decide and the fissure between principles and feelings) but split them apart. In the later drafts, the judge's lament over the case being brought at all was attributed not to his own moral or emotional qualms but to a quite different concern, his realization that many of his readers would see only the decision's harshness, and not the reasons for it:

> A judge cannot but lament when such cases as the present are brought into judgment. It is impossible that the reasons on which they go can be appreciated, but where institutions similar to our own exist and are thoroughly understood.

The long-standing commitment of the common-law judge to explain the reasons for a decision—a commitment the rough draft's beginning implicitly promised to carry out—was now disavowed as in principle hopeless. Slavery, we will realize by the time we have finished what these words begin, is so wholly beyond the world of constitutional and legal reason and order that one cannot even talk about it successfully in the terms of that world. Only the brutal facts of personal experience with it can render it comprehensible.

Such experience did not eliminate "the feelings of the man," to be sure, and Ruffin permitted himself in the later drafts to retain and even strengthen his claim to be emotionally torn over the decision. But he followed this claim with two new sentences depreciating the significance of his feelings: "It is *useless . . .* to complain of things inherent in our political state [and] *criminal . . .* to avoid any responsibility." Whatever the result in terms of external criticism or internal discomfort, a decision in the matter was the court's duty. Strikingly, by the third and final draft, Ruffin had moved the first draft's summary of the (good) reasons for the decision to the end of his opinion. What was originally introduced as an opinion about "the *rights* of the owner" that are "essential" to social order and indeed to the well-being of the slaves themselves, and even in the second draft was labeled an opinion about a "rule" relating to a "dominion of the Master, which is necessary" to fulfil the goals of "our law," had become in the final draft a flat statement about social reality, a virtual confession of "the extent of the dominion of the master over the slave in North Carolina." The rationale for the court's ruling, relocated to the end of the opinion, is almost an afterthought, and one that made no pretense of talking about anyone's rights. *State v. Mann* was not in the end about law, but about the necessary lawlessness at the heart of North Carolina society.

Ruffin's reworking of his original opening paragraph is illustrative of the other changes he made to the opinion in the later drafts. Throughout his effort was to eliminate anything that appeared to excuse or palliate the harshness of the court's ruling or of the institution that the court was upholding. Many of the edits are subtle. In a passage at the end of the opinion Ruffin described the social forces at work to ameliorate the inhumanity of slavery; in the second draft he had inserted here a motivation absent from the rough draft—"the private interest of the owner," and by the final draft Ruffin had made selfish interest the rhetorical key to social change—the owner's interest is "that all-powerful motive" at work. A central and much larger edit occurred in the second draft when Ruffin inserted a lengthy new discussion, entirely absent from the rough draft, responding to the question whether the court's ruling would not leave beyond punishment and thus beyond social control cruel mistreatment that on no fair view could be seen as necessary to the preservation of the master's authority. Ruffin's answer was a brutal yes:

> That there may be particular instances of cruelty and deliberate barbarity where, in conscience, the law might properly interfere, is most probable. The difficulty is to determine where a Court may properly begin. Merely in the abstract it may well be asked, which power of the master accords with right? The answer will probably sweep away all of them. But we cannot look at the matter in that light. The truth is that we are forbidden to enter upon a train of general reasoning on the subject. We cannot allow the right of the master to be brought into discussion in courts of justice.

The irony of referring to something as a "right" that neither accords with (true) right nor can even be discussed in a court of justice is underlined by a passage Ruffin included in the final draft. Where the second draft had spoken vaguely of the "danger" inherent in permitting a court to second-guess a master's decisions about the degree of punishment necessary, the final version laid the problem squarely at the feet of the slaveholder himself:

> No man can anticipate the many and aggravated provocations of the master which the slave would be constantly stimulated, by his own passions or the instigation of others, to give; or the consequent wrath of the master, prompting him to bloody vengeance upon the turbulent traitor—a vengeance generally practiced with impunity by reason of its privacy.

The master–slave relationship was of necessity a bloody tyranny, different only in scope from the most brutal of Old World dictatorships. It bore no resemblance whatever to the republican and constitutional legal order in which it was embedded in 1829 North Carolina. And that the reader should not overlook the enormous self-contradiction slavery posed in that legal order, Ruffin closed the passage just quoted with the following: "The Court, therefore, disclaims the power of changing the relation in which these parts of our people stand to each other."[41]

These parts of our people . . . . Ruffin had referred earlier in the opinion to the master's authority over the slave's body as "the curse of slavery to both the bond and free portion of our population." The earlier phrase is striking in its rhetorical inclusivity: slaves and slaveholders alike belong to "our population." The noun "population," however, might seem to maintain a certain ambiguity about what it is that the bond and the free share. Ruffin's later formulation is breathtaking in its simplicity and power: slavery is a relationship that exists between parts of the same *people*. This is the language of American constitution-making. Our people are the collective body politic that creates the legal order—We the people. The reader will recall Chief Justice Jay's comment in his opinion in *Chisholm v. Georgia:* "at the Revolution, the sovereignty devolved on the people; and they are truly the sovereigns of the country, but they are sovereigns without subjects (unless the African slaves among us may be so called) and have none to govern but themselves; the citizens of America are equal as fellow citizens, and as joint tenants in the sovereignty."[42] In *State v. Mann,* Ruffin collapsed the distinction that Jay tentatively posited in *Chisholm:* North Carolina's slaves are not "Africans . . . among us," but part of us and thus, in principle, sharers in the sovereignty that American independence conferred on the people.

It is impossible at this remove to determine Ruffin's exact purposes in crafting an opinion so damning of the institution it was upholding. His goal certainly was not to argue, in any direct sense, for the abolition of slavery; indeed, Ruffin's opinions, taken as a whole, rested on "a doctrine of stern necessity" in construing the legal limits and ramifications of slavery that "requir[ed] an unflinching, conscious disregard of natural justice" and led him to narrow views of, for example, the private right of emancipation.[43] More generally, Ruffin's opinions display no great sympathy for slaves or for African Americans. But at the same time Ruffin was unwilling to pretend that the customs necessary to the maintenance of slavery could be assimilated to the ordered social world of republican freedom and the rule of law. Twenty years after *Mann,* Ruffin denied that slavery bore any resemblance to the common-law traditions of that world: "[t]here is nothing analogous to it." Instead, the customs of slavery "must necessarily modify the rules of law" in order that the law not interfere with the existing relationship of "the two classes and races of our people":

> Such are the habits of the country. It is not now the question, whether these things are naturally right and proper to exist. They do exist actually, legally, and inveterately. Indeed, they are inseparable from the state of slavery; and are only to be deemed wrong upon the admission that slavery is fundamentally wrong.[44]

No one who has read *State v. Mann* can doubt Thomas Ruffin's private opinion on whether the "things" of slavery were "naturally right and proper."

Ruffin's rhetorical insistence that North Carolina's slaves were part of the people of North Carolina ran contrary to the dominant political and social sentiment of the time. Only a few years later, a state constitutional convention voted, by a slim majority to be sure, to abrogate the then-existing voting rights of *free* African American men over the objections of Ruffin's colleague William Gaston that African Americans "are part of the body politic."[45] To a majority of the 1835 convention delegates, Africans were strangers to the constitutional system regardless of their status as free or slave.

State v. Mann is not usually understood as a constitutional case, but I believe that its value in reflecting on American constitutionalism is profound. Let us begin with the aspect of Ruffin's opinion that led Harriet Beecher Stowe to admire it and him—Ruffin's candor. Ruffin makes little pretense that the institution of slavery is in any sense beneficial for the slave. In a passage dismissing as foolish the notion that there are any "moral considerations" that could lead a slave to obey his or her master, Ruffin added in his final draft the sardonic observation that it "can never be true" that the slave labors "for the sake of his own personal happiness." If we are to have the institution, he implied, let us at least be clear-sighted and honest about what it is. In this regard, we should emulate Ruffin. A willingness to be realistic and truthful, both about the world in which constitutional norms are to be applied and about their impact on that world, ought to be seen as a fundamental duty of the interpreter. The temptations to shirk this duty are strong. It is often difficult to know exactly how the social world and constitutional arguments intersect, and correspondingly easy to build arguments on premises the empirical validity of which is questionable. But a constitutionalism that is to be worthy of its claims to "establish Justice . . . and secure the Blessings of Liberty" cannot rest on ideological slogans or comfortable fictions. The care with which Ruffin wrote and rewrote his opinion in *State v. Mann* stands in sharp contrast to the practice of most contemporary appellate judges, whose opinions are primarily the product of law clerks and, especially on the Supreme Court, are in large measure a patchwork of quotations from earlier judicial opinions.

In another respect, Ruffin is an object lesson in how not to do law, and especially constitutional law. In crafting a rhetorically and emotionally compelling indictment of slavery, Ruffin created a judicial masterpiece that can almost lead the reader to forget that the decision in *State v. Mann* undergirded if it did not increase the horrors of slavery. Ruffin's great object lesson in the incompatibility of slavery with an American constitutional order was written on the back of Lydia and all of the other North Carolina slaves to whom Ruffin said that no brutality, no matter how egregious even in the eyes of a slaveholding society, could provoke a legal response as long as the master stopped short of murder. There was nothing predetermined about that conclusion. Ruffin and his colleagues were under no obligation of faithfulness to a document or tradition that required them to announce so brutal a rule. It was, rather, a choice.

State v. Mann presents in stark form a recurrent issue in American constitutional law: To what extent do American constitutional provisions assume the social status quo, and when should they be read to empower legislatures, or require courts, to demand changes in that status quo? This question, which we have already encountered in various ways, is especially pointed when the constitutional interpreter is dealing with those provisions the purpose of which was to end the institution of slavery that Ruffin was explicating. A strong tendency in federal constitutional law since the adoption of the Civil War amendments has been to limit their scope, and this impulse has strong arguments supporting it. At the same time, as *State v. Mann* starkly reveals, the legal and social aspects of slavery were deeply intertwined, and constitutional provisions intended to uproot it would seem to fall short of their purpose if they did not address, or permit government to address, those links. Where private power claims an exemption from public norms, the question must always arise whether the logic of the claim is to the sort of privileged lawlessness that Ruffin described in *Mann*.

PART FOUR

Judge Thomas Ruffin's opinion in *State v. Mann* posed in the sharpest possible manner the incongruity of slavery with the American claim to live in republican polities characterized by the rule of law and (in most states) an increasingly democratic political system. Furthermore, constitutional issues rooted in sectional tensions over slavery dovetailed with questions dating back to the 1790s about the scope of national power and the role of the states under the federal Constitution. For most of the antebellum period there was a loose correlation between nationalist views of federal authority and ambivalence or hostility to slavery. In the 1850s, in the wake of the Compromise of 1850 and its harsh Fugitive Slave Act, for many Americans this earlier tendency was reversed: as administered by federal instrumentalities, federal law both constitutional and statutory seemed increasingly the tool of slavery's proponents. As a consequence, some of their opponents saw in the states the only secure location for the constitutional value of personal liberty traditionally associated with the U.S. Constitution. With the election of a president from a newly formed antislavery party that laid claim to the time-honored mantle of Republicanism, leading proslavery politicians in the South believed that the relationship between constitutional federalism and the institution of slavery had shifted once again, and unfavorably from their perspective.

The intellectual consequences of these events were as explosive in constitutional terms as the events themselves were literally cataclysmic in the Republic's history: secession and Civil War were paralleled by profound struggles over the meaning of American constitutionalism. The potential weight of the federal government as an engine of domestic change, long recognized but generally deflected after the demise of the Federalists, came to the forefront as first proslavery and then antislavery forces sought to harness national power to their own ends. In decisions such as the infamous Dred Scott case and *Ableman v. Booth,* the U.S. Supreme Court staked out a strongly nationalist interpretation of federalism (see section XVI) that found its reverse image in Radical Republican constitutional reform efforts after the war. The postwar Court struggled to reconcile the mixed heritage of the antebellum period with the nation's adoption of the thirteenth, fourteenth, and fifteenth amendments (see section XVIII), with questionable success; modern federal constitutional law is the heir of the resulting tensions even as it has been shaped by the failure of some constitutional initiatives to find a secure footing in the tradition. (See section XVII.)

As a formal matter, one of the most striking trajectories in American constitutional history has been the extension of the political franchise. With many hesitations and partial reversals, the long-term tendency has been to include ever larger percentages of the adult population within the body of those vested with formal political authority. The significance—and the limitations—of written constitutionalism can be seen vividly in the fact that the early twentieth century witnessed the effective disenfranchisement of virtually the entire African American male population of the southern states, even while the fifteenth amendment with its prohibition on race-based denials of the vote remained inscribed (or entombed) in the Constitution's official text. This process did not go unnoticed, of course, by the instrumentalities of the national government. In a 1903 opinion written by Justice Oliver Wendell Holmes Jr., the U.S. Supreme Court announced its self-diagnosed (and self-protective) inability to give any effective meaning to enforce the fifteenth amendment,[1] a decision that aided and abetted Congress and the federal executive branch in their decades-long acquiescence in the denial by white southerners of rights to blacks.

Irony is a regular concomitant of human action, and American constitutional history is no exception to this principle. The inclusive and democratic ideals that the Court betrayed in 1903 have nonetheless played a regular part in shaping constitutional debate on and off the Court in the modern era. Indeed (heightening the irony), some of the most eloquent early-modern statements of those ideals are found in the work of Justice Holmes (see section XIX), who was himself far from being an unalloyed devotee of either democracy or equality. Despite Holmes's oft-repeated private disdain for idealism in politics,[2] moreover, he joined in one of the modern era's clearest statements of the democratic vision of American constitutionalism, Justice Louis D. Brandeis's concurrence in *Whitney v. California*. (See section **XX**.) It took little more than a decade for the Supreme Court as an institution to endorse the account of the Constitution Brandeis presented in his *Whitney* opinion, and that account has retained its centrality down to the present. For those like me who think this politically good, it is sobering to remember that *Korematsu v. United States*, the 1944 decision upholding the World War II internment of law-abiding residents of this country solely on the basis of their race, was the work of a Court unanimously "committed" to Brandeis's vision. American constitutionalism must be more than a mere intellectual exercise, or it is nothing.

XVI. 1859: The Supreme Court and the Metaphysics of Supremacy

Article IV, section 2 of the Constitution states that "[n]o person held to Service or Labour in one State, under the Laws thereof, escaping into another, shall, by Consequence of any Law or Regulation therein, be discharged from such Service or Labour, but shall be delivered up on Claim of the Party to whom such Service or Labour may be due." Like all other provisions of the original Constitution that related to the institution of slavery, this clause squeamishly avoided use of the term "slave," but no doubt has ever existed about its intention, which was to require the return to their legal masters of fugitive slaves who escaped into states that had abolished slavery. The clause is located at the end of a series of provisions imposing duties on the states, only one of which (the full faith and credit clause of Article IV, section 1) expressly empowers Congress to enact legislation relating to those duties. Applying our old friend, the maxim *expressio unius exclusio alterius est*, we could sensibly conclude that Congress had no power with respect to the fugitive slave clause. Nonetheless, without recorded hesitation or debate, in February 1793 the Second Congress passed and President Washington signed into a law a bill implementing the clause. (The law also established a procedure for carrying out the states' obligation, under the preceding clause of Article IV, to return fugitives from justice.) The Fugitive Slave Act of 1793 empowered "the person to whom such labor or service may be due" (the title of the Act was blunter and referred to "masters") or "his agent or attorney, . . . to seize or arrest such fugitive from labor, and to take him or her before any" federal judge or local magistrate. If the master proved "to the satisfaction of such Judge or magistrate" that the fugitive was bound to service "under the laws of the State or Territory from which he or she fled," the judicial officer was to issue a certificate of removal that would serve as a warrant for the master to return the fugitive slave to captivity. The Act made deliberate interference with this process a federal crime.[3]

The history of enforcement of the Fugitive Slave Act, and the slow rise in resistance to the Act in the free states, is an important part of antebellum American legal history. From the 1830s on, as antislavery sentiment spread in the north and sectional hostilities deepened, several northern states enacted personal liberty laws that interfered in various ways with the ability of masters to reclaim fugitives. In an 1842 decision, *Prigg v. Pennsylvania,* the Supreme Court intervened in the controversy. *Prigg's* legal import, beyond the fact that it upheld the federal Act and invalidated the state's personal liberty law, was unclear. While Justice Joseph Story's opinion described itself as the opinion of the Court, even a casual reading of the six separate opinions by other justices made it clear that the Court was badly divided over the constitutional issues involved.[4] *Prigg's* practical impact was equally blurred, with many antislavery lawyers and legislators reading the decision (erroneously) to have held that state officers could not enforce the federal Act, and the defenders of slavery arguing (plausibly) that Story's opinion undermined the efficacy of the Act by its conclusion that Congress had no authority to require state officers to enforce it.

In 1850, Congress returned to the issue by passing a new fugitive slave bill as part of the great political compromise by which it attempted to allay the sectional crisis of that year. The proposed Act responded to the practical problems created by *Prigg* by providing for a nationwide system of federal commissioners, appointed by the federal district courts, to conduct rendition proceedings. Proceedings under the new Act were to be ex parte, with the fugitive denied even the right to testify in his or her behalf; in a blatant tilting of the scales, the Act awarded a commissioner a ten-dollar fee for each certificate of removal he issued but only five dollars if he denied the certificate. Preliminary proceedings to enforce the Act's heightened criminal penalties for interference with the process of rendition were also to be held before the commissioners. The bill's sharp curtailment of the modest procedural safeguards to accused fugitives available under the 1793 Act raised serious questions about its constitutionality even among those who supported a strengthened fugitive slave law, among them President Millard Fillmore, an avid proponent of sectional reconciliation along terms acceptable to slaveholding interests, who nonetheless privately expressed concern over the Act when it was presented to him for his signature.

Fillmore was particularly troubled about section 6 of the Act, which provided that a certificate of removal issued by one of the new federal commissioners "shall prevent all molestation of [the master or agent] by any process issued by any court, judge, magistrate, or other person whomsoever." In light of Article I, section 9, which states that "[t]he privilege of the Writ of Habeas Corpus shall not be suspended, unless in Cases of Rebellion or Invasion the public Safety may require it," Fillmore asked Attorney General John J. Crittenden whether he could in good conscience sign the bill into law. Crittenden, a political moderate from slaveholding Kentucky, assured Fillmore that the Act's general constitutionality was clear under *Prigg.* The Act, Crittenden continued, did not purport to suspend habeas corpus, and because the Act vested the new commissioners with competent jurisdiction, habeas corpus would not lie to free a fugitive held under a commissioner's certificate. "Whenever [the commissioner's] judgment is made to appear it is conclusive on the right of the owner to retain in his custody the fugitive . . . [i]f it is shown upon the application of the fugitive for a writ of habeas corpus, it prevents the issuing of the writ—if, upon the return, it discharges the writ and restores or maintains the custody."[5] Crittenden's opinion did not discuss what courts might conceivably be tempted to issue writs of habeas corpus in fugitive slave cases, but his discussion and indeed the language of the Act itself clearly assumed that state judges were the likely culprits.

Reassured, Fillmore signed the bill, but his personal willingness to approve and enforce the new Act was not shared by many of his fellow northerners. Signs of trouble weren't long in coming. By December 1850, Fillmore was asking Crittenden whether he ought to remove the U.S. marshal in Massachusetts, Charles Deven (later to be attorney general himself), for "neglect and dereliction of duty" in enforcing the Act. (Crittenden opined that he need not.)[6] Deven's offense, as Crittenden described it, was merely that he had displayed little "activity and energy" in arresting an alleged fugitive, but the inhabitants of other free states reacted with a cascade of intimidation, riots, and physical resistance to enforcement of the Act that rendered it increasingly a nullity in parts of the north.

The most famous judicial decisions to which the Fugitive Slave Act of 1850 gave rise involved not the Act's harsh dealings with alleged fugitives, but with its ancillary criminal provisions intended to prevent private interference with the rendition process. In the spring of 1854 a Missouri resident named Benammi Garland went to Wisconsin in an attempt to capture Joshua Glover, allegedly his slave. With Garland's assistance, the federal marshal Stephen Ableman was able to capture Glover in Racine, but the day after the capture, a mob led by an abolitionist named Sherman Booth among others broke Glover out of the jail in which he was being held. Glover escaped to Canada, leaving behind a judicial donnybrook. Even before the rescue, Marshal Ableman was served with a state writ of habeas corpus on Glover's behalf, which Ableman ignored; immediately after the rescue, the local sheriff, Timothy Morris, arrested Garland for assault and battery. In a proceeding on habeas corpus, the federal district judge ordered Garland's release,[7] and the federal commissioner subsequently ordered the arrest of Booth for violating the Fugitive Slave Act. In a state habeas proceeding, a justice of the state supreme court, Abram Smith, held the Act unconstitutional and the commissioner without valid jurisdiction to order Booth's detention, and accordingly ordered Booth's release from federal custody. The Wisconsin high court sitting en banc affirmed Justice Smith's decision,[8] but when the federal district judge issued a warrant for Booth's arrest, the Wisconsin justices denied his petition for habeas corpus, holding that the writ did not lie because the district court properly had jurisdiction over Booth and the legal issues, including the constitutionality of the Act, arising out of his arrest.[9] Booth and another member of the Racine mob, John Rycraft, were convicted after a jury trial of violating the Act. On yet another application for habeas corpus, the Wisconsin Supreme Court held that the counts on which Booth and Rycraft were convicted were not offenses against the Act, and that the federal court therefore lacked jurisdiction to detain or sentence them.[10]

A unanimous U.S. Supreme Court reversed the Wisconsin court's decisions sustaining state court authority to review the legality of Booth's (and in the later case Rycraft's) detention by federal authorities. In a brief paragraph, Chief Justice Roger Brooke Taney's opinion for the Court upheld the constitutionality of the 1850 Act and the legality of the commissioner's actions in the proceedings against Booth, but Taney focused virtually all of his and the reader's attention on what he saw as a more fundamental question of constitutional supremacy. At the "foundation" of the state courts' decision, Taney argued, was the Wisconsin court's assertion of "the supremacy of the State courts over the courts of the United States." The Wisconsin decisions implicitly laid claim to "the paramount power of the State court," a power that, if admitted, would leave the federal government helpless before the discordant judgments of the various states' judiciaries. In answer to this vision of constitutional anarchy, Taney invoked the supremacy of federal law, which the "language of the Constitution" asserts in terms "too plain to admit of doubt or to need comment." From the supremacy of federal law, Taney reasoned, it followed that federal judicial authority must be institutionally supreme: "But the supremacy thus conferred on this Government could not peacefully be maintained, unless it was clothed with judicial power, equally paramount in authority to carry it into execution." As a consequence, Taney concluded, in a case where state habeas is issued with respect to someone held under federal judicial order, once "the State judge or court [is] judicially apprized that the party is in custody under the authority of the United States, they can proceed no further." Any state court attempt to interfere further with "the dominion and exclusive jurisdiction of the United States" over the prisoner ought to be met with "any force that might be necessary to maintain the authority of law against illegal interference." "No state judge or court . . . has any right to interfere with" someone "imprisoned under the authority of the United States."[11]

The precise implications of *Ableman v. Booth* were the subject of discussion in many cases in the years following the decision, although the occasion of almost all of the decisions was the Civil War, not the enforcement of the Fugitive Slave Act. Courts sharply disagreed whether Chief Justice Taney had intended to preclude state habeas corpus in all cases where the individual detained was held by a federal *officer*, or only when the detention was pursuant to the order of a federal *court*. Taney's language, including his ambiguous references to the "dominion" or "authority" of the United States, was susceptible to either reading,[12] and the latter, narrower interpretation of his opinion accorded not only with the facts of *Ableman* but with the long-standing practice of state courts exercising habeas jurisdiction over individuals detained by federal officials without authorization by a federal court.[13] On this view, the fundamental error of the Wisconsin court had been its officious intrusion into a controversy over which another court already had jurisdiction, and most of Taney's discussion of federal supremacy was beside the point:

> [*Ableman v. Booth*] decides only that a prisoner cannot be taken out of the custody of the judicial department of the Federal government by means of a habeas corpus issued by a State court. I do not understand the Chief Justice of the United States to have meant more than this; and if he did, he meant more than the case called for, and all beyond is mere obiter dictum, and cannot be taken by itself as sufficient authority for so important a principle.[14]

Various federal and state cases read *Ableman* in this manner.[15]

Others understood *Ableman*'s holding to rest on Taney's broad language about federal supremacy.[16] Particularly against the background of secession and civil war, Taney's opinion seemed almost prophetic in its equation of state opposition to the exercise of federal power with "lawless violence":[17]

> The disaffected, at different times, and in various sections of the Union, have earnestly sought for some legal mode of resisting legitimate authority. But it has been in vain. There is no such anomalous middle ground between submission and rebellion; and this last extreme has at length been reached. Secession is but another name for revolution; for it is vain to contend for a constitutional right to overthrow the constitution, and a legal right to destroy all law.[18]

The Court's vindication of national authority in *Ableman*, as these constitutionalists read the decision, was a necessary implication not only of national supremacy, but of "the fundamental principle of free government, viz. the supremacy of law."[19]

The issue of how to interpret *Ableman v. Booth* came before the Wisconsin Supreme Court in an 1870 case in which a minor who had enlisted unlawfully in the U.S. Army sought a state writ of habeas corpus to secure his discharge. Although the membership of the state court had entirely changed in the fifteen years since it had entered the judgments reversed by *Ableman*, two of the court's three justices joined in an opinion flatly rejecting the authority of *Ableman* on any reading of Taney's meaning. There was, Justice Byron Paine stated for the court, "no solid distinction between" "cases of detention under the judgment of a judicial tribunal and those of detention by mere ministerial officers. . . . [T]he doctrine of Ableman v. Booth, if true at all, is as applicable to one as to the other." *Ableman*, however, was wrong, root and branch, and the evidence of the founders' intentions, the course of congressional legislation, and judicial precedent alike demonstrated that its predecessors had been on solid ground in asserting their jurisdiction to free persons held under the order or sentence of a court with no valid jurisdiction over them. Taney's insinuations that the Wisconsin decision was lawless and would lead to violence got the truth exactly backward: in fact, it was Taney, with his exhortation to local federal officials to resist state court orders with force, who was the proponent of conflict as a means of resolving constitutional dispute. The Wisconsin decision, which left ultimate resolution of the legality of the federal detention to the federal Supreme Court through its power of appellate review, reconciled American constitutionalism's fundamental commitment to individual freedom—"the facilities for the protection of liberty cannot be too great"—

with "the conceded supremacy of the constitution and laws of the United States."[20]

The U.S. Supreme Court reacted to this abrupt dismissal of its own unanimous decision by reversing the Wisconsin decision in an equally uncompromising opinion by Justice Stephen J. Field. *Tarble's Case* eliminated any ambiguity about the correct understanding of *Ableman* by opting decisively for the broader reading: *Ableman* "disposes alike of the claim of jurisdiction by a State court, or by a State judge, to interfere with the authority of the United States, whether that authority be exercised by a Federal officer or be exercised by a Federal tribunal." The independence of both the federal and state governments, and their reciprocal autonomy from interference by the other, which Field conceded as a general proposition, has a necessary limitation: state autonomy must give way "so far as such intrusion may be necessary on the part of the National government to preserve its rightful supremacy in cases of conflict of authority." But this compromise in the principle of federal–state independence is not reciprocal:

> Whenever . . . any conflict arises between the enactments of the two sovereignties, or in the enforcement of their asserted authorities, those of the National government must have supremacy until the validity of the different enactments and authorities can be finally determined by the tribunals of the United States.

A state habeas corpus proceeding can proceed no further, therefore, as soon as the state court learns that "the prisoner is held by an officer of the United States under what, in truth, purports to be the authority of the United States; that is, an authority, the validity of which is to be determined by the Constitution and laws of the United States." However illegal such a detention may be—"whether such illegality consist in the character of the process, the authority of the officer, or the invalidity of the law under which [the prisoner] is held"—it is "for the courts or judicial officers of the United States, and those courts or officers alone, to grant him release."[21]

Chief Justice Salmon P. Chase was the lone dissenter in *Tarble's Case*. Chase, whose tireless representation of fugitives before the Civil War had earned him the nickname "attorney general for runaway slaves," retained from his antebellum labors a sense of the utility of state habeas corpus in the defense of liberty. "I have no doubt," he announced, of a state court's power to release from custody a federal prisoner sentenced by a court without jurisdiction, and "still less doubt, if possible, that a writ of habeas corpus may issue

from a State court to inquire into the validity of imprisonment or detention . . . by an officer of the United States" acting without a judicial order. The
Supreme Court's appellate jurisdiction was the adequate and congressionally
prescribed means of ensuring the supremacy of federal law and protecting the
interests of the federal government, and the real effect of the majority's decision was "to deny the right to protect the citizen by habeas corpus against
arbitrary imprisonment in a large class of cases." *Tarble's Case* was in direct
contradiction to the sweeping command of Article I, section 9 that "the privilege of habeas corpus shall not be suspended" except under the most exigent
of circumstances.[22]

Ableman v. Booth and *Tarble's Case* are not especially well-reasoned decisions: In
particular, Chief Justice Taney's argument that the supremacy of national law
implies exclusivity of national jurisdiction seems a non sequitur, while Justice
Field's brusque dismissal of all state habeas jurisdiction over persons held by
federal officials simply ignored widespread and long-standing practice as well
as the considered opinion of many lawyers who were no fans of the Wisconsin
court's contumacy. The state court's 1855 order that someone convicted and
sentenced by a federal court with statutory jurisdiction over the case was an
extraordinary assertion of power and, as the chief justice of Pennsylvania
later sniffed, the legal issues surrounding the prosecution of Sherman Booth
were "disputed in Wisconsin in a very disorderly way, and out of that dispute
that decision [*Ableman*] arose." The facts that the Wisconsin court had declared unconstitutional a federal statute that most of the federal justices were
deeply committed to, and then refused to cooperate with the process of
Supreme Court review, may have played a role as well.[23] The state decision in
Tarble loudly and expressly defied a national judicial decision a scant few years
after the nation had fought a great war to overcome state defiance.

Nevertheless, *Ableman* and *Tarble* have generally fared well in subsequent es-
timation, at least once one goes beyond the turmoil of the years immediately
after them. Virtually all modern constitutionalists accept as a given the asymmetrical relationship between the federal and state judicial systems that *Ableman* and *Tarble* played a significant role in constructing. Not only does the
federal Supreme Court exercise appellate review over state court decisions involving federal questions, but the lower federal courts enjoy a wide jurisdiction
over cases that would otherwise be in state court and, indeed, through the
mechanism of removal, that sometimes commence in state court. Since the
1950s, finally, the federal courts have engaged in substantial appellate-type re-

view of federal issues arising out of state criminal prosecutions through the device of federal habeas corpus.[24] In such a legal universe, the exclusion of state courts from involvement in reviewing the legality of the federal detention of individuals seems natural.

Natural perhaps, but not, I think, necessarily correct in principle. As a preliminary matter, let us note a fact that, if we were closer in time to the decisions, might render their authority questionable: both decisions arose out of situations that were understandably alarming to the justices of the federal Supreme Court and thus may have provoked the Court to hasty and overbroad reactions. In 1854 and 1855 the Wisconsin court sought to use state habeas corpus in the least defensible posture possible, where a federal judicial officer had asserted a jurisdiction granted by a federal statute over a legal controversy, while in 1870 the state court flagrantly contested the authority of Chief Justice Taney's *Ableman* opinion. Consider the following argument. (1) The suspension clause of Article I, section 9 is indisputable proof that the Constitution presupposes that judicial tribunals will exist possessing the jurisdiction to issue writs of habeas corpus. (2) It is a nontextual but almost equally undeniable inference that the object of the writs of habeas corpus the Constitution contemplates are, or at least include, persons held under federal authority. (3) The Constitution does not require Congress to create lower federal courts. (4) Therefore, nothing about the Constitution in itself precludes state habeas jurisdiction over federal detainees, and indeed in the absence of any federal courts such jurisdiction would have to exist; any federal mandate to the contrary would be invalid unless it met the suspension clause's narrow exception for "Cases of Rebellion or Invasion." (5) Any suggestion that the creation of lower federal courts would of its own force strip state courts of the habeas jurisdiction they would otherwise possess is both a violent assumption without textual basis, and ignores Congress's power to define and limit the jurisdiction of the federal courts and thus preclude federal habeas. (Perhaps state habeas jurisdiction would flicker in and out of existence depending on the contents of Congress's federal court legislation.) Some constitutional theorists reject my step (3) and believe, against both a reasonable textual argument and the weight of historical understanding, that Congress is obliged to create a system of lower federal courts. Of course, for that view materially to affect the argument one must also assume, as some theorists argue, that step (5) is also wrong and Congress is required to vest the entirety of Article III jurisdiction in the federal courts (contrary to what Congress actually did prior to 1875).

The reader may or may not be intrigued by this little exercise in constitutional logic. The case against *Ableman* and *Tarble* can draw on another and perhaps more fundamental argument as well. As Justice Paine suggested in *In re Tarble*, American constitutional law is not evenhanded or indifferent as between liberty and power. However paradoxical its attempt to harness power to protect liberty, and however deep its commitment to the use of power in service to the common good, American constitutionalism's most basic value is liberty. Unlike judicial review of legislation, through which courts may exercise their own power in opposition to broad programs or decisions of the political branches of government, habeas corpus operates on what is basically a one-by-one basis, ensuring the individual that someone other than the governmental entity that is depriving her of liberty has questioned the legitimacy of that deprivation. State habeas jurisdiction over federal prisoners would ensure that the federal government has no power to preclude the existence of this protection for freedom no matter what constitutional theory the government or the Supreme Court may espouse. If state habeas were confined to circumstances in which no federal court has asserted jurisdiction, the danger that Chief Justice Taney trumpeted of armed conflict between state and federal officials would be virtually nonexistent, while the supremacy and integrity of federal law would be protected in the first instance by the ability of federal officers with legitimate reasons to detain someone to obtain a federal judicial order, and ultimately by Supreme Court review of state decisions. While it is undeniable that recognizing the legitimacy of state habeas would interfere theoretically, and to some extent practically, with the efficiency of the federal government, efficiency is not as central a constitutional value as liberty.

I believe that *Ableman v. Booth* and *Tarble's Case* exemplify a problem in constitutional law that we first encountered in our reading of *Chisholm v. Georgia*. In *Chisholm*, the reader will recall, Justice Wilson and Chief Justice Jay argued, convincingly in my judgment, that using the term "sovereignty" in discussions about the legal contours of American federalism is deeply confusing and improperly accorded to state governments a hazy but potent status that obscures the realities of a given dispute. A mirror image of the error they were attacking was at work in *Ableman* and *Tarble's Case*. Rather than focusing on the human and institutional realities of the issues before them, the justices (with the honorable exception of Chief Justice Chase, a greatly underrated constitutionalist) treated the issues as posing a grand theoretical question of who or what is supreme in our system. National supremacy, rather than being treated as a practical question of ensuring that the dictates of the supremacy clause are enforceable, acquired a pseudo-ontological quality that drove out of consideration the fact that the Constitution contains the suspension clause as well. American federalism, as Wilson and Jay recognized and Taney and Field did not, is best understood as a practical set of political arrangements controlled by the constitutional text, not an exercise in political metaphysics.

XVII. 1862: Four Attorneys General and the Meaning of Citizenship

The issue of whether African Americans were to be counted as members of the body politic that Judge Ruffin raised suggestively through his language in *State v. Mann* was squarely addressed by his contemporaries in a variety of settings, not least in a series of opinions by federal attorneys general stretching from eight years before *Mann* until a month before the Emancipation Proclamation. In 1821, Attorney General William Wirt received a request for advice from the secretary of the treasury, William Crawford, acting on behalf of the collector of customs at Norfolk, Virginia. Federal law mandated that the master of an American-flag vessel be a "citizen of the United States," and Crawford's inquiry was whether a free African American resident in Virginia satisfied this requirement. Wirt began his opinion by assuming that Congress had intended its statutory use of the expression to carry the same meaning as in the Constitution. On that assumption, he wrote, "it seems very manifest that no person is included in the description . . . who has not the full rights of a citizen of the State of his residence." Wirt demonstrated that this conclusion "manifestly" followed by giving what he regarded as two examples of the unacceptable consequences of denying it: if someone can be a "citizen of the United States" without enjoying "the high characteristic privileges of a citizen of [his] State," then free black Virginians are entitled to the protections of Article IV, section 2 of the Constitution ("Citizens of each State shall be entitled to all Privileges and Immunities of Citizens in the several States"), and are eligible to serve as president or member of Congress.

Wirt was confident, no doubt correctly, that Secretary Crawford would agree that federal citizenship must not be defined so broadly as to require such unthinkable results. The solution to the general question of constitutional (and thus statutory) construction, in Wirt's view, was to define citizenship of the United States in terms of citizenship in the individual states: only those possessed of "the full and equal privileges of white citizens in the State of their residence" are citizens of the nation. The answer to Crawford's immediate question then became simple. "[F]ree people of color in Virginia are not citizens of the United States . . . for such people have very few of the privileges of the citizens of Virginia." Instead, they are in essence resident aliens in Virginia, with only that connection and "allegiance which . . . a sojourning stranger owes—the mere consequence and return for the protection which he receives from the laws."[25]

Both in what it said and what it did not, Wirt's citizenship opinion mirrored well his own attitudes as well as those common in his social class. Like most children of the Revolutionary era (Wirt was born in 1772), he was opposed in the abstract to slavery without being in practice an active proponent of the institution's abolition. At the same time, he was respectful of the variations in race-related policy among the states. His opinion carefully avoided any suggestion that a state that wished to accord full citizenship to African Americans was precluded from doing so, and indeed his language clearly implied without stating so outright that an African American so enfranchised by "the State of his nativity" would be a citizen of the United States with all of the constitutional and statutory privileges that attach to that status.

The next attorney general to address the question was a generation younger than Wirt. Hugh Swinton Legaré (born in 1797) was a distinguished South Carolina lawyer and man of letters, and held the office for two years in the early 1840s. Like many white southerners of his day, Legaré rejected the founding era's theoretically antislavery ethics for a more accommodating moral perspective, and one might have predicted that his views on the idea of African American citizenship would be at least as negative as Wirt's. Rather surprisingly, however, Legaré took a different and more liberal approach. The issue arose out of a question of statutory construction posed in 1843 by Secretary Crawford's successor John C. Spencer. The statute in question accorded a preemptive right to purchase public lands on which he or she had made improvements to "every person being the head of a family, or widow, or single man, over the age of twenty-one years, and being a citizen of the United States, or having filed his declaration of intention to become a citizen." If Legaré had followed the logic of Wirt's 1821 opinion this statutory right would have been limited to African Americans who were full citizens in their state of residence, but Legaré took a different tack.

His first point was to reject Wirt's equation of citizenship with the possession of the broadest category of legal rights and privileges. At least for the purposes of construing the preemption statute, Legaré reasoned, Congress's intent in limiting the right to citizens was evidently to distinguish aliens from what Legaré called "denizens." "Now, free people of color are not *aliens*; they enjoy universally . . . the rights of denizens. Even in the slaveholding States they are capable of all of the rights of contract and property."[26] Indeed, Legaré went on, "even the *slave* is distinguished from the *alien*":

> He is a part of the family, and as soon as he passes into the class of freemen, is considered at once capable of all the *rights* which mere birth, under the *ligeance* of a country, bestows. How far a political *status* may be acquired is a different question, but his civil *status* is that of a complete denizenship.

Unlike Wirt, Legaré did not think that African Americans were analogous to sojourning foreigners and he did not treat federal citizenship (at least in a statutory setting) as derivative of state citizenship. For him African Americans were "a part of the family," and thereby (when free) part of the mass of individuals for whom Congress legislated when it accorded civil rights and privileges to American citizens.

The third attorney general to opine on the concept of national citizenship was Caleb Cushing. Like both Wirt and Legaré, Cushing was an author with broad intellectual interests as well as a skilled lawyer. Born in 1800 he was a near-contemporary of Legaré but was far more heavily involved in the politics both of his native Massachusetts and of the national capital. By the time he served as attorney general (1853–57), Cushing was a proslavery Democrat, and he seized on a question raised in 1856 by Secretary of the Interior Robert McClelland to correct what he saw as Wirt's and Legaré's differing and equally dangerous misunderstandings of the issues at stake. Secretary McClelland's inquiry concerned the preemption rights (under the same statute Legaré had interpreted) of a Native American who had maintained his identity as a member of a tribe with a treaty relationship to the United States, but, as Cushing candidly admitted, "it involves the much more serious question of the constitutional *status*, relatively to the question of citizenship of the African race in the United States."

A national citizen, Cushing argued, is "an elemental part of the *sovereign* people, the body politic, of the United States." The status did not depend on place of birth—Native Americans are born in the United States but are subjects rather than citizens unless made so by statute or treaty; neither did status depend on the right to vote—women, minors, and those disfranchised by criminal conviction or inability to pay a poll tax may be citizens but not voters. Nor, in Cushing's view, could national citizenship be a matter for state-by-state determination as Wirt had thought, for Cushing was unwilling to admit the possibility that Wirt had implicitly accepted, that a free state could make its African American residents citizens and thereby clothe them with the privileges of membership in the national body politic, including, he noted ominously, the rights conferred by "that unexplored clause of the Constitution" in Article IV, section 2:

> Can it be, that New York may impose on Virginia, or Virginia on New York, any person whom either of them shall choose to call a citizen? It would seem not. It would seem that the determination of what shall be deemed citizenship in all the States must be matter of Federal jurisdiction, residing only in the General Government.[27]

Legaré, then, had been right to uncouple state and federal citizenship, but had erred in including free African Americans within the body for whom Congress legislates when it speaks of citizens. (Legaré "had . . . been carried away in argument by a generous disposition to protect in the given case the claim of a free African.") As a matter of statutory construction, Cushing argued that Legaré had mistaken the effect of the preemption law's grant of the privilege to an alien who had filed the proper declaration of an intent to seek citizenship. By doing so the statute "pointedly excludes all other non-citizens." On its face, this invocation of the *expressio unius* canon begged the question since Legaré had denied that free African Americans were noncitizens in the relevant sense. What gave Cushing's argument its logical traction was his assumption that citizenship is necessarily linked with political membership in the nation. For Cushing (implicitly), as for Chief Justice Roger Brooke Taney the following year in his opinion in *Scott v. Sandford,* the consequence of giving federal citizenship a federal definition was to put a check on the ability of slavery's opponents to accord free African Americans privileges inconsistent with the maintenance of slavery.

The question of African American citizenship arose yet again, and with respect to the same statute Wirt had construed in 1821, in the midst of the Civil War. In 1862 another secretary of the treasury, Salmon P. Chase, requested the advice of Attorney General Edward Bates. In response Bates wrote a lengthy and learned opinion that ranged over ancient history, American politics, and, not least, the opinions of his predecessors before concluding that a free African American born in the United States satisfied the statutory requirement that the master of an American-flag vessel be a citizen of the United States.

Even after "[e]ighty years of practical enjoyment of citizenship, under the Constitution," in Bates's view the nature and meaning of American citizenship remained unclear. "For aught I see to the contrary, the subject is now as little understood in its details and elements, and the question as open to argument and speculative criticism, as it was at the beginning of the Government." Bates identified three reasons for the confusion surrounding the subject. First, he believed that most prior discussions of "the matter of citizenship" had in fact concerned "the claim of some right or privilege" that is not intrinsic to citizenship itself; by failing to notice this distinction, "we are easily led into errors both of fact and principle." Secondly, Bates thought the tendency to look to other legal systems, particularly those of the ancient world, for illumination on the nature of American citizenship was an error because of "the organic differences between their governments and ours." Finally, Bates noted that concern over the relationship between national citizenship and race had plainly "embarrassed and obscured" the "discussion of this great subject." He proposed in his own analysis to avoid the difficulties each of these factors had created.

Bates began with the text of the Constitution, which, as he correctly observed "does not declare who are and who are not citizens, nor does it attempt to describe the constituent elements of citizenship." (The reader will recall that Bates was writing before the framing and adoption of the fourteenth amendment.) Read carefully, however, the text creates a presumption that "every person born in the country is, at the moment of birth, prima facie a citizen; and he who would deny it must take upon himself the burden of proving some great disfranchisement strong enough to override the 'natural-born' right as recognized by the Constitution [in Article II, section 5]²⁸ in terms the most simple and comprehensive":

> In my opinion, the Constitution uses the word citizen only to express the political quality of the individual in his relations to the nation; to declare that he is a member of the body politic, and bound to it by the reciprocal obligation of allegiance on the one side and protection on the other. . . . The phrase, "a citizen of the United States," means neither more nor less than a member of the nation. And all such are, politically and legally, equal—the child in the cradle and its father in the Senate, are equally citizens of the United States.²⁹

National citizenship is not dependent on state recognition, nor indeed, with respect to those born within the United States, is it created by federal law. "The Constitution itself does not *make* the citizens; it is, in fact, made by them."

Bates then turned to what he saw as the real issue: the claim that persons of African descent are incapable of being citizens of the United States. "As far as the Constitution is concerned, this is a naked assumption; for the Constitution contains not one word upon the subject." Bates unequivocally repudiated both Wirt's conclusion that national citizenship depends on state citizenship and Chief Justice Taney's claim, in *Scott v. Sandford*, that under the Constitution no African American can become a U.S. citizen. Wirt's error, in Bates's view, was twofold: he had confused the political status of citizen with the possession of particular civil and political rights, and he had failed to recognize that the supremacy of national law entailed the logical priority of national to state citizenship. Without naming Taney, Bates rejected the arguments of those who would limit U.S. citizenship on racial grounds as based not "on the Constitution as it is, but upon what, in their own minds and sentiments, they think it ought to be." *Scott v. Sandford* did not provide judicial precedent for racial arguments, Bates insisted, because the Supreme Court's holding was necessarily limited to a point of jurisdiction far narrower than the dicta contained in the majority justices' opinions. Nothing in the Constitution draws any distinction along racial or color lines, and the existence of racial distinctions in the laws governing civil and political rights no more deprives the native-born African American of citizenship than the various disabilities imposed on women and children imply that they are not citizens. "Citizenship of the United States is an integral thing, incapable of legal existence in fractional parts. Whoever, then, has that franchise is a whole citizen, and a citizen of the whole nation."

Despite some internal argument over Bates's conclusion, Bates's opinion on citizenship was soon adopted by the Lincoln administration as its official position. Previous executive practices not in conformity with the opinion were changed—the secretary of state, for example, began issuing passports to African Americans. When the Civil Rights Act of 1866 was introduced in Congress, its leading proponents claimed that the proposed Act's declaration that all persons born in the United States enjoyed national citizenship was "merely declaratory of what the law is now," and cited Bates's opinion ("the ablest and most exhaustive ever given on the subject") as authority.[30] Although the fourteenth amendment subsequently incorporated Bates's view into the text of the Constitution, many and perhaps most of its supporters believed that doing so was a means of ensuring that the correct view of the Constitution was beyond dispute, rather than a change in the instrument's proper construction.

Years ago the great constitutional scholar Alexander Bickel wrote that "the concept of citizenship plays only the most minimal role in the American constitutional scheme."[31] Bickel thought this a happy, if somewhat accidental, fact, chiefly because he viewed the notion of citizenship as "a legal construct, an abstraction, a theory":

> No matter what the safeguards, it is at best something given, and given to some and not to others, and it can be taken away. It has always been easier, it always will be easier, to think of someone as a noncitizen than to decide he is a non-person, which is the point of the *Dred Scott* case.[32]

On this view it is fortunate that the Supreme Court rejected the fourteenth amendment's invitation to conceptualize the national protection of individual rights in terms of "privileges and immunities of citizens of the United States," for by doing so the Court (unintentionally) ensured that the issue would be seen as one involving the rights of "people" or "persons."

Attorney General Bates's 1862 citizenship opinion, with which Bickel was apparently not familiar, suggests that the essential desuetude of "citizenship" in constitutional law may not be an unmixed blessing. As Bates interpreted the concept, it does not leave the rights of native-born citizens (by far the largest group, then and now) subject to governmental denial or disparagement. The government, indeed the Constitution itself, must take the citizenship of this country's native inhabitants as a given, and thus whatever rights or privileges are inherent in citizenship are for them beyond legitimate governmental denial or interference. If we think of our constitutional law of individual liberty against the background of a Batesian understanding of citizenship, what we now think of as negative liberties might appear more readily to have an affirmative aspect as well. Citizenship is a relationship, not merely a legal shield against interference, one that imposes positive duties on both the citizen and the government. American constitutionalism is, at its heart, a shared, common effort at collective self-government. Bates's image of the United States as a national community held together by the correlative obligations of citizens and nation has the potential to enrich our understanding of what that means.

XVIII. 1873: *Slaughterhouse* Revisited

Perhaps no decision of the Supreme Court that is not perceived as morally evil in its result has been the subject of so much criticism as the *Slaughterhouse Cases*.[33] The Court's holding—that the state of Louisiana did not violate the Constitution of the United States by granting the Crescent City Live-Stock

Landing and Slaughter-House Company a monopoly over the operation of slaughterhouses within the city and environs of New Orleans—is seldom the object of great interest. What excites widespread censure are the constitutional misdeeds the Court allegedly committed in coming to its judgment. The central items of the usual bill of particulars are the assertion that the Court eviscerated the privileges or immunities clause of section 1 of the fourteenth amendment by giving it so narrow a construction that it has since been of virtually no practical importance, and that the Court manifested a fundamental hostility toward the Civil War amendments that led eventually to the judicial dismantling of Reconstruction and *Plessy v. Ferguson*'s tragic approval of Jim Crow segregation, judicial misdeeds that indefinitely delayed implementation of the nation's promise of freedom and equality to African Americans. These are serious accusations, and I do not deny that each contains a considerable degree of truth. In this section, however, I want to advance a thesis about the *Slaughterhouse Cases* that departs in certain respects from the usual condemnation of the decision.

Justice Samuel F. Miller wrote the opinion of the Court on behalf of the five-justice majority. Like every member of the Court by 1873, Miller had been appointed by a Republican president, in Miller's case Abraham Lincoln (in 1862); like most, his antebellum politics were decidedly antislavery in cast and thus he is generally, and perhaps rightly, seen as an example of the antislavery North's rapid loss of interest in the protection of African Americans during the Reconstruction era. The *Slaughterhouse Cases,* of course, did not involve that issue (a point Miller repeatedly emphasized), but the narrowminded approach his opinion evinced to the interpretation of the Civil War amendments is generally seen as at the root of the Court's subsequent attack on congressional Reconstruction. Miller, the argument goes, either blindly or hypocritically refused to see and acknowledge the enormous constitutional change the amendments were intended to effect. Instead, Miller insisted on reading the amendments as limited adjustments to a system basically sound in itself. "Was it the purpose of the fourteenth amendment," Miller asked rhetorically, "to transfer the security and protection of all the civil rights . . . from the States to the Federal government? And . . . was it intended to bring within the power of Congress the entire domain of civil rights heretofore belonging exclusively to the States?" Miller's answer, which he thought showed the unthinkable consequences of answering these questions affirmatively, is in his critics' minds a description of precisely what the amendments *were* meant to accomplish:

All this and more must follow, if the proposition of the plaintiffs in error be sound. For not only are these rights subject to the control of Congress whenever in its discretion any of them are supposed to be abridged by State legislation, but that body may also pass laws in advance, limiting and restricting the exercise of legislative power by the States, in their most ordinary and usual functions, as in its judgment it may think proper on all such subjects. And still further, such a construction followed by the reversal of the judgments of the Supreme Court of Louisiana in these cases, would constitute this court a perpetual censor upon all legislation of the States, on the civil rights of their own citizens, with authority to nullify such as it did not approve as consistent with those rights, as they existed at the time of the adoption of this amendment.[34]

When Miller concluded for the majority justices that they were "convinced that no such results were intended by the Congress which proposed these amendments, nor by the legislatures of the States which ratified them," the critics charge that he had the truth precisely backward.

This condemnation of Miller, that his opinion managed to make a molehill out of the mountain of the nation's reworking of the Constitution, was articulated forcefully at the time in the unjustly neglected dissenting opinion of Justice Noah Swayne. While Swayne joined in the much better-known dissents of Justices Stephen J. Field and Joseph P. Bradley, he wrote separately, in part to emphasize what he saw as the majority's failure to recognize the Civil War amendments for the constitutional revolution that Swayne believed them to be:

Fairly construed these amendments may be said to rise to the dignity of a new Magna Charta. . . . The language employed is unqualified in its scope. . . . This court has no authority to interpolate a limitation that is neither expressed nor implied. Our duty is to execute the law, not to make it. . . . It is objected that the power conferred is novel and large. The answer is that the novelty was known and the measure deliberately adopted. The power is beneficent in its nature, and cannot be abused. It is such as should exist in every well-ordered system of polity. Where could it be more appropriately lodged than in the hands to which it is confided? It is necessary to enable the government of the nation to secure to every one within its jurisdiction the rights and privileges enumerated, which, according to the plainest considerations of reason and justice and the fundamental principles of the social compact, all are entitled to enjoy. Without such authority any government claiming to be national is glaringly defective. . . . Nowhere, than in this court, ought the will of the nation, as thus expressed, to be more liberally construed or more cordially executed. This determination of the majority seems to me to lie far in the other direction.[35]

In Swayne's judgment, the majority's interpretation of the fourteenth amendment "defeats, by a limitation not anticipated, the intent of those by whom the instrument was framed and of those by whom it was adopted. To the extent of that limitation it turns, as it were, what was meant for bread into a stone."

My thesis is that both Justice Miller and Justice Swayne were right. Miller was correct in his concern that an overly broad interpretation of the Civil War amendments could lead to unintended and undesirable changes in constitutional law, and Swayne was correct in his assertion that the Civil War amendments worked a major transformation in the antebellum Constitution and ought to be interpreted accordingly. And—and here is the difficult part— there is a way to reconcile the two men's concerns that is substantially faithful to those concerns although it is not the approach that either historical figure took. First, Miller was right to worry about the consequences of making the Supreme Court "a perpetual censor upon all legislation of the States, on the civil rights of their own citizens, with authority to nullify such as it did not approve as consistent with those rights." In this regard, Miller's critics often forget the substantive constitutional arguments he was rejecting but which the dissents of Field and Bradley stated candidly and uncompromisingly.

As the *Slaughterhouse* dissenters construed the fourteenth amendment, it authorizes—indeed requires—the judiciary to subject state legislation to stringent judicial examination whenever the state law "encroach[es] upon the liberty of citizens to acquire property and pursue happiness."[36] Field's and Bradley's discussions of the various rationales offered in defense of the Louisiana monopoly statute read almost exactly like economic substantive due process opinions of the *Lochner* era: the statute, as Bradley summarized their reasoning "is onerous, unreasonable, arbitrary, and unjust." Therefore, he concluded, "[i]t has none of the qualities of a police regulation" and is, instead, an unconstitutional invasion of the liberty protected by the fourteenth amendment.[37] If the Court had adopted this approach to the amendment, it would have justified a similar form and degree of interference with state regulatory power to that which the Court practiced in cases such as *Lochner.* If *Lochner*-style judicial review of regulatory laws is inappropriate—a proposition that most contemporary constitutional lawyers would endorse—Miller was right at least in what he was rejecting.

Miller's objection to aggressive judicial review of the sort the dissenters proposed thus was grounded not only in his conservative vision of federalism but also in his objection to the great expansion in judicial power that they endorsed. (Justice Bradley even touted the accretion of power to the courts that the dissenters sought as a mark in their favor: by ensuring that objections to state legislation were "regularly raised, in a suit at law, and settled by final reference to the Federal court," the dissenters' view of the amendment would eliminate the threat of congressional interference. "Very little, if any, legislation on the part of Congress would be required to carry the amendment into effect.")[38] A few years after the *Slaughterhouse Cases*, Miller protested what he labeled a "strange misconception of the scope of [the due process clause] as found in the fourteenth amendment":

> In fact, it would seem, from the character of many of the cases before us, and the arguments made in them, that the clause under consideration is looked upon as a means of bringing to the test of the decision of this court the abstract opinions of every unsuccessful litigant in a State court of the justice of the decision against him, and of the merits of the legislation on which such a decision may be founded.[39]

Whatever else Miller got wrong, he was right to reject a reading of the fourteenth amendment that empowers the Court to invalidate state legislation simply because, in the opinion of a majority of the justices, the legislation is "onerous, unreasonable, arbitrary, and unjust."

At the same time, Justice Swayne's objection that "[t]he construction adopted by the majority of my brethren is . . . much too narrow" was well founded. As he shrewdly noted, the national experience with slavery, secession, and civil war that motivated and informed the Civil War amendments involved a profound rejection of the Jeffersonian suspicion of central government that had dominated earlier constitutional debates:

> These amendments are all consequences of the late civil war. The prejudices and apprehension as to the central government which prevailed when the Constitution was adopted were dispelled by the light of experience. The public mind became satisfied that there was less danger of tyranny in the head than of anarchy and tyranny in the members.[40]

To Miller's charge that the dissenters' position "radically changes the whole theory of the relations of the State and Federal governments to each other and of both these governments to the people," Swayne's response was that such was the nation's will:

> The first eleven amendments to the Constitution were intended to be checks and limitations upon the government which that instrument called into existence. They had their origin in a spirit of jealousy on the part of the States, which existed when the Constitution was adopted. . . . [The Civil War] amendments are a new departure, and mark an important epoch in the constitutional history of the country. They trench directly upon the power of the States, and deeply affect those bodies. They are, in this respect, at the opposite pole from the first eleven.[41]

Whatever else one might say about Swayne's views, he correctly rejected a reading of the fourteenth amendment that ignored or subverted the profound reordering of the American constitutional system of which the amendment is an important part.

In the (very) long run, our constitutional tradition has vindicated both Miller and Swayne on the issues that I believe they got right. Beginning in the 1930s, the Court has consistently rejected in principle any suggestion that the fourteenth amendment authorizes it to "sit as a super-legislature to determine the wisdom, need, and propriety of laws that touch economic problems, business affairs, or social conditions."[42] (The quotation is from a case that some would regard as a patent violation of the principle. My point here is about what we say we agree on, not on the fidelity of our practice to our commitments.) And from *Brown v. Board of Education*[43] on, the Court and later Congress have acted on an understanding of the Civil War amendments that acknowledges the profound constitutional change they embody. Nevertheless, in one area of constitutional law, the scope of Congress's power to enforce the Civil War amendments, a ghostly afterimage of the "bad" Miller and Swayne—the former's crabbed view of the amendments, the latter's judicial imperialism—continues to haunt, and in my judgment distort, our thinking. If Miller and Swayne were right in the ways the tradition has come to see that they were, the Court is in error when it treats congressional enforcement legislation as an exception to some norm of federal–state relations that must be carefully cabined in through stringent judicial examination. The Civil War amendments changed that norm, and in doing so empowered Congress to exercise the same broad discretion in protecting civil rights that it enjoys when regulating interstate commerce.

In what was probably the first federal court decision interpreting the scope of Congress's enforcement powers, Justice Swayne himself combined his own robust understanding of the revolutionary nature of the changes wrought by the Civil War with Justice Miller's concern to avoid judicial overreaching. Sitting on circuit in *United States v. Rhodes*, Swayne anticipated his *Slaughterhouse* discussion of the Civil War amendments by giving a broad reading of the purpose and effect of the thirteenth amendment. That amendment, he wrote, "trenches directly upon the power of the states and of the people of the states" and "consecrates the entire territory of the republic to freedom, as well as to free institutions." Swayne construed the second section of the amendment, which grants Congress "the power to enforce this article by appropriate legislation," as affording Congress the same wide discretion it enjoys in legislating pursuant to Article I, section 8. Swayne acknowledged, of course, that legislation enacted pursuant to section 2 of the amendment had to be "appropriate to the end" of the amendment but stressed that judicial review of such legislation was to be as restrained as in the case of statutes enacted under the Constitution's original grants of power:

> Any exercise of legislative power within its limits involves a legislative, and not a judicial question. It is only when the authority given has been clearly exceeded, that the judicial power can be invoked. Its office, then, is to repress and annul the excess; beyond that it is powerless.[44]

A series of later circuit court decisions, most decided by members of the Supreme Court, took the same approach in upholding enforcement legislation.[45] Perhaps the most lasting harm that the *Slaughterhouse Cases* did was to obscure for later constitutionalists the fact that the post–*Slaughterhouse* Court's hostility to congressional civil rights laws was in fact a reversal of the initial judicial response to the adoption of the thirteenth and fourteenth amendments.

The *Slaughterhouse Cases* exemplify a central feature of American constitutionalism: its reliance on power to defend freedom. By creating text-based liberties, privileges, and immunities, the written Constitution seeks to safeguard individuals against treatment deemed abusive or tyrannical by empowering some institution or institutions to enforce individual constitutional rights. But in the very act of doing so, by creating power the Constitution makes it possible for the "protecting" institution to abuse or overreach its authority. Section 1 of the fourteenth amendment, for example, imposes a series of restrictions on state governments that are (and were intended to be) judicially enforceable even in the absence of congressional legislation.[46] In doing so, the amendment expanded the power of one branch of the federal government, the Article III judiciary, at the expense of the states. Section 5's grant of power to Congress to enforce the amendment expanded the power of the other two branches of the federal government, Congress directly and the executive through its inevitable role in enforcing federal laws, once again at the expense of the states. In both cases, as Justice Miller feared, there is a danger that the various national institutions will exercise these powers in ways that are inimical to local autonomy and democratic self-government, to the federal structure, and to the liberty of those affected negatively by federal action. And by virtue of the existence of judicial review of federal legislation, the amendment has created a new possibility that the courts will overreach their authority at the expense of Congress's power. (The same observations could of course be made about the thirteenth and fifteenth amendments.)

There is no solution to this dilemma. It is inherent in our system, which depends in part on the clash of opposing institutions to give substance to individual liberty. The Civil War amendments, however, differ from earlier parts of the Constitution in one crucial respect. The rejection of Jefferson's generalized suspicion of congressional power by Republican nationalists following the War of 1812 was premised on their belief that national politics can produce legislative outcomes that serve the common good. The Marshall Court's endorsement of limited judicial review of such congressional legislation in *M'Culloch v. Maryland* demonstrated that Court's acceptance of the validity of the Republican nationalists' premise. The modern Court's continued unease with congressional enforcement legislation suggests that it is not entirely willing to accept as valid the belief underlying the Civil War amendments that the national democratic process can safeguard individual freedom.

XIX. 1904: Clay May, the Railroad, and Justice Holmes

In 1901 the Texas legislature enacted a law related to Johnson grass and Russian thistle, fast-spreading weeds that, if allowed to go unchecked, pose a threat to various cash crops. The statute provided for a penalty of $25 for allowing either plant to go to seed on one's property, recoverable by owners of contiguous plots of land as long as they were not guilty of the same fault. The law did not apply to all landowners, however: only railroad companies were subject to the penalty. A couple of years later, Clay May of Bell County, Texas, having noticed Johnson grass growing on an adjacent roadbed belonging to the Missouri, Kansas & Texas Railway Company, took the railroad to court and, apparently being a careful farmer with no Johnson grass on his land, obtained a judgment for the $25 penalty from the county court. The railroad, perhaps concerned about how many potential Clay Mays owned land adjoining its property, decided to appeal the case on federal constitutional grounds, and the case ended up in the U.S. Supreme Court. Before the Court, the railroad's argument was that the statute's limitation of liability to railroad companies drew a patently arbitrary distinction between those companies and all the many other landowners who might fail to control the spread of Johnson grass and Russian thistle. Such a distinction without "a fair ground for discrimination," the railroad contended, violates the command of the fourteenth amendment that no state shall "deny to any person within its jurisdiction the equal protection of the laws."[47]

Farmer May got to keep the $25. Over three dissents the Supreme Court upheld the constitutionality of the Texas statute in an opinion written by one of its most junior justices, Oliver Wendell Holmes Jr.[48] Less than two years into his service on the Court, Holmes had yet to make a significant mark (although an observer might have taken note of the brevity of his opinions, an oddity on a Court with a collective penchant for the elephantine in written expression), and *Missouri, Kansas, & Texas Railway Co. of Texas v. May* was hardly a major case on anyone's estimation, save perhaps the railroad and May. In retrospect, however, Holmes's opinion in *May* displayed in miniature (the opinion was brief even for Holmes: three paragraphs) most of the features of his mature constitutional thought.

Holmes disposed of the railroad's equal protection argument with celerity. "There is no dispute about general principles," he asserted: on the one hand the state may discriminate when there is a good reason for doing so, and on the other the fourteenth amendment prohibits distinctions when "there is no fair reason for the law that would not require with equal force its extension to others whom it leaves untouched." The question before the Court, Holmes therefore concluded, could be reduced to the issue of "whether this case lies on one side or the other of a line which is to be worked out between cases differing only in degree." The contention that distinctions in the law typically reflect not watertight categories but differing locations along a spectrum was one that Holmes had argued for years. In the context of equal protection litigation he believed that a court has no basis for invalidating a statutory discrimination unless it can "see clearly" that the distinction drawn has no fair basis. Holmes cited *M'Culloch v. Maryland* as recognizing a similar principle in reviewing Congress's exercise of implied powers. In both situations, Holmes intimated, the guiding principle was that "the legislature is the only judge . . . [whether] policy requires a certain measure." Courts must keep a tight rein on their review of issues such as the necessity of exercising an implied power, or the rationale for drawing a statutory distinction, in order to avoid intruding into the domain of political opinion and legislative power. Because several reasons could be imagined for the line the Texas legislature had drawn between railroads and other landowners with respect to weeds, the Court had no basis on which to invalidate the law.[49]

At the end of his opinion, Holmes added three observations that will be the focus of our interest:

> Great constitutional provisions must be administered with caution. Some play must be allowed for the joints of the machine, and it must be remembered that legislatures are ultimate guardians of the liberties and welfare of the people in quite as great a degree as the courts.[50]

Each major clause in these two sentences makes a separate and interesting assertion that deserves some discussion.

(1) Why is it that great—I take Holmes to mean something like "broadly phrased"—constitutional provisions have to be "administered with caution"? In the context of *May*, Holmes surely had in mind the judiciary's administration of the Constitution through judicial review. His point, then, was one he had already made in his previous paragraph, that a court should exercise its power of judicial review in a manner that avoids overleaping the bounds of judicial decision and acting as if it possessed the policymaking discretion of a legislature. The Constitution's more general and broadly worded provisions present greater temptations to forget this caution because their wording provides correspondingly less guidance for judicial decision making. (Contrast the ex post facto clauses, as construed by Justice Paterson in *Calder*, with the equal protection clause that was at issue in *May*.) Holmes understood that it followed from his insistence that legal distinctions are differences of degree that there is no absolute, categorical difference between the political and policy-driven discretion of a legislature and the legal and norm-driven discretion of a court— he later wrote that "I recognize without hesitation that judges do and must legislate."[51] The absence of absolute difference, however, was in his mind no more a justification for collapsing the distinction between legislative and judicial decisionmaking than it is for refusing to give content to the myriad of substantive distinctions that law necessarily draws:

> When a legal distinction is determined, as no one doubts that it may be, between night and day, childhood and maturity, or any other extremes, a point has to be fixed or a line has to be drawn, or gradually picked out by successive decisions, to mark where the change takes place. Looked at by itself without regard to the necessity behind it the line or point seems arbitrary. It might as well or nearly as well be a little more to one side or the

other. But . . . a line or point there must [despite the fact that] there is no mathematical or logical way of fixing it precisely.[52]

Judges unavoidably legislate, but it is intrinsic to their particular role in our constitutional order that "they can do so only interstitially; they are confined from molar to molecular motions."[53] Caution in the judicial ascription of meaning to inexact constitutional language is necessary in order to preserve the separation of powers that is an undeniable feature of the system.[54]

(2) In a famous antebellum decision, Judge William Gaston wrote that "[c]onstitutions are not themes proposed for ingenious speculation; but fundamental laws ordained for practical purposes."[55] Gaston's view was also Holmes's, and it was for this reason Holmes insisted that courts must allow for "play in the joints" of the constitutional mechanism. The judicial role in our self-governance through a written Constitution is not one of simply rubber-stamping whatever perhaps transient policies political actors may wish to pursue, but neither should courts see themselves as champions of the people, or law, or liberty, standing entirely outside the institutions and concerns of government. (Contrast Judge Roane's 1794 understanding of the judicial role, and Secretary Jefferson's 1791 suspicion of legislative, or at least federal legislative, power.) In interpreting the Constitution the courts are, and act as, a part of the government that the Constitution establishes. They are administering the fundamental law of this polity, not handing down philosophical rules of justice or transcendental political norms. As Holmes apparently said to Judge Learned Hand, the judge's task is not a general commission to "do justice" but a specific obligation "to play the game according to the rules."[56]

(3) "Legislatures are ultimate guardians of the liberties and welfare of the people in quite as great a degree as the courts." Holmes was no romantic believer in democracy as an ideal or the mass of voters as political decisionmakers, and he had a lively, from many perspectives exaggerated, skepticism about the chances that legislation will benefit the common good. To a great extent (recall the two points above), Holmes's commitment to the constrained exercise of judicial review was a product of his understanding of his role as a judge. There is no logical reason why the same role could not be accepted and acted upon by judges in a polity with less or entirely nondemocratic means of making public policy. On this interpretation of Holmes, his remark in *May* about legislatures as guardians of the liberty and welfare of the people (itself rhetorically a bit undemocratic) might simply be a notional stipulation stemming entirely from the Constitution's assignment of political tasks: if the Constitution is, as its preamble asserts, devoted to liberty and the general welfare,

then by definition its coordinate instrumentalities have a role in serving those goals.

All of this said, Holmes's advocacy of judicial restraint was not entirely a matter of role differentiation. It also rested on two propositions, each of which Holmes held deeply. One was what is often viewed as his skepticism, an attitude that with equal accuracy could be termed an epistemological modesty, a recognition that judges are individuals with limited knowledge and abundant biases—like all individuals—and that their views on great moral and political issues enjoy no intrinsic superiority over those of others. The "marketplace of ideas" metaphor from his first amendment opinion in *Abrams v. United States* is the best known instance in which Holmes linked this attitude about knowledge to the Constitution, but its influence on his constitutional thinking was pervasive. And such a modesty about one's wisdom supports, even if it does not entail, an enhanced respect for the political processes of representative democracy.

Holmes stated the other proposition on various occasions both in constitutional and broader, rather sociological terms. In his famous dissent in *Lochner v. New York*, Holmes made the point as an observation about the fundamental character of the Constitution. Some legal regulations of the economy, he wrote,

> embody convictions or prejudices which judges are likely to share. Some may not. But a Constitution is not intended to embody a particular economic theory, whether of paternalism and the organic relation of the citizen to the state or of laissez faire. It is made for people of fundamentally differing views, and the accident of our finding certain opinions natural and familiar, or novel, and even shocking, ought not to conclude our judgment upon the question whether statutes embodying them conflict with the Constitution of the United States.[57]

The Constitution is inclusive, "made for people of fundamentally differing views." Constitutional interpretation cannot depend on or wait for consensus; but the importation into it of contested policy choices not clearly founded on its text, or on "fundamental principles as they have been understood by the traditions of our people and our law," risks the implicit exclusion of some of the people to whom it belongs. "Otherwise," Holmes said in the first opinion he wrote for the Supreme Court, "a constitution, instead of embodying only relatively fundamental rules of right . . . would become the partisan of a particular set of ethical or economical opinions, which by no means are held *semper ubique et ab omnibus*."[58]

Holmes himself held what today might be called a nonfoundationalist view of moral values, although it is wrong to characterize him a relativist. At times he put his *Lochner* claim about the Constitution being made for people with differing views in terms of this broader understanding of the meaningfulness of norms in human life. In a letter to his friend Alice Stopford Green, for example, Holmes wrote critically of the "attitude of absoluteness" that he detected in Henry James's novel *The Ambassadors,* one that "exclud[ed] from the heights all those who do not share his scale of values. As against that, I think that values like truth are largely personal. There is enough community for us to talk, not enough for anyone to command."[59] Holmes thought that this broad-minded acceptance of the fact that other people are truly *other,* and that some of the differences of opinion and principle that arise from that otherness are incorrigible, was essential to a constitutional interpreter whose task it is to interpret and safeguard the fundamental law that constitutes our political community. "I believe . . . that we need more democratic feeling—I like to multiply my scepticisms—for in administering constitutional law one cannot realize too clearly the possibility of different points of view for all of which there ought to be room . . . if the constitution is not to be a Procrustean bed."[60]

Holmes's willingness from 1919 on to extend strong judicial protection to freedom of speech, sometimes seen as inconsistent with his general attitude of judicial deference to legislation, in fact was deeply consistent with the views that informed his concepts of the judge's role and of the inclusive nature of the constitutional community. In part the consistency rested on Holmes's belief that constitutional protection for free speech was deeply rooted in both the constitutional text and the American political tradition. He wrote, for example, of "the sweeping language [of the first amendment] that governs or ought to govern the laws of the United States," and referred on one occasion to the nineteenth century's near-consensus that the Republican position on the Sedition Act was correct.[61] In part, however, he had come to connect his democratic conviction that "there is enough community for us to talk, not enough for anyone to command" with seeing the first amendment as a prohibition on governmental attempts to substitute command for talk. For Holmes, a robust doctrine of constitutional free speech did not depend on any assumption that the better argument always wins or on a libertarian theory of free expression; it was rather the translation into a legal interpretation of the first amendment of the entire Constitution's commitment to creating a political community that can encompass men and women of sharply divided views without stifling those views or excommunicating those who lose in the political struggle. "If there is any principle of the Constitution that more imperatively calls for attachment than any other it is the principle of free thought—not free thought for those who agree with us but freedom for the thought that we hate."[62]

Justice Holmes seems to be of perennial interest to legal scholars, but my sense is that his influence as a constitutional lawyer is at a fairly low ebb. His seminal first amendment opinions have long ago been absorbed into the foundations of modern free speech doctrine and his resistance to the *Lochner* era's heightened judicial protection for property and contract rights is broadly shared, but as a general matter Holmes gets fairly low marks for his constitutional reasoning as opposed to his occasional insights and rhetorical flourishes. (Holmes himself would probably see nothing in any of this to trouble him overmuch. He often remarked that in his view systems of thought become boring as they age, and that it is only the aperçus of the past that live on.) We err if we dismiss him as having nothing further to say for constitutional law, however, for better than any other single figure in our history Holmes expressed the judge's place in the American constitutional order. As readers of this work have seen, American constitutionalism from its beginning has wrestled with the irony that adopting a written Constitution does not end dispute or controversy over fundamental matters, it only provides a language and a process for debating them. Over time, as we have also seen, the issues in dispute shift: on some matters we reach a practical agreement (recall judicial review and the repeal debates of 1802), on others social conflict dies away for reasons having little to do with law, and still others arise that excited little disagreement or were not even contemplated at an earlier stage of our constitutional tradition. Conflict and disagreement are tiring, and the urge to seek an end to them is understandable. But they are inseparable from any common life that is not entirely structured by the use of force, as Madison saw long ago.[63] The judicial role is intrinsically one of command, not (in the end) of dialogue; and judicial review would be an unacceptable anomaly in our democracy if it were uncoupled from a constitutional tradition that is in some sense the property of all. Holmes's mind set is essential if judges, whose role in the American constitutional order is necessary but not sufficient to its goals, are to avoid narrowing improperly the range of political discussion and action possible in the political community.

Part of the enduring value of Justice Holmes's constitutional thought lies in his careful refusal to claim too much for the processes of democratic decisionmaking. In an essay written to honor the memory of Chief Justice Harlan

Fiske Stone, who served (as an associate justice) with Holmes from 1925 until Holmes retired in 1932, Judge Learned Hand summarized what he saw as the understanding of democracy Stone shared with Holmes, and which he clearly endorsed himself:

> These men believed that democracy was a political contrivance by which the group conflicts inevitable in all society should find a relatively harmless outlet in the give and take of legislative compromise after the contending groups had a chance to measure their relative strength; and through which the bitterest animosities might at least be assuaged, even though that reconciliation did not ensue which sometimes follows upon an open fight.[64]

Hand, like Holmes, made no use of tropes common in romantic accounts of democracy such as "the popular will" or "the People." Democracy in the sense it is practiced in the American constitutional order does not depend on such notions; indeed, its social realism and its commitment to the maintenance of political community through and within sharp political conflict is on a deep level antithetical to the romantic vision of democracy as the great common endeavor of an organic people. Democracy is, instead, "a political contrivance" enabling people of fundamentally differing views to get by together with as much attention to the general welfare as their disagreements will permit. But it is precisely in the modesty of its claims about the degree of social unity that our constitutionalism expects that Holmes's vision of a community with room for talk but none for command displays what is morally attractive about American constitutionalism.

XX. 1927: Justice Brandeis and the Final End of the State

In 1927, Justice Louis Brandeis wrote a justly famous opinion, which Justice Holmes joined, concurring in the Court's judgment in *Whitney v. California*. *Whitney* sustained a conviction under a California law prohibiting participation in the formation of a society to advocate criminal syndicalism, a concept the legislature defined as "any doctrine or precept advocating, teaching or aiding and abetting the commission of crime, sabotage (which word is hereby defined as meaning willful and malicious physical damage or injury to physical property), or unlawful acts of force and violence or unlawful methods of terrorism as a means of accomplishing a change in industrial ownership or control or effecting any political change."[65] Brandeis and Holmes thought the conviction a violation of the freedom of speech that the majority had assumed to be protected against state interference by the fourteenth amendment in *Gitlow v. New York*.[66] (They concurred in the majority's affirmance of the *Whitney* conviction on procedural grounds.) In explaining their constitutional reasoning, Brandeis remarked that "to reach sound conclusions on these matters, we must bear in mind why a state is, ordinarily, denied the power to prohibit dissemination of social, economic and political doctrine which a vast majority of its citizens believes to be false and fraught with evil consequence." His explanation invoked the founders:

> Those who won our independence believed that the final end of the state was to make men free to develop their faculties, and that in its government the deliberative forces should prevail over the arbitrary. They valued liberty both as an end and as a means. They believed . . . that public discussion is a political duty; and that this should be a fundamental principle of the American government. They recognized the risks to which all human institutions are subject. But they knew that order cannot be secured merely through fear of punishment for its infraction; that it is hazardous to discourage thought, hope and imagination; that fear breeds repression; that repression breeds hate, that hate menaces stable government; that the path of safety lies in the opportunity to discuss freely supposed grievances and proposed remedies; and that the fitting remedy for evil counsels is good ones. . . . Recognizing the occasional tyrannies of governing majorities, they amended the Constitution so that free speech and assembly should be guaranteed. Fear of serious injury cannot alone justify suppression of free speech and assembly. Men feared witches and burnt women. It is the function of speech to free men from the bondage of irrational fears. . . . Those who won our independence by revolution were not cowards. They did not fear political change. They did not exalt order at the cost of liberty. . . . If there be time to expose through discussion the falsehood and fallacies, to avert the evil by the processes of education, the remedy to be applied is more speech, not enforced silence. Only an emergency can justify repression. Such must be the rule if authority is to be reconciled with freedom. Such, in my opinion, is the command of the Constitution.[67]

What is the significance of this passage, beautifully written as it is? As a formal matter, it is a description of the views of the founders, a group of historical figures who can be identified—at least if we may confine ourselves to the group's prominent leaders—with considerable precision (in the broad sense Brandeis obviously intends, Washington, Madison, Jefferson, and Sam and

John Adams were all founders, but Justice Story [too late] and Benedict Arnold [wrong side] were not). But the passage makes no real pretense at being the distillation of historical research into that group's views. There are two quotations from Jefferson in a footnote that I have omitted, but that is all. Brandeis is not making an argument about original meaning in the sense common in contemporary constitutional scholarship and judicial opinions. It would miss the point to cite historical evidence that Jefferson was willing to countenance seditious libel prosecutions under state authority.

Nor is this simply a purple passage, stirring rhetoric intended to ease down the bitter tonic of the doctrinal discussion in which it is embedded. In the paragraph immediately before the quoted passage begins, Brandeis noted that the Court had "not yet fixed the standard by which to determine" when speech meets the "clear and present danger" test (derived from Holmes's opinion in *Schenck v. United States*) and can therefore be penalized. The quoted passage is the foundation for Brandeis's proposal that "the command of the Constitution" requires the Court to insist that the government establish in any case in which it wishes to suppress speech that the danger it seeks to avert is genuinely imminent and serious, that it goes beyond advocacy of law-breaking to direct and immediate incitement to violation of the law. The majority justices thought, quite reasonably, that such a standard permits incendiaries immunity from interference until a point that might be just short of a political conflagration. It is the passage we are considering that was Brandeis's explanation of why and how the Constitution can require such extensive tolerance of political "doctrine which a vast majority of [the state's] citizens believes to be false and fraught with evil consequence."

In this passage, Brandeis was neither engaged in historical scholarship nor indulging in literary ornamentation. Rather he was proposing a way to understand the significance, for free speech, of the historical enterprise that "those who won our independence" set underway. Isn't this the compelling, the morally and politically attractive way to understand our constitutional tradition, Brandeis implicitly asks his reader. There are, doubtless, other ways to interpret that tradition, each involving the same interplay between history—the gritty past reality of other persons, other times—and present-day moral, political, and social thought. A reader who believes that the Republic's roots lie more in authority and social order than in liberty and political openness will find Brandeis unpersuasive, just as a reader troubled by the threat posed by political radicalism to the political community might find the doctrine Brandeis proposed too risky to implement. Nothing about the passage we are discussing compels assent, as if to a geometric proof. Instead, Brandeis invites us to see the Republic in a certain light, and interpret the Constitution in that light.

Justice Brandeis's invitation has been universally accepted. As early as *Stromberg v. California* in 1931, the Court began treating his *Whitney* concurrence as an authority in free speech cases, and by 1964 the Court could refer to his opinion as providing the "classic formulation" of the fundamental principle underlying the first amendment's guaranty of freedom of speech.[68] While the doctrinal formulations through which the courts enforce the first amendment have proliferated enormously since 1927, there has been for several decades a consensus on the Supreme Court and more generally that Brandeis's robustly libertarian vision of the role of speech in American society is normative. It is now the basis on which one can make arguments rather than an issue in contention. The legitimacy of easy governmental resort to the suppression of political expression viewed as dangerous is no longer a viable constitutional position.[69]

Justice Brandeis's interpretation of the place of freedom of speech in the American constitutional order is so familiar that it is easy to miss part of the significance of its victory. It did not prevail because Brandeis was a better historian than those advocating narrower understandings of constitutional free speech, for as we noted he did not present an historical argument. Nor was his interpretation successful because no other view gives a coherent picture of democracy, freedom, or the words of the first amendment. Brandeis's argument was rhetorical in nature, and thus asked for assent on the basis of its attractiveness as a vision of constitutional meaning. The questions asked by someone attempting to decide whether to accept or reject such an argument include its fit with text and history, but also, unavoidably, its implicit projection of the future: if we accept this vision of constitutional meaning, what will the United States become? What are the implications of this vision for American government and society? Such questions cannot be answered in a mechanical or value-neutral manner. They necessarily involve the moral and political commitments of the person trying to answer them, and these commitments may conflict with those of other Americans. All that Brandeis strove to do in *Whitney*, all that anyone can do in similar circumstances, is state his or her vision clearly, and hope that enough others find it compelling.

In making an argument of this kind, Brandeis was in good company, for constitutionalists have been making such arguments from the beginning of the Republic. (Think of the debate between Jefferson and Hamilton over the national bank legislation, or of the arguments for a broad reading of the first amendment that Jefferson's allies advanced during the Sedition Act crisis.) The prevalence of such arguments in constitutional discussion is unsurprising, given the close interconnections we have observed between constitutional views and moral, political, and ideological commitments. They mark American constitutionalism for what it is: a tradition of attempting to persuade one another—and, especially where that proves impossible, posterity—that one or the other clashing vision of the Republic's meaning is more attractive, morally and politically. Brandeis's vision in *Whitney* is normative for the simple reason that over time it proved more persuasive than its competitors.

XXI. 1944: Constitutional Injustice

At the time of the attack on Pearl Harbor that brought the United States into World War Two, three federal agencies, the FBI, the Office of Naval Intelligence, and Army Intelligence, were engaged in surveillance of, and investigation into the loyalty of, residents of the United States who were of Japanese origin or descent. These investigations focused on Japanese Americans living on the West Coast and in Hawaii, but did not differentiate between citizens and resident aliens. As a result of their work, the agencies were "confident that they had identified all potential subversives," and within three weeks of Pearl Harbor, the majority of these suspects had been arrested. "With the completion of these arrests, the FBI and the Justice Department were satisfied that Japanese-Americans no longer posed any threat to national security."[70]

Enter, stage right, racism and xenophobia. The military officer responsible for security on the Pacific coast, Lieutenant General John L. DeWitt, a racist whose dislike for people with Japanese ancestry was patent, militated for more far-reaching measures including the removal of all such people from the area of his command. (General Delos C. Emmons, DeWitt's analogue in endangered Hawaii, resisted calls there for the internment of Japanese Americans.) DeWitt's internal remonstrations were seconded publicly by prominent California politicians and influential journalists including, on February 12, 1942, Walter Lippmann. Resistance to an internment program within the administration of Franklin D. Roosevelt crumbled, as senior officials scrambled guiltily to avoid personal responsibility for the idea, and on February 19, President Roosevelt signed Executive Order No. 9066, which authorized Secretary of War Henry Stimson to take broad steps ensuring "every possible

protection against espionage and against sabotage." Congress hurriedly enacted, over little opposition, a statute providing criminal penalties for violations of orders pursuant to 9066, and by early June most Japanese Americans
on the West Coast had been confined to internment camps. Eventually "some
112,000 men, women, and children would be held for an average of 900 days
under harsh conditions in rural areas and wastelands."[71]

No one today defends the confinement of thousands of persons, most of
them American citizens, to concentration camps. The Civil Liberties Act of
1988 states that "Congress recognizes that . . . a grave injustice was done to
both citizens and permanent resident aliens of Japanese ancestry by the evac-
uation, relocation, and internment of civilians during World War II."[72] The
Supreme Court's two decisions upholding the constitutionality of convictions
for violating military orders issued pursuant to Executive Order No. 9066,
Hirabayashi v. United States and *Korematsu v. United States*,[73] are generally viewed
as among the Court's greatest disasters, and rightly so. The entire episode was
a massive betrayal of the vision of inclusive democracy the previous section of
this work discussed. But despite this betrayal—or rather because of it—these
events, and (for our purposes) in particular the opinions in *Korematsu*, are of
enormous significance for understanding American constitutionalism.

The defendant in *Hirabayashi* was convicted of violating a curfew order,
and Chief Justice Stone's opinion for the Court sustaining the conviction
stressed the narrowness of the holding: "we decide only that the curfew order
as applied, and at the time it was applied, was within the boundaries of the
war power."[74] In *Korematsu*, however, the Court was confronted with a direct
challenge to the constitutionality of General DeWitt's order that "all persons
of Japanese ancestry should be excluded from" an area including San Lean-
dro, California, the defendant's home town. For the Court, Justice Hugo Black
announced that "all legal restrictions which curtail the civil rights of a single
racial group are immediately suspect" and subject to "the most rigid scrutiny"
by the courts. "Pressing public necessity may sometimes justify the existence of
such restrictions; racial antagonism never can." While he admitted that "exclusion from the area in which one's home is located is a far greater deprivation than" the imposition of an evening curfew, Black concluded that
Hirabayashi required the Court to sustain the exclusion order. "[E]xclusion
from a threatened area, no less than curfew, has a definite and close relationship
to the prevention of espionage and sabotage. . . . Here, as in the *Hirabayashi*
case, we cannot reject as unfounded the judgment of the military authorities
and of Congress that . . . the national defense and safety" required the government's draconian measures.[75]

Three justices dissented. Justice Frank Murphy straightforwardly invoked the inclusivity of American constitutional democracy in rejecting what he termed "this legalization of racism":

> Racial discrimination in any form and in any degree has no justifiable part whatever in our democratic way of life. It is unattractive in any setting but it is utterly revolting among a free people who have embraced the principles set forth in the Constitution of the United States. All residents of this nation are kin in some way by blood or culture to a foreign land. Yet they are primarily and necessarily a part of the new and distinct civilization of the United States. They must accordingly be treated at all times as the heirs of the American experiment and as entitled to all the rights and freedoms guaranteed by the Constitution.[76]

Justice Robert H. Jackson agreed with Murphy's conclusion but thought the constitutional issue was that Toyosaburo Korematsu had been convicted of a "crime" defined by a military order that made his "guilt" turn entirely on a fact having no connection to anything he had done or not done: "here is an attempt to make an otherwise innocent act a crime merely because this prisoner is the son of parents as to whom he had no choice, and belongs to a race from which there is no way to resign." "Now, if any fundamental assumption underlies our system, it is that guilt is personal and not inheritable."[77]

Jackson and Murphy sharply disagreed on the response the Court should have made to the government's argument that the race-based exclusion order was legally justified by exigent military need. For Murphy, however unusual the circumstances, the argument was a perfectly ordinary one, to be analyzed through a version of the familiar judicial inquiry into the reasonableness of governmental action:

> [L]ike other claims conflicting with the asserted constitutional rights of the individual, the military claim must subject itself to the judicial process of having its reasonableness determined and its conflicts with other interests reconciled. . . . The judicial test of whether the Government, on a plea of military necessity, can validly deprive an individual of any of his constitutional rights is whether the deprivation is reasonably related to a public danger that is so "immediate, imminent, and impending" as not to admit of delay and not to permit the intervention of ordinary constitutional processes to alleviate the danger. . . . In adjudging the military action taken in light of the then apparent dangers, we must not erect too high or too meticulous standards; it is necessary only that the action have some reasonable relation to the removal of the dangers of invasion, sabotage and espionage.

DeWitt's order, and thus Korematsu's conviction for violating the order, failed this quite lenient test in Murphy's view because he thought it simply illogical to assume that "all persons of Japanese ancestry may have a dangerous tendency to commit sabotage and espionage."[78] The majority had gone astray through its failure to notice or acknowledge the irrationality—and hence the racism, whether intentional or not—of the exclusion program.

Jackson, in contrast, thought the Court's error lay in entertaining the government's argument in the first place. The actions of military commanders dealing with a military emergency are not and cannot be governed by law as a civil court understands that term:

> It would be impracticable and dangerous idealism to expect or insist that each specific military command in an area of probable operations will conform to conventional tests of constitutionality. . . . No court can require such a commander in such circumstances to act as a reasonable man; he may be unreasonably cautious and exacting. Perhaps he should be. But a commander in temporarily focusing the life of a community on defense is carrying out a military program; he is not making law in the sense the courts know the term. He issues orders, and they may have a certain authority as military commands, although they may be very bad as constitutional law.[79]

This being the case, Jackson thought the entire enterprise of purporting to subject the reasonableness of DeWitt's order to judicial scrutiny was a vain and empty pretense. "In the very nature of things military decisions are not susceptible of intelligent judicial appraisal." Dependent on the military's own "self-serving" assertions of facts often beyond proof by the rules of evidence (and which it would often be completely imprudent to disclose to a court), "courts can never have any real alternative to accepting the mere declaration of the authority that issued the order that it was reasonably necessary from a military point of view."

Such judicial rubber-stamping of military action that is a prima facie violation of the Constitution is, Jackson asserted, itself "a far more subtle blow to liberty than the promulgation of the order itself," for by "rationaliz[ing] the Constitution to show that the Constitution sanctions such an order," the Court introduces into the Constitution the very evil it is meant to prohibit. By upholding DeWitt's order as constitutional because justified militarily, the Court had "validated the principle of racial discrimination in criminal procedure and of transplanting American citizens." The Court, not the military, had transformed what were, before its decisions, absolute constitutional prohibitions into limitations subject to being overridden by a strong enough claim of governmental necessity. "The principle then lies about like a loaded weapon ready for the hand of any authority that can bring forward a plausible claim of an urgent need." The conversion of a prohibition into a defeasible limitation is an invitation to justify other, perhaps harsher invasions of the constitutional right whenever the government is willing to assert a weighty enough interest, as *Korematsu*'s reliance on *Hirabayashi* showed.

Jackson therefore believed that the Court should have refused to bend constitutional principle to the claims of military need. The question of whether DeWitt's actions were reasonable militarily was for the military (and presumably its civilian commander in chief, although Jackson neglected to mention the president) to determine.[80] Jackson's "duties as a justice" were quite different. "I should hold that a civil court cannot be made to enforce an order which violates constitutional limitations even if it is a reasonable exercise of military authority. The courts can exercise only the judicial power, can apply only law, and must abide by the Constitution, or they cease to be civil courts and become instruments of military policy." Having taken Korematsu to the civil courts, the military authorities should have received the only response a court is commissioned to give, that the law does not permit criminal convictions based on race.

Justice Felix Frankfurter took issue with the distinction Jackson drew between the requirements of military action and the demands of the law. "Within their sphere, military authorities are no more outside the bounds of obedience to the Constitution than are judges within theirs." Frankfurter thought farcical Jackson's notion that there might be actions a military commander could or even ought to take, and legitimate therefore from a military perspective, that would nonetheless be violations of the Constitution. "To recognize that military orders are 'reasonably expedient military precautions' in time of war and yet to deny them constitutional legitimacy makes of the Constitution an instrument for dialectic subtleties not reasonably to be attributed to the hard-headed Framers, of whom a majority had had actual participation in war." Jackson was confusing a holding that the Constitution does not forbid a given exercise of "the war power of the Government" with judicial approval of "that which Congress and the Executive did. That is their business, not ours."[81]

Korematsu v. United States raises issues of the deepest significance for American constitutionalism. One stems from the dispute between Justices Frankfurter and Jackson over the latter's proposal that the Court cabin off an area of military action (and perhaps other governmental activity, at least during wartime) that is simply beyond judicial review. Frankfurter was surely right that governmental actors are not absolved from their constitutional responsibilities simply because they are acting in a military capacity, or in wartime. To the extent that Jackson's proposal might seem to license disregard for constitutional principles by military authorities, its effects might be pernicious, and indeed self-defeating, since Jackson's concern was to safeguard the Constitution. The president as commander in chief, and *a fortiori* his uniformed subordinates, have no power that does not come directly or immediately from the Constitution and as a result is beyond the Constitution's limitations. On the other hand, Jackson's observations about the impact on constitutional law of judicial decisions that create exceptions to constitutional principles protecting liberty based on governmental necessity seem to me entirely correct. It may be that on rare occasions it is morally and politically right for the executive to take actions that cannot be defended constitutionally. Two of our most constitutionally sophisticated presidents, Jefferson and Lincoln, were inclined to hold this opinion.[82] Jackson, on the other hand, was undoubtedly correct to see courts as invariably limited to the commands of the Constitution.

As important as these matters are, *Korematsu* reveals an even deeper truth about the American constitutional system: the potential within it for procedural and substantive regularity to coexist with, and even to validate, injustice. Today's universal—and entirely justified—abhorrence at the government's actions should not be allowed to obscure the fact that those actions were approved by the national legislature and reviewed and upheld by an independent judiciary. In striking contrast with President Lincoln's actions at the outbreak of the Civil War, the Roosevelt administration neither prevented Fred Korematsu from challenging the exclusion order nor suggested any inclination to disobey the writ of the federal courts. The Supreme Court's rejection of his challenge was freely decided by life-tenured judges far from any physical danger, and rested on the principle, acknowledged from the beginning of the Republic, that the Constitution creates "an efficient national Government" with the power to protect the nation "against *hostilities* from abroad." The Court said nothing surprising when it wrote in *Hirabayashi* that "it is not for any court to sit in review of the wisdom of their action or substitute its judgment" for the decisions of "those branches of the Government on which the Constitution has placed the responsibility of warmaking."[83] Lacking the benefit of hindsight, Justice Black and his colleagues in the majority were well within the bounds of existing legal thought in declining to substitute their judgment for the government's on the justification for the exclusion order at issue in *Korematsu*. The American constitutional order functioned smoothly . . . and thousands of people suffered needlessly and unjustly. Constitutionalism is a means for seeking to do justice, not a guarantee that we will have the wisdom or vision to do so.

.

PART FIVE

The constitutional history of the United States is not the inexorable working out of some deep historical process carrying this society along toward
a predestined goal, however that goal might be described. It is something less,
and more: the ongoing process by which men and women in the United States
have made arguments, structured disputes, and reached decisions in the pursuit of their moral and political objectives—their selfish interests, yes; but also
their ideals of liberty and community. In that process many things have happened that seem to me wrong and regrettable, but to acknowledge this does
not mean that I think the story is an entirely repellent one. Close attention to
the history of constitutional discussion, I have tried to show, can bring to light
the ways in which constitutionalism has served as a means to maintain the
American political community across time and in the midst of partisan strife.
Beyond that, furthermore, I believe that we can identify some themes that are
common ground for contemporary constitutional debate. These themes are,
to be sure, no more invulnerable to modification or displacement than any
other principles that have held sway in our history, and they leave unanswered
the questions that most trouble us today, as they must: they are the starting
points for contemporary constitutional argument, not its conclusions. For us,
as for our predecessors, the conclusions we reach will not, cannot, be dictated
by our premises; they are decisions that we must make. But it is something, I
think, to understand better those premises, and the means by which they came
to assume that role.

XXII. 2002: Common Ground after Two Centuries

As the reader will recall, already in 1818 Henry St. George Tucker unhappily identified one feature of a system of government founded on a written Constitution, the destabilizing manner in which the instrument's existence renders possible future challenges to present-day understandings of the Constitution's meaning:

> Do gentlemen suppose that if, which Heaven permit! this confederation of States shall last for a century, we shall, throughout that period, be continually mooting Constitutional points; holding nothing as decided; admitting no construction to have been agreed upon; and, instead of going on with the business of the nation, continually occupied with fighting, over and over again, battles a thousand times won?[1]

In some measure, the answer to Tucker's question turns out to be yes. Our constitutional history is replete with issues and themes that emerge again and again regardless of how clearly they seem settled on any given occasion.

At the same time, it would be a mistake to infer (as Tucker feared his opponents thought or implied) that everything is perpetually up for grabs, that we "admit no construction to have been agreed upon." Issues that were once subjects of debate do—sometimes—achieve a resolution that becomes a presupposition, not a question, in subsequent constitutional debate. Certain options in how to understand and apply the Constitution that were alive become foreclosed by decisions or events or, on rare occasions, formal amendments of the text. Other options that would once have seemed farfetched become live questions for discussion and decision. There is nothing inevitable or inexorable about this process, and the principles that seem agreed upon at one point may always be narrowed, transformed, or (infrequently) repudiated at a later time. But the longer a principle is accepted, the more difficult its repudiation, both because it becomes part of the bedrock assumptions that all constitutionalists bring to the task, and because the practical implications of repudiation become extremely weighty. Regardless of whether one is persuaded by the arguments of Madison and others for the normative significance of constitutional practice, I think there can be no doubt that as a pragmatic matter, long-standing practice comes to share in substantial measure in the axiomatic authority of the text.

With that historical observation in mind, where do we stand, at the beginning of the twenty-first century, with respect to the Constitution of the United States? What broad principles beyond the undisputed if ambiguous authority of the text seem decided in such a fashion as to preclude serious challenge in any practical setting? What is the common ground on which present-day constitutionalists stand as we come to rhetorical blows over the hotly disputed issues of our day? A number of years ago, the distinguished philosopher Alasdair MacIntyre argued that American constitutional law is empty at its center. In any contentious constitutional case, he wrote, the Supreme Court "play[s] the role of a peace-making or truce-keeping body by negotiating its way through an impasse of conflict, not by invoking our society's shared moral first principles. For our society as a whole has none."[2] MacIntyre's assertion begs the question of what relationship can or ought to exist between *moral* first principles and the principles embodied in a constitution of government; but even with respect to constitutional law itself, MacIntyre's accusation is in error. The United States does have a set of shared constitutional first principles. What follows is my attempt to identify them, even if admittedly at a very high level of generality and with no thought of exclusivity.

(1) *No political or social dispute—none, not any, not ever—is to be resolved by military means.* The crucial "decision" here is, of course, the Civil War, in which the national government used military force to reject the proposition that it is legitimate to withdraw from the national political community and to seek to maintain that stance of secession by force. The irony of attributing this principle to "the constitutional experts on Missionary Ridge" (as Professor Black once referred to the Union army) is obvious, but the success of their efforts in eliminating force as a factor in American political controversies is profoundly important.

(2) *The electoral processes ordained for selecting the president and members of Congress must be followed regardless of circumstance or consequence.* Some people think that one or more presidential elections have been stolen, and there is no doubt that has been true in some indeterminate number of congressional races. But the principle that we hold the constitutionally ordained elections on time, during war or peace, and that we abide by their outcomes is now unshakable, however unhappy many of us sometimes are over the outcome.[3]

(3) *Each and every action of the federal government, its branches, its components, its officers and its agents must be authorized by the Constitution.* This principle brings with it a necessary corollary: *There are no extraconstitutional sources of federal power.* The contrary argument has occasionally been advanced, most notably by Justice George Sutherland in an opinion for the Supreme Court in 1936. (Sutherland thought that the president's authority with respect to foreign affairs derived

from national sovereignty rather than the Constitution, although even he admitted that the Constitution controls the president's exercise of that authority.) It is quite clear that Sutherland's argument has been rejected by the Supreme Court, the executive branch, and generally,[4] and it is broadly considered a settled matter that all parts of the federal government are entirely dependent on the Constitution, and subsidiary sources of law authorized by the Constitution (statutes and treaties), for the power to act. It is thus always germane, with respect to any federal action, to ask whether it is duly authorized under the Constitution.

(4) *With exceptions relating to the federal government, the state governments need not demonstrate that their actions are authorized by the Constitution.* As a matter of federal constitutional law, state governments presumptively have authority to legislate on any matter not forbidden to them by the Constitution of the United States, including those matters that the Constitution assigns to the jurisdiction of the federal government. It may be the case that on some matters relating to the states' role in selecting the president and Congress the states' powers derive from the Constitution, an issue on which the Supreme Court sharply divided in 1995.[5] With that important but very limited possible exception, state governmental power is a product of some other source of political authority, and its exercise is not subject to challenge on the ground that the federal Constitution does not affirmatively authorize it.

(5) *The federal government is not omnicompetent.* Put another way, the federal government's authority does not extend to all conceivable governmental actions not prohibited by the Constitution. The Supreme Court's recent decisions striking down federal statutes on the grounds that they were not affirmatively authorized by Article I or the fourteenth amendment were and are controversial, but the principle is unchallenged. An application of it that is not currently controversial is the rule that federal courts sitting in diversity (because the litigants are citizens of different states) must apply the substantive law of the relevant state.[6]

(6) *State governments and state officers must obey federal rules of law and federal commands that are consistent with the Constitution.* Recent Supreme Court decisions limiting Congress's power to "commandeer" state officials or allow federal legal actions against unconsenting states may have obscured the fact that this principle remains unquestioned. The debate has in every case been over whether the particular federal rule or command was consistent with the Constitution.

(7) *The exercise of constitutionally authorized (or permitted) powers is subordinate to constitutional prohibitions and guarantees of individual liberty: in short, constitutional rights trump constitutional powers.* Founding-era constitutionalists were uncertain

whether to understand constitutional rights as simply areas that lie beyond the affirmative power of a particular government, or to see them as prohibitions on certain exercises of power that as an original matter might be within the scope of the government's authority. It has long been settled that the latter is the proper interpretation: it would be unconstitutional for Congress to forbid the transportation of copies of the Bible in commerce among the several states not because the statute would be outside the scope of the commerce clause but because it would violate the first amendment.

(8) *Some constitutional rights are absolute; some are not, and their scope is defined in part with respect to social need.* The right not to be subject to a governmental imposition and not to be denied a governmental benefit on the basis of one's theological beliefs is absolute; the right to enforce contractual obligations owed one without retrospective interference by government is not. There are many and difficult questions with the modern Supreme Court's tendency to treat almost all rights as defined by a judicial balancing of governmental and individual interests, but the principle, as I have stated it, seems secure.

(9) *As a matter of constitutional law, American executive officers must obey judicial orders, at least once affirmed at the highest level.* President Madison's 1809 pronouncement that the executive's duty is to enforce judicial decisions is constitutional orthodoxy. The only clear counterexample is President Lincoln's instruction to his subordinates to disregard a writ of habeas corpus issued by Chief Justice Taney during the early days of the Civil War.[7]

(10) *As a matter of constitutional morality, American legislatures ought to respect settled judicial views about the meaning of the Constitution, unless they undertake the task of amending the Constitution.* The reader is familiar with the idea that the Constitution generates norms of political conduct that ought to be observed even though they are not legally enforceable and may even be, in some sense, not rules of law at all. In recent decades, state legislatures have sometimes skirted if not openly violated this principle, but I believe that only illustrates the obvious point that at times human beings will disobey even a settled principle governing their conduct. Congressional practice is more respectful of the courts, and the principle is an important one. If legislatures disregarded it as a general matter they could simply overwhelm the judicial system with repeated, calculated violations of constitutional rules the courts are committed to maintaining.

(11) *The judiciary is not infallible; therefore, the people and the political branches of the federal government ought to take appropriate steps to change the constitutional views of the judiciary, when they believe the courts have erred, through constitutional amendment, litigation, and the appointments process.* The most formal means of correcting perceived

judicial error, the amendment process created by Article V, is also the most cumbersome, and I believe that our history legitimates efforts to persuade the courts to change their views on constitutional matters through the litigation process and by appointing, as opportunity arises, judges likely to take a different position. The use of the appointments process for this purpose raises some hard questions in application, but despite the occasional protest by those substantively opposed to whatever change is sought, the principle is settled.

(12) *The Constitution assigns the resolution of some constitutional questions to the political branches of the federal government; therefore, the judiciary must abstain from addressing these questions.* There is no (nonacademic) dispute over this principle in the abstract. My own view is that the judiciary is not sensible enough of its importance in practice, and that this in turn generates or contributes to a sense on the part of electorally responsible officials that they need not worry overmuch about constitutional issues as long as they avoid trouble with the courts. Others will disagree with that opinion, but the disagreement is over the scope of a precept, not its validity.

(13) *There are no (federal) extraconstitutional sources of legal limitation on the political branches or the states; therefore, a court exercising the power of judicial review under federal law must invoke a rule of law ultimately derived from the Constitution.* If Justice Chase meant to suggest in *Calder v. Bull* that courts can invalidate statutes on grounds unrelated to a written constitution, he long ago lost the argument. There is no "general constitutional law" on the basis of which a federal court can invalidate the action of one of the political branches or of a state government. If the court cannot show that the action contravenes some legal rule based on the Constitution immediately or indirectly (by being contained in a valid statute or treaty), it has no power to interfere. Similarly, a state court cannot invalidate federal or state governmental action, on federal grounds, unless it can make a similar showing. The power of a state court to invalidate state governmental action on state grounds is not generally a matter of federal constitutional law.[8]

(14) *In constitutional argument it is legitimate to invoke text, constitutional structure, original meaning, original intent, judicial precedent and doctrine, political-branch practice and doctrine, settled expectations, the ethos of American constitutionalism, the traditions of our law and our people, and the consequences of differing interpretations of the Constitution.* Eclecticism in the modalities of argument recognized as constitutional has been standard in American constitutional law since the founding. The array of arguments that are acceptable can change over time: for example, the importance of political-branch interpretation, at least in the courts, has waned somewhat without becoming irrelevant, while the saliency of arguments based on alleged elements of our constitutional ethos tends to ebb and flow

over time (compare early-twentieth-century freedom of contract with late-twentieth-century privacy). Thus the principle has a corollary: *The Constitution does not ordain a fixed set of legitimate forms of argument.* Academic constitutional lawyers and the occasional Supreme Court justice sometimes make arguments that the list of legitimate modalities ought to be drastically shortened, which is itself a legitimate form of argument but ought to be recognized for what it is, a proposal for radical reform. As the traditionally accepted, longish list of legitimate methods suggests, constitutional law is not the logical working-out of any unitary theory. Hence a second corollary: *The Constitution does not ordain a particular moral or political theory.*

(15) *The Constitution is a practical instrument of governance: its grants of power and its guarantees of individual liberty are to be construed, to the extent reasonably possible, to create a coherent political system capable of achieving the goals stated in its preamble.* This principle underlies a great many discrete features of modern constitutional law. One example: the Supreme Court long ago rejected both the argument that Congress's power over interstate commerce is exclusive (so that a state is precluded entirely from regulation affecting such commerce) and the argument that in the absence of affirmative congressional action, the states are free to take whatever steps they wish, including outright and parochial protectionism. The resulting "dormant" commerce clause doctrine is untidy but workable.

(16) *The Congress is constitutionally authorized to regulate the national economy.* Despite the historical and other arguments that can be mounted against the New Deal era decision fully to accept this principle, it remains firmly in place. The Supreme Court's recent efforts to set some judicially enforceable limit to the scope of Congress's power over interstate commerce have been hotly contested on the Court, and only one justice has given any indication that he questions this principle as a general matter.[9]

(17) *American governments must respect an extremely broad realm of free expression.* The struggle to define the basic scope of the first amendment's guarantee of freedom of speech and press, which began in earnest in 1790s, has been settled for at least fifty years and arguably longer. Our sometimes bitter disputes over the application of this principle in particular cases can easily overshadow the remarkable degree of consensus on a fundamental level.

(18) *American governments must not compel religious or—save in fairly rare circumstances—political expression.* The principle that theological matters are wholly beyond the competence and cognizance of government is so familiar that it is easy to forget how important a constitutional accomplishment it represents. Justice Jackson stated the principle in even wider terms in 1943 when he wrote

that "[i]f there is any fixed star in our constitutional constellation, it is that no official, high or petty, can prescribe what shall be orthodox in politics, nationalism, religion, or other matters of opinion or force citizens to confess by word or act their faith therein."[10] Read too literally, that might be seen as something of an exaggeration: the Constitution does not prohibit the president from choosing his or her advisors or the military from precluding convinced pacifists from occupying positions of command over combat troops. In general, however, government may no more concern itself with a citizen's political opinions than with her religious commitments.

(19) *American governments must not enforce or condone racial caste.* The constitutionality of race-based affirmative action, and the related question of race-conscious electoral redistricting, are currently among the five or six major constitutional issues that evoke the most serious and far-reaching disagreement among constitutionalists and citizens generally. The illegitimacy of governmentally sponsored discrimination against racial minorities, on the other hand, is axiomatic.

(20) *American governments must obey judicially defined processes when they inflict (at least many forms of) injury on individuals.* The presupposition lying behind *State v. Munn,* that there can be a domain of public life beyond the reach of the rule of law, is as a general matter gone from constitutional law. There are partial exceptions, particularly with respect to the treatment of some illegal aliens, and the precise scope of judicially enforceable limitations on such matters as police procedure remains in flux. But the principle seems clear and unquestioned.

At the beginning of the twenty-first century, there are enormously important constitutional issues that are both current and contentious: the constitutionality of governmental restrictions on abortion is the paradigmatic example. We Americans are, as we have always been, divided on humanly significant questions of public policy, some of which are of constitutional dimension. At the same time, our disagreements take place against the backdrop, and in the presence of, hard-won agreement on the Constitution's meaning for many issues. While we indeed have spent the almost two centuries since Henry St. George Tucker asked his question, quoted at the beginning of this section, in continually mooting constitutional points, we have also come to see much as decided, many constructions as agreed upon. In midst of our ongoing battles over the meaning of the Constitution and of the Republic that it constitutes, we have gone on with the business of the nation.

CONCLUSION

Is there any Constitution in constitutional law? To be sure, what I called in the introduction the "housekeeping details" in the written instrument are of great importance in structuring the American political process and the central institutions of the federal government. The election of 2000 illustrated the difficulties posed when a question of the sort usually resolved by the housekeeping provisions of the Constitution eludes determination in that manner. Almost by definition, however, these provisions are peripheral to the sort of controversies that are usually in view when we refer to constitutional law. And beyond them, once the thoroughgoing historicity of constitutional law becomes clear, lies a domain of political, moral, and social debate that is chaotic and (often) ideologically charged. Jefferson and Hamilton weren't wrangling over some narrow question of documentary interpretation in 1791; they were locked in disagreement over fundamental questions of what this country is and should be. The same could be said of most of the altercations we have considered in this book. Is there anything that can be said about American constitutionalism other than that it is an ongoing process by which a varying set of public questions are resolved, not by direct debate over the merits of competing policies, but instead in terms derived (sometimes remotely) from the written instruments that we call constitutions?

To be sure, the creation of a common language of debate and a tradition of political dispute resolution centered on judicial review is in itself no mean accomplishment. Language shapes human thought and decisionmaking in ways that go beyond and deeper than we consciously realize. The salience and dignity of arguments invoking "the Constitution" have been an important influence on the evolution of American social and political norms: the deep-rooted allegiance to the rule of law that Canadian philosopher George Grant attributed years ago to the tradition of "English-speaking justice" flows, in the United States, along constitutional channels. In recent years, to be sure, a powerful case has been made for the proposition that this influence has not been altogether benign: "rights talk," some contend, has contributed to the hegemony of an excessive and atomistic individualism in our culture. Whatever the specific mixture of good and evil in the way constitutional law assumptions and concepts have become rooted in American thought, I believe that they play a significant role in sustaining the American political community's sense of unity. The distinguished American writer E. L. Doctorow made this point in an essay he wrote in 1987, the bicentennial of the Philadelphia convention that framed the U.S. Constitution:

> [T]he great genius of the convention of 1787 . . . was its community of discourse. The law it designed found character from the means of its designing. Something arose from its deliberations, however contentious, and that was the empowering act of composition given to people who know what words mean and how they must be valued. Nobody told anybody else to love it or leave it; nobody told anybody else to go back where they came from; nobody suggested disagreement was disloyalty; and nobody pulled a gun. Ideas, difficult ideas, were articulated with language and disputed with language and took their final fate, to be passed or rejected, as language. . . . This is what we cherish and honor, a document that gives us the means by which we may fearlessly argue ourselves into clarity as a free and unified people.[1]

Doctorow was no apologist for the American status quo or for the federal government of that time—in his essay he opined that the United States was "evolving . . . into a national military state"—but he was profoundly optimistic about the manner in which the Constitution and constitutional law have contributed to the American attempt to build a political community not on the basis of a shared religion, homogenous ethnicity, or moral consensus, but rather through words, the maintenance and expansion of an ongoing tradition of debate and disagreement among *our* people.

The idea that a political community can be built on words is, from many perspectives, chimerical or even farcical. Mao Tse-tung wrote that "political power grows out of the barrel of a gun,"[2] and the history of the American Republic could supply abundant evidence for his dictum, from the Revolutionary War that made the Republic possible on. The maintenance of the constitutional Union itself during the crisis of 1860 to 1865 was the product of a bloody civil war, and many provisions of the Constitution's text are a reminder that this was no aberration, that as law the Constitution rests ultimately on the willingness of men and women to enforce it by violent means. *State v. Mann* and *Korematsu v. United States* bear witness to the fact that Americans are no more immune than any other human beings from the temptation to refuse to talk, to exclude others from what Doctorow called the "community of discourse." And from a very different moral stance than Mao's, some contemporary communitarians view American constitutionalism's reliance on talk as a mistake, a product of the Enlightenment's hubristic overconfidence in the power of rationality. Political community, these critics argue, must have deeper roots and stronger ties. A polity built on talk is too thin in moral substance to evoke or deserve commitment; it conduces to atomism and anomie.

Perhaps so. Justice Holmes wrote that the Constitution is an experiment. There are many ways to characterize what the experiment is about and how it is going. In this book, through engagement with a series of controversies in our constitutional history, I have argued that one way to interpret American constitutionalism is as a tradition of talk in which a persistent theme has been the inclusion of people within the conversation, within the community of discourse that the Constitution announces and constitutional law, at its best, safeguards. Rather than suppressing disagreement by force, delegitimizing it by fiat, or wishing it away by fantasy, American constitutionalism can be read as an ongoing proposal to maintain political community in the teeth of, and indeed through means of, robust disagreement.

The Constitution provides no guarantee that the outcomes of our disagreements will be wise or just or good. Whether our political actions deserve those accolades or their opposites will depend on our wisdom, justice, and virtue. And since the very question of which course of action would be wise or just or good is often precisely what is in dispute, a central aspect of our constitutional history is ongoing debate over what we have done. American constitutional law provides no haven from controversy; all it offers is the means by which people of fundamentally different views, beliefs, origins, and visions can become and remain a political community.

NOTES

Abbreviations and Shortened Titles Used in the Notes

Annals   Annals of the Congress of the United States (Joseph Gales & William
Seaton ed., 1834 ff.)

DHFFC   Documentary History of the First Federal Congress 1789–1791 (Charlene
Bangs Bickford et al. ed., 1972–95)

DHRC   Documentary History of the Ratification of the Constitution (Merrill
Jensen et al. ed., 1976–)

Federalist   The Federalist (Jacob E. Cooke ed., 1961).

Va. Rep.   The Virginia Report of 1799–1800 . . . together with the Virginia
Resolutions of December 21, 1798, the Debate and Proceedings Thereon
in the House of Delegates of Virginia, and several other documents
illustrative of the Report and Resolutions (J. W. Randolph ed., 1850)

I have not provided pinpoint citations to relatively short documents from which I quote
extensively.

Introduction

1. *Olsen v. Nebraska ex rel. Western Reference & Bond Assoc.*, 313 U.S. 236, 246–47 (1941).

2. L. H. LaRue, Constitutional Law and Constitutional History, 36 Buff. L. Rev. 373
(1987). Professor LaRue's brilliant essay is an unjustly neglected gem of constitutional
scholarship.

3. Charles L. Black, On Worrying about the Constitution, 55 U.Colo. L. Rev. 469
(1984).

4. Finley Peter Dunne, Mr. Dooley's Opinions 26 (1900)

5. An Impartial Citizen, A Dissertation upon the Constitutional Freedom of the Press
(1801), in 2 American Political Writing during the Founding Era, 1760–1805, 1126,
1128 (Charles S. Hyneman & Donald S. Lutz ed., 1983).

6. L. H. LaRue, The Constitution: Will It Survive? 62 Washington & Lee Alumni Mag. No. 5, at 9 (1987).

Part One

1. Morris, Letter to Timothy Pickering (December 22, 1814), in 3 Max Farrand, Records of the Federal Convention 419–20 (rev. ed. 1966). Morris did go on to except part of Article III from his general description of the convention's work. With respect to those provisions, on which "conflicting opinions had been maintained with. . . much professional astuteness," Morris explained that he used his position as stylist "to select phrases, which expressing my own notions would not alarm others, nor shock their self-love, and to the best of my recollections, this was the only part which passed without cavil."

2. This anecdote is quoted without attribution to a source in Alpheus T. Mason, The States Rights Debate 107 (2d ed. 1972). For an earlier citation, still without attribution, see Edward S. Corwin, Court over Constitution 228 (1938).

3. *Marbury v. Madison,* 5 U.S. (1 Cranch) 137, 178, 177 (1803); 9 Annals 3002 (February 25, 1799).

4. *United States v. Butler,* 297 U.S. 1, 62 (1936).

5. Marshall, Letter to Patrick Henry (August 31, 1790), in 2 Papers of John Marshall 61 (Herbert A. Johnson ed., 1974); Jefferson, Letter to Wilson C. Nicholas (September 7, 1803), in 10 Writings of Thomas Jefferson 419 (Albert E. Bergh ed., 1907)

6. Washington, Address to the United States Senate and House of Representatives (January 8, 1790), in 4 Papers of George Washington (Presidential Series) 543–44 (Dorothy Twohig et al. ed., 1996).

7. See, e.g., 5 Annals 1488 (May 30, 1796) (Robert Goodloe Harper in the House) ("in the courts of Europe it is a thing of consequence that Ministers of a proper grade were sent to them").

8. 12 DHFFC 82 (January 26, 1790) (House).

9. Summary of debate as reported in the Gazette of the United States (January 26, 1790), id. at 71.

10. Washington instructed Jefferson to reassure Congress about his commitment to frugality. Washington, Diary Entry (March 26, 1790), in 6 Diaries of George Washington 54 (D. Jackson & D. Twohig eds., 1979). William Maclay of Pennsylvania interpreted the thrust of Jefferson's conversation with the Senate committee rather differently. Jefferson, he thought, "has been long enough abroad to catch the tone of European folly. he gave Us a sentiment which seemed to Savour rather of quaintness. 'It is better to take the highest of the lowest, than the lowest of the highest' Translation. it is better to appoint A Chargé des affaires with an handsome Salary, than a Minister Plenipotentiary with a small One." See Diary Entry (May 24, 1790), in 9 DHFFC 275.

11. Washington, Diary Entry (April 27, 1790), in 6 Diaries of George Washington at 68.

12. Jefferson, Opinion of the Secretary of State (April 24, 1790), in 5 Papers of George Washington (Presidential Series) at 342–43.

13. 12 DHFFC 77–78 (January 26, 1790) (House); 12 DHFFC 36 (January 19, 1790) (House).

14. 1 Blackstone, Commentaries on the Laws of England *245 (1765). Determining the exact grade of minister to send was treated as a part of the king's general prerogative.

15. The Federalist No. 67 (A. Hamilton), at 453.

16. 1 Blackstone, Commentaries at *253.

17. See, e.g., speeches by John Smilie and William Findley in the Pennsylvania ratifying convention (December 6, 1787), 2 DHRC 508, 512.

18. In 1798, the House considered a proposal to limit President John Adams's discretion in the employment of ministers plenipotentiary. The debaters closely tracked the arguments made on both sides in 1790, and in the end the House rejected the proposal. See 7 Annals 848 ff. (January 18, 1798).

19. The maxim's limits were understood in Jefferson's time. See, e.g., *Commonwealth v. Ronald*, 8 Va. (4 Call.) 97 (1786), where the Virginia court of appeals rejected an *expressio unius* argument as immaterial when other law or practical necessity demands additional exceptions to a supposedly general rule.

20. See generally Jefferson, Circular to Heads of Departments (November 6, 1801), in 4 Writings of Thomas Jefferson 415–17 (H. A. Washington ed., 1854); Jefferson, Letter to Antoine L. C. Destutt de Tracy (January 26, 1811), 5 id. at 566; The Federalist No. 70 (Alexander Hamilton), at 471; James Madison (June 16 & 17, 1789), 11 DHFFC 866–69, 895–99 (House).

21. *Springer v. Government of the Philippine Islands*, 277 U.S. 189, 211 (1928) (Holmes, J., dissenting). Justice Holmes, to be sure, was writing of the Smithsonian Institute.

22. *M'Culloch v. Maryland*, 17 U.S. (4 Wheat.) 316, 401–2 (1819).

23. John Marshall, 4 Life of George Washington 243 (reprint 1983) (1805).

24. See George C. Christie, The Notion of an Ideal Audience in Legal Argument (2000).

25. 14 DHFFC 390, 392 (February 3, 1791) (House).

26. Randolph, Letter to Washington (February 12, 1791). I have relied on the edition of Randolph's opinions and cover letter Walter Dellinger and I published. See Dellinger and Powell, The Constitutionality of the Bank Bill: The Attorney General's First Constitutional Law Opinions, 44 Duke L.J. 110 (1994). The letter is on page 121, and the opinions at 122–30.

27. "The Congress shall have Power . . . To make all Laws which shall be necessary and proper, for carrying into Execution the foregoing Powers. . . ."

28. Randolph actually referred to the "twelfth" amendment as he was writing before it became clear that a constitutional majority of the states would approve only the third through twelfth of the amendments Congress had proposed. Here and elsewhere I use our enumeration. In 1992, of course, the second of the original proposals finally obtained the required number of ratifications, and became the twenty-seventh amendment, creating an interesting if ultimately minor debate over its legitimacy.

29. Jefferson, Opinion on the Constitutionality of the Bill for Establishing a National Bank (February 15, 1791), in Jefferson Powell, Languages of Power: A Source Book of Early American Constitutional History 41–43 (1991).

30. Letter to James A. Bayard (January 16, 1801), in 25 Papers of Alexander Hamilton 319 (Harold C. Syrett ed., 1961–87).

31. Ames (February 3, 1791), 14 DHFFC 393 (House).

32. Hamilton, Opinion on the Constitutionality of an Act to Establish a Bank (February 23, 1791), in 8 Papers of Alexander Hamilton at 63.

33. *United States v. Lopez*, 514 U.S. 549 (1995), held (for the first time since the New Deal) that a federal statute was unconstitutional simply because it exceeded the reach of Congress's commerce power.

34. 2 U.S. (2 Dall.) 419 (1793).

35. Article V requires ratification by three-fourths of the states in order to adopt an amendment. That figure was reached when North Carolina became the twelfth state to ratify what is now the eleventh amendment in February 1795. As a result of the failure of several state legislatures to notify the federal government of their actions, the amendment's adoption was not officially noted and promulgated until January 1798. See 5 Documentary History of the Supreme Court of the United States, 1789–1800, at 627, 637–38 (Maeva Marcus ed., 1994).

36. *Hollingsworth v. Virginia*, 3 U.S. (3 Dall.) 378 (1798).

37. At the time of writing, the justices are narrowly divided over whether to read the eleventh amendment as reflecting a broad constitutional limitation on the authority both of the federal courts and of Congress, or as a specific rejection of the 1793 ruling that the Court could entertain a private individual's action against a state other than his own in the absence of congressional authorization. See, e.g., *Alden v. Maine*, 527 U.S. 706 (1999). The justices holding the former view see *Chisholm* as simply erroneous when decided, while those who read the amendment narrowly believe that *Chisholm* was a sound decision in principle that fell victim to widespread fears about the practical consequences of state amenability to actions in federal courts.

38. 3 Joseph Story, Commentaries on the Constitution of the United States § 1677 n.1 (1833).

39. 2 U.S. (2 Dall.) at 449–50. Iredell's published opinion did not discuss the constitutional question, noting only that Iredell's "present opinion" was that the Constitution did not impair the state's immunity. In a separate manuscript Iredell outlined his reasons for this view, and may in fact have delivered them orally although he did not ultimately include them in the opinion he provided the reporter Alexander Dallas. See the edition of his unpublished comments in 5 Documentary History of the Supreme Court at 186–93.

40. Edmund Randolph, Letter to James Madison (August 12, 1792), 14 Papers of James Madison 349 (Robert A. Rutland et al. ed., 1983).

41. 2 U.S. (2 Dall.) at 454.

42. Id. at 455.

43. Id. at 471–72.

44. Id. at 472–73.

45. Oliver Wendell Holmes Jr., Law in Science and Science in Law (1899), in Collected Legal Papers 238 (1920).

46. 505 U.S. 144, 155 (1992) (citations omitted).

47. *Principality of Monaco v. Mississippi*, 292 U.S. 313, 322 (1934).

48. Historically, a fourth rationale for the use of state sovereignty language has enjoyed significant support: recognizing that the states are sovereign, it was said, locates the

constitutional power to resolve disputes between federal and state authority. This idea is an old one, with roots in the famous Kentucky and Virginia Resolutions of 1798 (drafted by Jefferson and Madison, respectively), and took center stage during the nullification crisis of the late 1820s and early 1830s. John C. Calhoun and other nullificationists contended that because the Constitution originated as a compact among sovereign states, each state necessarily possesses, within its jurisdiction, final interpretive authority over such constitutional conflicts. As the aged Madison pointed out at the time, such a position assumed that "sovereignty is a unit, at once indivisible and inalienable," an assumption that Madison thought unmistakably contrary to the "the law and the testimony of the fundamental charter." (Debating how to characterize the Constitution's origins was a red herring, in Madison's opinion, concerning "an historical fact of merely speculative curiosity.") Madison, Notes on Nullification (ca. 1835–36), in The Mind of the Founder (Marvin Meyers rev. ed., 1981) 436–37, 440. Quite apart from its intellectual flaws, as a practical matter this argument (which was invoked once again in the 1950s and early 1960s by white southerners opposed to desegregation) is not a viable one at this point in our history.

49. 1 Blackstone, Commentaries *162.

50. 5 U.S. (1 Cranch) at 176.

51. 3 Va. (1 Va. Cas.) 20 (1793).

52. Id. at 30.

53. Id. at 79.

54. *Turpin v. Locket*, 10 Va. (6 Call.) 113, 172–73 (1804). I discuss this case in section IX.

55. 3 Va. (1 Va. Cas.) at 24.

56. 3 U.S. (3 Dall.) 386 (1798).

57. *Satterlee v. Mathewson*, 27 U.S. (2 Pet.) 380, 416 note (1829) (appendix by Johnson, J.).

58. 3 U.S. (3 Dall.) at 388–89.

59. Id. at 399.

60. Madison's notes actually recorded the motion as referring to "retrospective" laws, which, as Max Farrand (the editor of the convention's proceedings) noted, was a mistake. See 2 Max Farrand, Records of the Federal Convention of 1787, 440 n.19 (reprint 1966) (1911).

61. Madison's notes state that Mason moved to strike the reference to ex post facto laws, while the convention's Details of Ayes and Noes described it as a motion "to reconsider" the clause. Farrand's suggestion that the latter is correct and the motion a general one to reconsider the clause is plausible and would explain the otherwise odd alliance between Mason and Gerry.

62. Mason's pamphlet inspired many rebuttals. See, e.g., Winchester Virginia Gazette (January 25, 1788); 8 DHRC 327 (term refers only to criminal laws); id. at 338 (same); Virginia Independent Chronicle (March 12, 1788), 8 DHRC 488 (term covers civil legislation); Norfolk and Portsmouth Journal (February 20, 1788), 16 DHRC 164 (same).

63. Mason (June 17, 1788),10 DHRC 1361.

64. All of the anti-Federalist (opposition to ratification) commentary I have seen interprets the term to include civil laws, but the issue split the Federalist defenders of the

Constitution. For anti-Federalist comments, see Letters of Centinel, Herbert Storing, The Complete Anti-Federalist 2.7.168; Aristocritis, id. at 3.16.18; Patrick Henry, Remarks in the Virginia Convention (June 17, 1788), id. at 5.16.39; William Findley, Remarks in the Pennsylvania Convention (December 7, 1787), 2 DHRC 522. For Federalist discussions, see the documents cited in note 62 above and, additionally, 2 DHRC 417 (term limited to criminal laws); id. at 724 (term includes civil laws); 8 DHRC 371 (same). Madison's recorded comments during the ratification period were slightly ambiguous, although each one I have read appears to assume the broader interpretation that he had propounded at Philadelphia. See 9 DHRC 730; id. at 1408; The Federalist No. 44, at 301. On the other hand, Randolph supported his argument that "ex post facto" referred solely to criminal matters with the observation that "my honourable colleague tells you it was so interpreted in [The Philadelphia] Convention," and the editors of the Documentary History comment that this unnamed colleague "was probably" Madison. 10 DHRC 1359 n.15. In a late number of The Federalist, Hamilton construed the clauses as prohibiting retrospective penal laws without mentioning civil legislation. See The Federalist No. 84, at 577.

65. 3 U.S. (3 Dall.) at 397.

66. The Federalist No. 83, at 560.

67. See *Satterlee v. Mathewson*, 27 U.S. (2 Pet.) at 416 note (1829) (appendix by Johnson, J.).

68. Opinion on the Constitutionality of an Act to Establish a Bank (February 23, 1791), in 8 Papers of Alexander Hamilton at 111.

69. "It is obvious *from the specification of contracts in the last member of the clause,* that the framers of the Constitution, did not understand or use the words in the sense contended for." The following two sentences make the same connection: it is "[t]he arrangement of the distinct members of this section" that "necessarily points to" the conclusion that the framers "understood and used the words" to refer to criminal laws only.

70. See *Hylton v. United States,* 3 U.S. (3 Dall.) 171 (1796) (seriatim opinion) (refusing to extend the scope of the apportionment clause of Article I, section 9, clause 4 "by construction" because the principle of the clause "is radically wrong; it cannot be supported by any solid reasoning"); *Cooper v. Telfair,* 4 U.S. (4 Dall.) 14 (1800) (seriatim opinion) (inferring existence of legislative power from "the very nature of the social compact"); *Vanhorne's Lessee v. Dorrance,* 28 F. Cas. 1012 (C.C.D. Pa. 1795) (deriving limitations on the legislature's eminent domain power from the role of property in a free society); *Lyon's Case,* 15 F. Cas. 1183 (C.C.D. Vt. 1798) (basing the jury's incompetence to consider constitutional issues on the consequences of permitting it to do so).

Part Two

1. Stanley Elkins & Eric McKitrick, The Age of Federalism 104 (1993). Elkins and McKitrick consider and reject recent attempts to discern in the Hamilton–Madison alliance of the 1780s foreshadows of their political hostility in the 1790s. Id. at 103–4.

2. Hamilton, Letter to Edward Carrington (May 26, 1792), in 11 Papers of Alexander Hamilton 427 (Harold C. Syrett ed., 1961–87).

3. Id. at 441.

4. Madison, A Candid State of Parties, National Gazette (September 26, 1792), in 14 Papers of James Madison 371 (Robert A. Rutland et al. ed., 1983).

5. Ch. 74, 1 Stat. 596.

6. 8 Annals 2139 (July 10, 1798).

7. 8 Annals 1959 (June 16, 1798).

8. Samuel W. Dana (July 5, 1798), 8 Annals 2112 (U.S. House).

9. Robert Goodloe Harper (July 10, 1798), 8 Annals 2167 (U.S. House).

10. Blackstone concluded his discussion of the subject with the remark that "to censure the licentiousness, is to maintain the liberty of the press." 4 Blackstone, Commentaries on the Laws of England *153 (1769). Numerous Federalist speeches echoed his argument and borrowed his terminology.

11. George K. Taylor (December 21, 1798), Va. Rep. 136 (Virginia House of Delegates). In December 1798, the Virginia legislature debated a motion to adopt resolutions condemning the Sedition Act and other Federalist legislation. The quality of the discussion in the House of Delegates was little if any less than that in the federal House of Representatives. See also [U.S. House] Report of a select committee on petitions for a repeal of the Alien and Sedition Acts (February 25, 1799), 9 Annals 2989–90.

12. Va. Rep. 107 (December 20, 1798) (Henry Lee in the Virginia House).

13. 8 Annals 2147 (July 10, 1798).

14. Id. at 2146–47.

15. Va. Rep. 74 (December 18, 1798) (Archibald Magill in the Virginia House paraphrasing Blackstone).

16. George Taylor (December 21, 1798), Va. Rep.137.

17. [U.S. House] Report of a select committee on petitions for a repeal of the Alien and Sedition Acts (February 25, 1799), 9 Annals 2992.

18. Nathaniel Macon (July 10, 1798), 8 Annals 2151 (U.S. House). Republican John Nicholas answered the argument that the amendment's disallowance of laws *abridging* press freedom implied its tolerance of laws *respecting* in the same manner. "It is plain, the writer of the amendment intended to indulge his copiousness of expression, or that he had been accustomed to use certain words in a particular connexion." 9 Annals 3011 (February 25, 1799) (U.S. House).

19. 8 Annals 2144 (July 10, 1798) (John Nicholas in the U.S. House).

20. [Va. House] Report of a committee on responses to the Virginia Resolutions of 1798 (January 8, 1800), Va. Rep. 227 (drafted by Madison).

21. John Nicholas (July 5, 1798), 8 Annals 2104 (U.S. House). See also 8 Annals 2110 (July 5, 1798) (Albert Gallatin in the U.S. House): "if you put the press under any restraint in respect to the measures of members of government; if you thus deprive the people of the means of obtaining information of their conduct, you in fact render their right of electing nugatory."

22. [Va. House] Report of a committee on responses to the Virginia Resolutions of 1798 (January 8, 1800), Va. Rep 220 (drafted by Madison).

23. John Nicholas (July 10, 1798), 8 Annals 2140–41 (U.S. House).

24. John Taylor (December 20, 1798), Va. Rep. 119 (Virginia House).

25. 9 Annals 3008–9 (John Nicholas in the U.S. House); [Va. House] Report of a committee on responses to the Virginia Resolutions of 1798 (January 8, 1800), Va. Rep. 220 (drafted by James Madison).

26. "I thought the Constitution had assigned cognizance of that question to the courts, and so it has." 8 Annals 2096 (July 5, 1798) (Federalist John Allen). "[H]is opinion was that an appeal must be made to another tribunal, to the Judiciary." Id. at 2111 (July 5, 1798) (Republican Albert Gallatin). "[The question whether] this is an unconstitutional law [should be left] to be determined, where it ought to be determined, by the Judiciary." Id. at 2136 (July 9, 1798) (Federalist James A. Bayard). "[H]e could only hope that the Judges would exercise the power placed in them of declaring the law an unconstitutional law, if upon scrutiny, they find it to be so." Id. at 2152 (July 10, 1798) (Republican Nathaniel Macon). In January 1801, after several lower federal courts had upheld the Sedition Act, Federalist Jonas Platt told the House of Representatives that the congressional majority's original conclusion that the Act was constitutional now enjoyed "the solemn decision and concurrence of the judiciary." In response, Republican Thomas T. Davis argued that those decisions were "hasty adjudications" not to be treated as settling the issue either in court or in the public mind:

> Had the decisions of the courts been made with all moderation and solemnity that usually attend judicial decisions, he might answer that there had been proceedings in the courts of the United States calculated to establish the constitutionality of that law, as far as the opinions of the Judges went. For he must acknowledge that the Judges had the power of deciding the constitutionality of a law under which they were supposed to act; but he denied that those deliberate decisions had been made under it, that ought to establish it as a Constitutional law with the Judges generally. . . . But a Judge of the United States having determined the law to be Constitutional, did not bring conviction to his mind.

10 Annals 916, 917–18 (January 21, 1801). Federalists, unsurprisingly, happily agreed with Platt in reiterating their commitment to judicial review. See Va. Rep. 71 (December 18, 1798) (Archibald Magill in the Virginia House); 10 Annals 407 (January 23, 1800) (James A. Bayard); id. at 417 (January 23, 1800) (Harrison Gray Otis); id. at 932 (January 21, 1801) (John Rutledge); id. at 960 (January 23, 1801) (Henry Lee).

27. As a candidate for Congress, Marshall issued a public statement announcing his intention to oppose any extension of the Sedition Act, although he refrained from directly stating an opinion on the Act's constitutionality. Once in Congress, Marshall consistently voted with the Republicans during the latter's January 1800 effort to secure the Act's repeal. See 10 Annals 419–25. Other Federalists may have harbored private doubts about the validity of the Act. See Alexander Hamilton, Letter to Oliver Wolcott Jr. (June 29, 1798), in 21 Papers of Alexander Hamilton at 522 (objecting to an early Senate version of a sedition bill as containing "highly exceptionable" provisions: "Let us not establish a tyranny.").

28. U.S. Ministers, Letter to Charles-Maurice Talleyrand-Perigord (April 3, 1798), in 3 Papers of John Marshall 447 (Herbert A. Johnson ed., 1974).

29. Va. Rep. 119 (December 20, 1798) (John Taylor in the Virginia House). A leading congressional Republican made almost exactly the same point: "This subject has been so

well handled by our Envoys in their reply to Mr. Talleyrand, that he wondered an attempt of this kind [to defend the constitutionality of the sedition bill] should have been made. Nothing he could say would be half so well said as were their observations on the subject. They met with his entire approbation." 8 Annals 2106 (July 5, 1798) (Nathaniel Macon in the U.S. House)

30. The correspondence was first edited and published by Frank W. Grinnell, Hitherto Unpublished Correspondence between Chief Justice Cushing and John Adams in 1789, 27 Mass. Law Q. 11–16 (October 1942).

31. "[I]f all men are restrained by the fear of jails, scourges and loss of ears from examining the conduct of persons in administration and where their conduct is illegal, tyrannical and tending to overthrow the Constitution and introduce slavery, are so restrained from declaring it to the public *that* will be as effectual a restraint as any *previous* restraint whatever." Cushing, Letter to Adams (February 18, 1789), 27 Mass. Law Q. at 14.

32. Cushing's language wavered between suggesting that he thought falsity ought to be proved by the prosecution and implying that truth needed to be established as an affirmative defense. For the quotations from Cushing in the text, see 27 Mass. Law Q. at 12–15; Adams's response is from Adams, Letter to Cushing (March 7, 1789), id. at 16.

33. Another good example is an anonymous pamphlet, published in Boston in 1801, discussing the issue. See An Impartial Citizen, A Dissertation upon the Constitutional Freedom of the Press, 2 American Political Writing during the Founding Era 1760–1805, at 1126–69 (C. Hyneman & D. Lutz ed., 1983). Impartial Citizen does not seem to have been a Republican, and at any rate harshly criticized the Republican view of the first amendment, but he or she was equally dismissive of the argument that the common law or Blackstone defined the scope of the American liberty. "The freedom of the press . . . depends, for its constitutional definition, upon natural, simple principles; there is no abstruse learning on the subject." Id. at 1126. As Impartial Citizen applied those principles, they permitted prosecutions for defamation of the personal character of government officials, whether true or false, while the constitutional provisions required an absolute bar on interference with true reports about official (and officials') actions and on statements of political opinion whether true or not.

34. The Federalist No. 37, at 236. Cf. No. 82 (Hamilton), at 553 ("'Tis time only that . . . can liquidate the meaning of all the parts"). There is no serious doubt that the view expressed in these passages was a commonplace.

35. 11 Annals 104–5 (January 15, 1802).

36. 17 U.S. (4 Wheat.) 518, 644 (1819).

37. 10 Annals 533.

38. Marshall, Speech (March 7, 1800), in 4 Papers of John Marshall at 95.

39. Id. at 103–4.

40. Id. at 95.

41. Jean Edward Smith, John Marshall: Definer of a Nation 262 (1996); Jefferson, Letter to Madison (March 8, 1800), in 17 Papers of James Madison (Rutland ed.), at 368

42. See 9 Annals 2799–2800 (January 30, 1799); id. at 2887–88 (February 12, 1799).

43. Ch. 20, 1 Stat. 73 (September 24, 1789).

44. John Blair, Letter and memorandum to John Jay (August 5 [?], 1790), in 2 Docu-

mentary History of the Supreme Court of the United States, 1789–1800, at 84 (Maeva Marcus ed., 1994).

45. Ch. 4, 2 Stat. 89 (February 13, 1801).

46. We will not stop to recount the familiar story of how the Constitution's original arrangements threw the presidential election into the House after the Republicans' intended candidates for president and vice president, Jefferson and Aaron Burr, each received an identical number of electoral votes.

47. 10 Annals 917 (January 21, 1801).

48. Jefferson, Letter to John Dickinson (December 19, 1801), in 10 Writings of Thomas Jefferson 302 (Albert E. Bergh ed., 1907). Jefferson used almost identical language only days after his inauguration. See Jefferson, Letter to Joel Barlow (March 14, 1801), id. at 223.

49. Gerry, Letter to Jefferson (May 4, 1801), in 1 Charles Warren, The Supreme Court in United States History 193 (2d ed. 1928).

50. 11 Annals 15 (December 8, 1801); id. at 25 (January 8, 1802).

51. At least one Republican senator, Abraham Baldwin of Georgia, suggested that the repeal resolution "sa[id] nothing about what shall be done with the present judges," and that "they may get their full salaries during life, if it is their Constitutional right." 11 Annals 107 (January 15, 1802). But while Baldwin dismissed the salary issue as "of very small importance in the argument," his fellow Republicans silently disagreed, in part for the practical debater's reason that they were relying heavily on the alleged financial extravagance of the circuit courts as a justification for the repeal.

52. 11 Annals 822 (February 27, 1802).

53. 11 Annals 823 (February 27, 1802).

54. 11 Annals 39 (January 8, 1802).

55. 11 Annals 131–32 (January 19, 1802).

56. 11 Annals 574 (February 18, 1802).

57. Wright "had not supposed the judges were intended to decide questions not judicially submitted to them, or to lead the public mind in Legislative or Executive questions." He did condition his willingness to rely on state court judicial review on the availability of appellate review of state decisions on federal questions by the federal Supreme Court. 11 Annals 115–16 (January 15, 1802).

58. 11 Annals 178–80 (February 3, 1802).

59. 11 Annals 645 (February 20, 1802) (Bayard); id. at 181 (February 3, 1802) (Morris). It was standard Republican rhetoric in the 1790s to accuse the Federalists of seeking a "consolidation" of the federal union into a unitary national government that would inevitably become a monarchy or worse. In the 1802 repeal debates, Bayard, Morris and their colleagues skillfully melded this trope with the traditional Federalist accusation that the Republicans sought to make the House of Representatives supreme.

60. 11 Annals 529 (February 16, 1802). See also id. at 183 (February 3, 1802) (Jonathan Dayton in the Senate) ("those newly professed though secretly harbored doctrines"); id. at 542 (February 16, 1802) (Joseph Hemphill in the House) ("a doctrine new and dangerous"); id. at 919 (March 1, 1802) (Samuel Dana in the House) ("gentlemen would now decide, for the first time, that the Constitutional validity of the acts of Con-

gress is to be determined only by the result of elections; and that the judges, as compos-
ing a Constitutional department, have nothing to do with such questions").

61. 11 Annals 920 (March 1, 1802). The following is not intended to be an exhaustive
list of the Federalists' citations of authority. (All speakers were in the House, the Senate
debate having concluded soon after Breckinridge's notorious speech.)

U.S. Supreme Court:
> Samuel Dana (March 1, 1802), 11 Annals 924–26 (*United States v. Yale Todd* and
> *Hylton v. United States*).

Lower federal courts:
> Joseph Hemphill (February 16, 1802), 11 Annals 543 (Justice Paterson's opinion
> in *Vanhorne's Lessee v. Dorrance*).
> John Stanley (February 18, 1802), 11 Annals 575 (*Hayburn's Case*).
> Samuel Dana (March 1, 1802), 11 Annals 920–23 (*Hayburn's Case*).

State courts:
> Thomas Morris (February 17, 1802), 11 Annals 565–67 (quoting at length from
> the opinions of Judges Roane, Tyler, and Tucker in *Kamper v. Hawkins*).
> John Stanley (February 18, 1802), 11 Annals 575 (1788 remonstrance of the Vir-
> ginia judges).

Other authorities:
> James Bayard (February 20, 1802), 11 Annals 647–48 (quoting section 25 of the
> 1789 Judiciary Act, which provided for Supreme Court review of state court de-
> cisions finding a federal statute or treaty invalid).
> Joseph Hemphill (February 16, 1802), 11 Annals 543 (Virginia ratifying conven-
> tion and Governor M'Kean's veto).
> John Rutledge (February 24, 1802), 11 Annals 737–38 (quoting "General Mar-
> shall, the present Chief Justice," in the Virginia ratifying convention and
> Tucker's lectures).
> Benjamin Huger (February 18, 1802), 11 Annals 679–82 (quoting Tucker's lec-
> tures at length).

62. Representatives Robert Williams and John Randolph went the furthest in denying the existence of any sort of judicial review, although in both cases their remarks, at
least as recorded, fall short of asserting a judicial obligation to enforce laws against the
judge's conscientious view of the Constitution. See, respectively, 11 Annals 531–32 (February 16, 1802) and id. at 661 (February 20, 1802).

63. John Bacon (March 3, 1802), 11 Annals 982 (House). Israel Smith explained to
the House that

> [i]t is true your judges have authority, derived from the nature of their power as
> judges, to decide in this way [i.e., "to decide your laws unconstitutional"] . . . it
> is . . . [the judge's] duty to decide a law void, which directly infringes the Constitu-
> tion. When there is a constitution of government, this principle is inseparably
> united with the judiciary authority; but prudent judges will exercise this right with
> great caution, knowing the Legislature has an equal right to put constructions; they
> will also consider the Legislature are obliged to precede them in their construction.
> The evil resulting from a difference in opinion cannot escape them.

Id. at 698 (February 23, 1802). See also id. at 182 (February 3, 1802) (James Jackson in the Senate) (rejecting Morris's argument that the repeal bill would undermine the judiciary's resistance to congressional self-aggrandizement by noting that whatever "may be done by the inferior courts . . . there is always an appeal to the Supreme Court" that, he implicitly assumed, could not be abolished).

64. Philip R. Thompson (February 17, 1802), 11 Annals 558 (House). Thompson identified "Judge Patterson" as the author of the offensive phrase, presumably picking up on Federalist Joseph Hemphill's quotation the previous day of Justice Paterson's opinion in *Vanhorne's Lessee v. Dorrance*. Paterson made a similar comment in a notorious prosecution under the Sedition Act and it is also possible that Thompson had that in mind. See *Lyon's Case*, 15 F. Cas. 1183, 1185 (C.C.D. Vt. 1798).

65. 11 Annals 558 (February 17, 1802).

66. At least one Republican, Philip R. Thompson, indicated that the distinction's practical significance was that a law invalidated by the courts need not be reenacted if the judicial view of its constitutionality changed: the courts "may, to be sure, for a while impede the passage of a law, by a decision against its constitutionality; yet, notwithstanding the law is in force, is not nullified, and will be acted upon whenever there is a change of opinion." 11 Annals at 553 (February 17, 1802). Ironically, Breckinridge himself may have meant little more than this. See id. at 179–80 (February 3, 1802) (conceding the power of courts "to impeach the constitutionality of a law, and thereby, for a time, obstruct its operation" without specifying in what manner Congress could or should compel the judiciary to submit).

67. Two years later, in private correspondence with Abigail Adams, President Jefferson made it clear that he did not accept Breckinridge's rejection of judicial review and was in agreement with the views expressed by many Republican members of the House during the 1802 debate:

> You seem to think it devolved on the judges to decide on the validity of the Sedition Act. But nothing in the Constitution has given them a right to decide for the executive, more than to the executive to decide for them. Both magistrates are equally independent in the sphere of action assigned to them. The judges, believing the law constitutional, had a right to pass a sentence of fine and imprisonment, because the power was placed in their hands by the Constitution. But the executive, believing the law to be unconstitutional, were bound to remit the execution of it, because that power has been confided to them by the constitution.

Jefferson, Letter to Adams (September 11, 1804), in 11 Writings of Thomas Jefferson (Bergh ed.), at 50–51. The last sentence referred to Jefferson's actions, as president, in pardoning people convicted of violating the Sedition Act. Jefferson rejected Adams's suggestion that the constitutionally based pardons were improper in light of the consistent rejection by the courts of attacks on the Act's validity: "the opinion which gives to the judges the right to decide what laws are constitutional and what not, not only for themselves in their own sphere of action but for the Legislature and executive also in their spheres, would make the Judiciary a despotic branch."

68. Burr, Letter to Bidwell (February 1, 1802) 2 Political Correspondence and Public Papers of Aaron Burr 659 (Mary-Jo Kline ed., 1983).

69. 5 U.S. (1 Cranch) 299 (1803). Chief Justice Marshall recused himself because he had presided in the circuit court, where he rejected Lee's challenge to the repeal.

70. Or, to be complete, a private individual (under the thirteenth and twenty-first amendments). The state action doctrine, on this view, is an auxiliary set of predictions about the circumstances in which a constitutional actor (usually a court) will limit ostensibly private actors on grounds ordinarily invoked only against governmental entities.

71. 11 Annals 543 (February 16, 1802) (Joseph Hemphill in the House); id. at 645 (February 20, 1802) (Bayard in the House).

72. See, e.g., 11 Annals 698 (February 23, 1802) (Israel Smith in the House) (judicial review is "derived from the nature of their power as judges, to decide in this way. . . . It might as well be said, this was an evil inseparable from judicial authority, as to call it a salutary principle of the Constitution.").

73. 11 Annals 637 (February 20, 1802).

74. *Vanhorne's Lessee v. Dorrance*, 28 F. Cas. 1012 (C.C.D. Pa. 1795). Virginia's renowned chancellor George Wythe is reported to have described judicial review in the same terms even earlier: "here is the limit of your authority; and, hither, shall you go, but no further." *Commonwealth v. Caton*, 8 Va. (4 Call.) 1, 8 (1782). There is some question about Wythe's exact words. See William M. Treanor, The Case of the Prisoners and the Origins of Judicial Review, 143 U. Pa. L. Rev. 491, 530–34 (1994).

75. Founding-era constitutionalists often used the term in this sense. See, e.g., 1 DHFFC 392 (February 3, 1791) (Fisher Ames in the House) (Congress must exercise "our discretion with regard to the true intent of the constitution"). See also my discussion of the concept of discretion in The Political Grammar of Early Constitutional Law, 71 N.C. L. Rev. 949, 996–1008 (1993).

76. Act III, 2 Va. Hening's Stat. 45 (1661).

77. Act XI, 3 Va. Hening's Stat. 151 (1696).

78. Va. Const. Decl. Rights art. 16.

79. Ch. 34, 12 Va. Hening's Stat. 81 (1785).

80. Ch. 2, 9 Va. Hening's Stat. 164 (1776); Ch. 49, 11 Va. Hening's Stat. 532 (1784).

81. Ch. 47, 12 Va. Hening's Stat. 705 (1788); 1799 Va. Acts, Ch. 248.

82. An Act Concerning the Glebe Lands and Churches within the Commonwealth, 1802 Va. Acts, Ch. 289.

83. 10 Va. (6 Call) 113 (1804).

84. Charles T. Cullen's doctoral dissertation on Tucker's career up to his election to the court of appeals skillfully traces the complicated story. See Cullen, St. George Tucker and Law in Virginia, 1772–1804, at 247–62 (University of Virginia 1971).

85. *Turpin*, 10 Va. at 165–66.

86. Roane's view of the 1802 Act's exemption of glebes in parishes with incumbent ministers was similar to Tucker's. "[T]he most that could be contended for [is] that the legislature should have permitted the *life interest* of the then incumbents to run out, in tenderness to those engaged in their functions, under a reasonable expectation of the continuance of the then system."

87. 10 Va. at 174.

88. 5 U.S. (1 Cranch) 299 (1803).

89. Id. at 302–6.

90. As we have already seen, Carrington and Lyons believed that "the continuation of the establishment" was consistent with article 16. It is unclear whether they believed that the legislature could enact an entirely new religious establishment limited to a particular church. Their discussion of article 4 suggests that they may have thought that in any new system "similar benefits" would have to be conveyed on all (presumably Protestant) churches "so as to produce a general equality." Such "a *general* establishment of religion," as Roane termed it, was the objective of Patrick Henry's failed 1784 bill for religious assessments.

91. At one point Roane cited another 1776 statute as legislative support for the proposition that the legislature has the constitutional power to eliminate certain future interests in property, but he was careful to note that this statute had "received the sanction of our courts" and, especially "of this court, upon great consideration. Is it not then a high authority?"

92. 10 Va. at 185.

93. *Selden v. Overseers of the Poor of Loudoun*, 38 Va. (11 Leigh) 127 (1840) (opinion of Stanard, J.).

94. Despite his almost ostentatious refusal to mention the Virginia judges' discussion of the issues in *Turpin*, Story's opinion at several points seems to betray knowledge of the case. At one point, for example, Story's argument responds quite directly to Roane's remarks about the legal consequences of the Revolution and disestablishment. "The revolution might justly take away the public patronage, the exclusive cure of souls, and the compulsory taxation for the support of the church. Beyond these we are not prepared to admit the justice or the authority of the exercise of legislation." 13 U.S. (9 Cranch) 43, 50.

95. Story's flamboyant language concealed both his apparent strategy of resting the Supreme Court's judgment on legal grounds unassailable by the Virginia court of appeals and the exact federal constitutional basis of his decision. Subsequent decisions and commentators treated the federal law holding in *Terrett* as based on the contracts clause of Article I, section 10.

96. One cannot, of course, be certain, even at the beginning of the nineteenth century, that the positions an attorney took in litigation represented his personal views, but my sense is that lawyers in the early Republic were fairly unlikely to argue constitutional positions with which they were in fundamental disagreement.

97. In this passage, "occasionally" probably means something like "on particular occasions" rather than "rarely," as it usually does for us.

98. 11 Va. (1 Hen. & M.) 134 (1806).

99. The Wrights' choice of Taylor to represent them may have had as much to do with his sympathy for suits like theirs as to his legal acumen. See *Pegram v. Isabell*, 12 Va. (2 Hen. & M.) 193 (1808) (under an exception to the hearsay rule Taylor was permitted to testify about third-party descriptions of the plaintiff's Native American ancestry).

100. See *Trent v. Trent's Executrix*, 21 Va. (Gilmer) 174 (1821) (describing the writ). See also *Didlake v. Hooper*, 21 Va. (Gilmer) 194 (1820) (*ne exeat* was properly sought in a case involving the construction of a will directing alternative dispositions of the testator's slaves

when the party in possession intended to take them out of state); *Law v. Law*, 43 Va. (2 Gratt.) 366 (1845) (in dispute over ownership of slaves, *ne exeat regno* was proper when the plaintiff sought to prevent the opposing claimant from leaving the jurisdiction).

101. See *Coleman v. Dick & Pat*, 1 Va. (1 Wash.) 233 (1793). Edmund Randolph, arguing for Hudgins, claimed that the court of appeals had universally adhered to this principle, and suggested that Taylor had brought up the Wrights' appearance "more to excite the feelings of the court as *men*, than to address them as *judges.*"

102. *Hudgins*, 11 Va. at 134.

103. Tucker may have been referring to Randolph's argument, but as a description of counsel appearing before him this seems at odds with Tucker's well-known courtesy. I am inclined to think that Tucker had in mind public, or at least professional, criticism of Wythe's opinion.

104. 11 Va. at 144.

105. Robert M. Cover, Justice Accused 54 (1975).

106. 2 Tucker, Blackstone's Commentaries: with Notes of Reference to the Constitution and Laws, of the Federal Government of the United States; and of the Commonwealth of Virginia, app. H, 54–55 (1803).

107. The quotations in this paragraph are from Professor Cover. See Justice Accused at 44–49.

108. 11 Va. at 141.

109. A fact that the post-Reconstruction Supreme Court acknowledged, at least in theory. See, e.g., *Strauder v. West Virginia*, 100 U.S. 303, 307–8 (1879) ("The words of the [fourteenth] amendment, it is true, are prohibitory, but they contain a necessary implication of a positive immunity, or right, most valuable to the colored race,—the right to exemption from unfriendly legislation against them distinctively as colored,—exemption from legal discriminations, implying inferiority in civil society, lessening the security of their enjoyment of the rights which others enjoy, and discriminations which are steps towards reducing them to the condition of a subject race.").

110. *Plessy v. Ferguson*, 163 U.S. 537, 560–1 (1896) (Harlan, J., dissenting). The quotation in the following paragraph is at 557.

111. Gallatin, Letter to Jefferson (February 15, 1804), in 1 Writings of Albert Gallatin 177 (Henry Adams ed., 1879). The memorandum and the letter in which Plumer described Johnson are quoted in 1 Warren, Supreme Court in United States History at 287.

112. In *Ex parte Bollman & Swartwout*, 8 U.S. (4 Cranch) 75 (1807), Marshall concluded that the Court had the jurisdiction to issue writs of habeas corpus freeing from custody two of Burr's alleged confederates. Although by this time Johnson had been joined on the Court by a second Republican justice, Henry Brockholst Livingston, Livingston was ill and absent from the Court.

113. Richmond *Enquirer* (May 3, 1808), in Dumas Malone, Jefferson the President: Second Term, 1805–1809, at 583 (1974).

114. Ch. 46, 2 Stat. 499 (April 25, 1808).

115. *Gilchrist v. Collector of Charleston*, 10 F. Cas. 355, 356–57 (C.C.D.S.C. 1808).

116. 1 Warren, Supreme Court in United States History at 326.

117. Aurora, June 9, 1808, in 1 Warren, Supreme Court in United States History at 328.

118. Attorney General Caesar Rodney, Letter to Thomas Jefferson (July 15, 1808), in 1 William M. Goldsmith, Growth of Presidential Powers 558–61 (1974).

119. Johnson, Open Letter (August 26, 1808), 1 Goldsmith, Growth of Presidential Powers 563–74.

120. 3 Va. at 78.

121. Jefferson, Letter to John B. Colvin (September 20, 1810), 12 Writings of Thomas Jefferson (Bergh ed.), at 420.

122. Gallatin, Letter to William B. Giles (November 24, 1808), 1 Writings of Albert Gallatin at 43.

123. Adams, Letter to James Madison (June 3, 1811), in 3 Papers of James Madison (Presidential Series) 326 (J. C. A. Stagg et al. ed., 1996). The banquet's proceedings, and the most prominent of its attendees were described in various Federalist newspapers. See 24 Papers of Alexander Hamilton 579–80 & n.34.

124. John Quincy Adams, Letter to Ezekiel Bacon (November 17, 1808), 1 Warren, Supreme Court in United States History at 341–42; *United States v. The William,* 28 F. Cas. 614 (D. Mass. 1808).

125. See 1 Warren, Supreme Court in United States History at 343–45.

126. 28 F. Cas. at 615.

127. Id. at 615–16.

128. Id. at 620.

129. Davis discussed *Hayburn's Case,* 2 U.S. (2 Dall.) 409 (1792); Justice Paterson's opinion in *Vanhorne's Lessee v. Dorrance,* 2 U.S. (2 Dall.) 304 (C.C.D. Pa. 1795); *Hylton v. United States,* 3 U.S. (3 Dall.) 386 (1798); *Calder v. Bull,* 3 U.S. (3 Dall.) 386 (1798); and a Sedition Act prosecution, *United States v. Callender,* 25 F. Cas. 632 (C.C.D. Va. 1800).

130. Davis found one passage from The Federalist No. 44 (written by Madison) ambiguous on this point, but thought that if its (unclear) meaning was in fact at variance with the rest of The Federalist the cause would stem from "the circumstance, that those valuable papers were not all from the same pen." 28 F. Cas. at 620.

131. Id.

132. I do not think that Davis was begging the question when he described his third category as challenges to laws "bearing relation to a power with which Congress is vested." As we shall see shortly, the contrast Davis is suggesting with that phrase is to what he thought was the hypothetical case of a law patently beyond anything Congress is empowered to do.

133. In this regard, Davis quoted The Federalist No. 33 (written by Hamilton), which gave the example of a federal statute "vary[ing] the law of descent in any State." The Federalist No. 33, at 206.

134. 3 Joseph Story, Commentaries on the Constitution of the United States § 1286 (1833).

135. Adams, Letter to William Branch Giles (December 10, 1808), in 1 Warren, Supreme Court in United States History at 348; Adams, Letter to Madison (June 3, 1811), 3 Papers of James Madison (Presidential Series) at 326.

136. 19 Annals 541 (November 28, 1808).

137. *United States v. Peters,* 9 U.S. (5 Cranch) 115 (1809)

138. The eleventh amendment, Marshall pointed out, "simply provides, that no suit shall be commenced or prosecuted against a state," but Olmstead's action was against the Rittenhouses, for property within their (not the state's) possession, so that the action in no sense involved the exercise of jurisdiction over the state, even though in the process of deciding it the court would necessarily rule on the Commonwealth's claim to the money. Id. at 139–40.

139. Resolution in the Virginia House of Delegates (December 21, 1798), 17 Papers of James Madison (Rutland ed.) at 189.

140. Simon Snyder, Letter to Madison (April 6, 1809), 1 Papers of James Madison (Presidential Series) at 105.

141. Madison, Letter to Simon Snyder (April 13, 1809), id. at 114.

142. See Act of February 28, 1795, 1 Stat. 424, § 2 (authorizing the president to call forth state militia to suppress "combinations" opposing federal law or its execution).

143. Secretary of State Robert Smith wrote the state attorney general that Madison had decided that "in a case of so very serious a character" he would extend no act of clemency to the militiamen until he was given a very good reason to do so. Smith, Letter to Walter Franklin (April 24, 1809), id. at 131.

144. Madison, Letter to Caesar Rodney (April 22, 1809), id. at 131.

145. 1 Warren, Supreme Court in United States History at 383 (newspaper not identified); Jefferson, Letter to Madison (May 22, 1809), 1 Papers of James Madison (Presidential Series) at 197.

146. It should be noted that Madison's attitude in the Olmstead affair was identical to that privately expressed by Gallatin toward Johnson's *Gilchrist* decision. The events of the 1808–9 year were deeply intertwined.

Part Three

1. Wirt, Letter to James Monroe (May 5, 1823), in 2 John P. Kennedy, Memoirs of the Life of William Wirt 135 (1849).

2. 32 Annals 1371 (March 13, 1818).

3. 31 Annals 1123 (March 6, 1818).

4. Jefferson, Letter to Albert Gallatin (June 16, 1817), 15 Writings of Thomas Jefferson 133 (Albert E. Bergh ed., 1907).

5. 17 U.S. (4 Wheat.) 316, 423 (1819).

6. The adjective is odd but useful. The issue at stake in 1817, as Madison saw it, was not a threat of completely unlimited congressional power, but the lesser included question of whether there are any limits to Congress other than those arising from express prohibitions and affirmative constitutional requirements (Davis's first and second categories).

7. Madison, Letter to Spencer Roane (September 2, 1819), in The Mind of the Founder 360 (Marvin Meyers rev. ed., 1981).

8. *Champion,* 188 U.S. 321 (1903); *Kahriger,* 345 U.S. 22 (1953) (upholding the Gamblers' Occupational Tax Act). *Kahriger* also upheld the administration of the tax against a fifth amendment self-incrimination challenge and to that extent was overruled by *Marchetti v. United States,* 390 U.S. 39 (1968). See also *United States v. Butler,* 297 U.S. 1 (1936) (dictum); *South Dakota v. Dole,* 483 U.S. 203 (1987).

9. First Annual Message (December 2, 1817), 6 Writings of James Monroe 42 (S. M. Hamilton ed., 1902).

10. 31 Annals 1116 (March 6, 1818). I have reordered Sawyer's remarks.

11. 32 Annals 1361 (March 13, 1818).

12. 1 Tucker, Blackstone's Commentaries on the Laws of England, app. Note D, 145, 141, 143, 171, 154 (1803).

13. See 31 Annals 1160 (March 7, 1818). From Clay's remarks, I infer that Barbour may have made more extensive explicit use of Madison's Report of 1800 than the report of Barbour's speech in the Annals records.

14. 31 Annals 1165–66, 1168. In the last quotation, the text in the Annals actually reads "1797," which almost certainly is an error.

15. The Annals record only that he spoke for at least two hours. See 31 Annals 1282, 1284 (March 12, 1818).

16. See 32 Annals 1361 (March 13, 1818) (Henry Clay); 31 Annals (March 12, 1818) at 1305 (Charles F. Mercer).

17. 32 Annals 1319 (March 13, 1818) (Henry St. G. Tucker).

18. 32 Annals 1340 (March 13, 1818).

19. Pindall expressly cited "the second book of Vattel, chapter seventeenth," as an authority "which will surely be admitted by gentlemen who are determined to view our Constitution as an international treaty." 32 Annals 1349. See Emmerich de Vattel, 2 The Law of Nations (Joseph Chitty ed., 1797), at 264: "In a treaty of strict friendship, union, and alliance, every thing which, without being burdensome to any of the parties, tends to the common advantage of the confederacy, and to draw the bonds of union closer, is favorable."

20. 32 Annals 1341, 1343, 1349 (March 13, 1818).

21. 32 Annals 1380 (March 13, 1818).

22. 32 Annals 1384 (March 14, 1818) (William Lowndes) (hoping that the House "might be allowed to vote on the broad proposition").

23. The 1819 debate concerned a provision in a proposed military appropriation bill authorizing the expenditure of ten thousand dollars of extra pay for soldiers employed in the construction or repair of military roads. Alexander Smythe, a fervent opponent of federal internal improvements, argued (correctly) that despite its formulation as an appropriation of money the provision in practice authorized the direct federal construction of military roads. According to Smythe, the 1818 resolution had rejected a general congressional power to build roads, while approving the narrower power to appropriate funds. Tucker responded that the 1818 resolution was entirely consistent with the legislation then under consideration, and the House's approval of the bill suggests that Smythe was unpersuasive to most of his colleagues. See 33 Annals 495–96, 509–10, 530 (January 11, 1819). The Senate subsequently approved the bill and Monroe signed it into law.

24. The resolution quoted in the text was approved by a vote of ninety-five to seventy, and the other resolutions failed by varying margins. See 32 Annals 1385–89 (March 14, 1818). In contrast, in 1817 the House approved its version of the Bonus Bill eighty-six to eighty-four, and defeated a procedural attempt to prevent it from concurring in the Sen-

ate's amendments by an equally small margin, sixty-eight to sixty-six. See 31 Annals 934 (February 8, 1817); 1052 (March 1, 1817).

25. 1 Tucker, Blackstone's Commentaries, app. Note D, 172.

26. 39 Annals 1688 (April 26, 1822).

27. 32 Annals 1325–26 (March 12, 1818).

28. See *Callender*, 25 F. Cas. 632 (C.C.D. Va. 1800); and *Burr*, 25 F. Cas. 30 (C.C.D. Va. 1807).

29. *Ex parte Jochen*, 257 F. 200, 204 (D. Tex. 1919).

30. Office of Attorney General, 1 Op. Att'y Gen. 211 (1818); Duties of the Attorney General, 1 Op. Att'y Gen. 335, 337 (1820).

31. Office of Attorney General, 1 Op. Att'y Gen. 492, 493 (1821).

32. 19 U.S. (6 Wheat.) 204 (1821).

33. Duties of the Attorney General, 5 Op. Att'y Gen 720 (1820).

34. 19 U.S. (6 Wheat.) 204 (1821).

35. The President and Accounting Officers, 1 Op. Att'y Gen. 624, 626 (1823).

36. On rare occasions later constitutionalists have agreed with Wirt on this point. See *Cantwell v. Connecticut*, 310 U.S. 296, 307 (1940).

37. Harriet Beecher Stowe, The Key to Uncle Tom's Cabin 147 (reprint 1968) (1853).

38. The first and second drafts are reprinted in 4 Papers of Thomas Ruffin 249–54 (J. G. de Roulhuc Hamilton ed., 1920).

39. *State v. Mann*, 13 N.C. (2 Dev.) 263 (1829).

40. 9 N.C. (2 Hawks) 582, 583, 586 (1823).

41. 13 N.C. at 267.

42. 2 U.S. (2 Dall.) 419, 471–72 (1793).

43. Robert M. Cover, Justice Accused 77–78 (1975). Professor Cover wrote that Ruffin "was extraordinary (really very much like Holmes) in his eagerness to confront the reality of the unpleasant iron fist beneath the law's polite, neat language."

44. *State v. Caesar*, 31 N.C. (9 Ired.) 391, 421 (1849) (Ruffin, C.J., dissenting).

45. Proceedings and Debates of the Convention of North-Carolina, called to amend the Constitution of the State, which assembled at Raleigh, June 4, 1835 (1836), at 79. Gaston became a judge in 1833 and so was not a member of the court that decided *State v. Mann*.

Part Four

1. *Giles v. Harris*, 189 U.S. 475 (1903).

2. Professor Albert W. Alschuler recently made a powerful case for the conclusion that "Holmes apparently could not envision any basis for political, social, or personal action other than self-interest or devotion to an arbitrary, uncomprehended goal." Alschuler, Law without Values 25 (2000). Alschuler suggests that the influence of that unquestionable idealist Justice Brandeis may have been at work in those of Holmes's opinions that seem to rest on different premises. Id. at 53, 78, 82–83. See also Holmes, Letter to Frederick Pollock (October 31, 1926), in 2 Holmes–Pollock Letters 191 (2nd ed. 1961) ("I think [Brandeis] has done great work and I believe with high motives.").

3. Ch. 7, 1 Stat. 302 (February 12, 1793).

4. 41 U.S. (16 Pet.) 539 (1842).

5. Constitutionality of the Fugitive Slave Bill, 5 Op. Att'y Gen. 254 (1850).

6. Case of the Marshal of the District of Massachusetts, 5 Op. Att'y Gen. 272 (1850).

7. *United States ex rel. Garland v. Morris*, 26 F. Cas. 1318 (D. Wis. 1854).

8. *In re Sherman M. Booth*, 3 Wis. 1 (1854).

9. *Ex parte Sherman M. Booth*, 3 Wis. 145 (1854).

10. *In re Booth and Rycraft*, 3 Wis. 157 (1854).

11. 62 U.S. (21 How.) 506, 514, 517, 523–24 (1858).

12. As Attorney General Herbert Stanbery delicately put it, "[t]he language used in this opinion is not quite so specific as might have been expected." Gormley's Case—Habeas Corpus, 12 Op. Att'y Gen. 258, 272 (1867). Compare *Ex parte J. J. Hill*, 5 Nev. 154, 157–58 (1869) ("'the authority of the United States'" refers to cases "where process, regular on its face, has been issued from a Court of the United States") with *In re Farrand*, 8 F. Cas. 1070, 1073–74 (D. Ky. 1867) ("What the court obviously mean" refers to any case in which "the prisoner is in custody under what purports to be the authority of the United States" including "its custody as an enlisted soldier of the United States").

13. A federal district judge correctly noted in 1867 that before *Ableman* "the very decided preponderance of authority in the state courts sustains the jurisdiction of those courts to discharge upon habeas corpus prisoners who, in their judgment, are illegally held, though held under the authority of the United States." *In re Farrand*, 8 F. Cas. at 1071.

14. *Commonwealth ex rel. M'Lain v. Wright*, 3 Grant 437, 440 (Pa. 1863) (Lowrie, C.J., in chambers).

15. See, e.g., *Mims & Burdett v. Wimberly*, 33 Ga. 587 (1863); *In re Barrett*, 42 Barb. 479 (N.Y. Sup. Ct. 1863); *In re Bryan*, 60 N.C. 1 (1863); *In re McDonald*, 16 F. Cas. 33, 36 (D. Mass. 1866); *In re Reynolds*, 20 F. Cas. 592 (N.D.N.Y. 1867); *Ex parte Holman*, 28 Iowa 88 (1869).

16. See, e.g., *In re McDonald*, 16 F. Cas. 17 (E.D. Mo. 1861); *In the Matter of Jacob Spangler*, 11 Mich. 298 (1863) (seriatim opinion of Martin, C.J.); *In re Farrand*, 8 F. Cas. 1070, 1073–74 (D. Ky. 1867); Charge to the Grand Jury, 30 F. Cas. 1039 (D. Mass. 1861); Habeas Corpus, 13 Op. Att'y Gen. 451 (1871) (Bristow, Acting Att'y Gen.).

17. 62 U.S. (21 How.) at 524.

18. Charge to the Grand Jury, 30 F. Cas. at 1041. Judge Sprague appears to have been paraphrasing Daniel Webster's famous 1830 speech on "Liberty *and* Union, now and forever, one and inseparable": "I cannot conceive that there can be a middle course, between submission to the laws, when regularly pronounced constitutional, on the one hand, and open resistance, which is revolution or rebellion, on the other." Webster (January 26–27, 1830), 10 Reg. Deb. 80 (1830) (Senate).

19. *In re McDonald*, 16 F. Cas. at 18.

20. *In re Tarble*, 25 Wis. 390, 409–10 (1870). Chief Justice Luther Dixon dissented with a laconic statement that "jurisdiction of the writ of habeas corpus, in cases of this nature, is vested exclusively in the courts of the United States."

21. 80 U.S. (30 Wall.) 397, 403–4, 407, 411 (1871).

22. Id. at 412–13 (Chase, C.J., dissenting).

23. See *Commonwealth ex rel. M'Lain v. Wright*, 3 Grant 437, 440 (Pa. 1863) (Lowrie, C.J., in chambers). In 1855, the Wisconsin court apparently ordered its clerk "to make no return to the writ of error [Supreme Court order directing the state court to provide the Court with the record of the case] and to enter no [Supreme Court] order upon the journals or records of the [state] court concerning the same." 62 U.S. (21 How.) at 512. In *Tarble*, Justice Paine rudely but perhaps accurately speculated that it was this action along with the state court's decision "against the validity of a law passed to sustain the institution of slavery . . . that so shocked the nerves of the venerable members of the supreme court." 25 Wis. at 407.

24. Under the Judiciary Act of 1789, Ch. 20, 1 Stat. 73 (September 24, 1789), federal habeas jurisdiction was expressly limited to persons held under federal authority, although the occasional inventive judge found ways to skirt that limitation. See, e.g., *Elkison v. Deliessiline*, 8 F. Cas. 493 (C.C.D.S.C. 1823) (Johnson, C.J.) (holding that the circuit court could issue a writ of *de homine replegiando* in a case of state custody). Before the 1860s, Congress made relatively small incursions into this original limitation, but in 1867 it extended the habeas jurisdiction of the federal courts as a general matter to prisoners held under state authority. The contemporary federal writ reflects the confluence of this statutory expansion of jurisdiction, the judicial reinterpretation of the issues cognizable under federal habeas (mostly the doing of the Warren Court), the subsequent judicial imposition of sharp limitations on the writ's availability (mostly the doing of the Rehnquist Court), and, finally, Congress's curtailment of the federal judiciary's power to award relief to state prisoners who file successive petitions. See the Antiterrorism and Effective Death Penalty Act of 1996, 110 Stat. 1214 (April 24, 1996).

25. The Rights of Free Virginia Negroes, 1 Op. Att'y Gen. 506, 507–8 (1821).

26. Pre-Emption Rights of Colored Persons, 40 Op. Att'y Gen. 147 (1843).

27. Relation of Indians to Citizenship, 7 Op. Att'y Gen. 746 (1856).

28. "No Person except a natural born Citizen . . . shall be eligible to the Office of President." As Bates pointed out, the vast majority of American citizens by anyone's standard acquired that status by birth. "As far as I know, Mr. Secretary, you and I have no better title to the citizenship which we enjoy than the 'accident of birth'—the fact that we happened to be born in the United States."

29. Citizenship, 10 Op. Att'y Gen. 382 (1862).

30. 36 Congressional Globe 1115, 1116–17 (March 1, 1866) (James Wilson in the House). See also id. at 527 (January 31, 1866), 573–74 (February 1, 1866), and 756 (April 4, 1866) (Lyman Trumbull in the Senate). Wilson, indeed, also cited Legaré. Id. at 1116.

31. Alexander Bickel, The Morality of Consent 33 (1975).

32. Id. at 53.

33. 83 U.S. (16 Wall.) 36 (1873).

34. Id. at 77–78.

35. Id. at 129 (Swayne, J. dissenting)

36. Id. at 101 (Field, J., dissenting).

37. Id. at 119–20 (Bradley, J. dissenting).

38. Id. at 123–24 (Bradley, J., dissenting).

39. *Davidson v. New Orleans,* 96 U.S. 97, 104 (1877).

40. 83 U.S. (16 Wall.) at 128.

41. Id. at 124–25 (Swayne, J., dissenting).

42. *Griswold v. Connecticut,* 381 U.S. 479, 482 (1966).

43. 347 U.S. 483 (1954).

44. 27 F. Cas. 785 (C.C.D. Ky. 1866). Swayne cited *M'Culloch v. Maryland*'s description of the limited role of the courts in reviewing federal legislation as fully applicable to legislation enacted under the thirteenth amendment grant of power.

45. See *In re Turner,* 24 F. Cas. 337 (C.C.D. Md. 1867) (Chase, C.J.); *United States v. Hall,* 26 F. Cas. 79, 81 (C.C.S.D. Ala. 1871) (Woods, C.J., later Justice Woods) ("The extent to which congress shall exercise this power must depend on its discretion in view of the circumstances of each case."); *United States v. Given,* 25 F. Cas. 1324 (C.C.D. Del. 1873) (Strong, J.). Accord, *Smith v. Moody,* 26 Ind. 299 (1866); *People v. Washington,* 36 Cal. 658 (1869).

46. The history of how the fourteenth amendment, which was first proposed as a pure delegation of power to Congress, assumed the form in which it was adopted is succinctly rehearsed in William Nelson's important book The Fourteenth Amendment: From Political Principle to Judicial Doctrine 49–55 (1988).

47. A couple of decades earlier, the Supreme Court had held that corporations are "persons" within the meaning of the equal protection clause. See *Santa Clara County v. Southern Pacific Railroad,* 118 U.S. 394 (1886).

48. 194 U.S. 267 (1904). Justice David Brewer concurred in the judgment, while Justices Henry Brown, Edward Douglass White, and Joseph McKenna dissented.

49. Holmes was notably offhand in his speculations about legislative purpose:

> Approaching the question in this way we feel unable to say that the law before us may not have been justified by local conditions. It would have been more obviously fair to extend the regulation at least to highways. But it may have been found, for all that we know, that the seed of Johnson grass is dropped from the cars in such quantities as to cause special trouble. It may be that the neglected strips occupied by railroads afford a ground where noxious weeds especially flourish, and that whereas self-interest leads the owners of farms to keep down pests, the railroad companies have done nothing in a matter which concerns their neighbors only. Other reasons may be imagined.

Id. at 269–70. As Justice Brown protested in dissent, this was all speculation, and speculation he was not minded to indulge. Id. at 271. This was not, to be sure, all Holmes' fault—May was not represented before the Court. But *May* illustrates Holmes's usual though not invariable willingness to afford legislation the broadest imaginable scope.

50. Id. at 270.

51. *Southern Pacific Co. v. Jensen,* 244 U.S. 205, 221 (1917) (Holmes, J., dissenting).

52. *Louisville Gas & Electric Co. v. Coleman,* 277 U.S. 32, 41 (1928) (Holmes, J., dissenting).

53. *Southern Pacific Co. v. Jensen,* 244 U.S. at 221 (Holmes, J., dissenting).

54. "[C]ourts should be careful not to extend such prohibitions beyond their obvious meaning by reading into them conceptions of public policy that the particular court may

happen to entertain." *Tyson Brothers v. Banton,* 273 U.S. 418, 446 (1927) (Holmes, J., dissenting).

55. *State v. Manuel,* 20 N.C. (3 & 4 Dev. & Bat.) 144 (1838).

56. There are many versions of this well-known anecdote. I have followed the oldest common denominator as reconstructed by Professor Michael Herz in his valuable essay "Do Justice!" Variations of a Thrice-Told Tale, 82 Va. L. Rev. 111 (1996).

57. *Lochner v. New York,* 198 U.S. 45, 75–76 (1905) (Holmes, J., dissenting).

58. *Otis v. Parker,* 187 U.S. 606 (1903).

59. Holmes, Letter to Green (August 20, 1909), in The Essential Holmes 116 (Richard A. Posner ed., 1992).

60. Holmes, Letter to Richard T. Ely (June 18, 1906), in Benjamin G. & Barbara K. Rader, The Ely–Holmes Friendship, 1901–1914, 10 Am. J. Legal Hist. 128, 137 (1966).

61. "I wholly disagree with the argument of the government that the First Amendment left the common law as to seditious libel in force. History seems to me against that notion. I had conceived that the United States through many years had shown its repentance for the Sedition Act of 1798, by repaying the fines that it imposed." *Abrams,* 250 U.S. 616, 630 (1919) (Holmes, J., dissenting). The reference to the first amendment's sweeping language is from Holmes's dissent in *Gitlow v. New York,* 268 U.S. 652, 672 (1925) (Holmes, J., dissenting).

62. *United States v. Schwimmer,* 279 U.S. 644, 654–55 (1929) (Holmes, J., dissenting).

63. "Liberty is to faction, what air is to fire, an aliment without which it instantly expires. But it could not be a less folly to abolish liberty, which is essential to political life, because it nourishes faction, than it would be to wish the annihilation of air, which is essential to animal life, because it imparts to fire its destructive agency." The Federalist No. 10, at 58.

64. Learned Hand, Chief Justice Stone's Concept of the Judicial Function (1946), in The Spirit of Liberty 204 (3d ed. 1960). Hand's description of democracy in this passage is deliberately, almost ostentatiously, antiromantic.

65. 274 U.S. 357, 359 (1927) (quoting the statute).

66. 268 U.S. 652, 666 (1925).

67. 274 U.S. at 375–77 (Brandeis, J., concurring) (footnotes omitted).

68. *New York Times v. Sullivan,* 376 U.S. 254, 270 (1964). For early citations of Brandeis's concurring opinion as authority, compare *Stromberg v. California,* 283 U.S. 359, 368 (1931) (citing the concurrence on a par with the opinion of the Court in *Whitney*) with *United States v. Carolene Products,* 304 U.S. 144, 152 n.4 (1938) (citing the concurrence to the exclusion of the opinion of the Court).

69. As always in constitutional law, even the most stable intellectual position may be undercut or betrayed in practice. *Dennis v. United States,* 341 U.S. 494 (1951), which upheld the conviction of several members of the American Communist Party for advocating the violent overthrow of the United States government, is perhaps an example.

70. William O'Neill, A Democracy at War 231 (1993). A total of just over three thousand persons, virtually all of them noncitizens, were arrested on the basis of suspicion that they were actual or potential subversives. My discussion depends on Professor O'Neill's outstanding book.

71. Id. at 233.

72. Pub. L. No. 100-383, § 2(a), 102 Stat. 903 (August 10, 1988).

73. 320 U.S. 81 (1943); 323 U.S. 214 (1944).

74. 320 U.S. at 105.

75. 323 U.S. at 216, 217–18.

76. Id., at 242 (Murphy, J., dissenting). Justice Owen J. Roberts also dissented in a separate opinion.

77. Id., at 243 (Jackson, J., dissenting).

78. Id. at 234–35 (Murphy, J., dissenting).

79. Id. at 244 (Jackson, J., dissenting).

80. Jackson denied that the judiciary should have attempted to interfere with the military's actions in themselves, although he nowhere explained what he thought a court should have done if a Japanese American internee had petitioned for a writ of habeas corpus to secure release from an internment camp. See 323 U.S. at 248.

81. Id. at 224–25 (Frankfurter, J., concurring).

82. Jefferson expressly (if privately) endorsed this, although the two occasions on which he arguably acted on it (the Louisiana Purchase and certain U.S. Navy operations against Tripolitan corsairs) were both ambiguous in that in each case there was a clear argument supporting the legality of his actions. Lincoln defended as legal his unilateral suspension of habeas corpus in certain sensitive locations in early 1861, but also defended it as a legitimate action to save the Republic even if it was extralegal.

83. The Federalist No. 3 (J. Jay), at 14; *Hirabayashi*, 380 U.S. at 93 (quoting Chief Justice Charles Evans Hughes). See, e.g., *Stewart v. Kahn*, 78 U.S. (11 Wall.) 493, 506 (1870): "The measures to be taken in carrying on war and to suppress insurrection are not defined. The decision of all such questions rests wholly in the discretion of those to whom the substantial powers involved are confided by the Constitution."

Part Five

1. 32 Annals 1325–26 (March 12, 1818).

2. Alisdair MacIntyre, After Virtue 253 (2d ed. 1984).

3. The election of 2000 confirms rather than undercuts this principle. However deep the unhappiness on both sides over post–Election Day events, there was never any serious danger that the ultimate outcome of the process would be set aside by military or other unconstitutional means.

4. Compare *United States v. Curtiss-Wright Export Corp.*, 299 U.S. 304 (1936), with *Youngstown Sheet & Tube v. Sawyer*, 343 U.S. 579, 585 (1952) ("The President's power, if any, to issue the order must stem either from an act of Congress or from the Constitution itself."). See also Presidential Authority to Decline to Execute Unconstitutional Statutes, 18 Op. O.L.C. 199, 200 (1994) (Justice Department acknowledgment that the president's "office and authority are created and bounded by the Constitution").

5. See *U.S. Term Limits, Inc. v. Thornton*, 514 U.S. 779 (1995). The justices divided five to four.

6. See *Erie R. Co. v. Tompkins*, 304 U.S. 64 (1938) (holding the prior rule that federal

courts need not do so to be an unconstitutional assumption of power by the federal judiciary).

7. *Ex parte Merryman*, 17 F. Cas. 144 (C.C.D. Md. 1861). Even *Merryman* is not an exception as a technical matter to the principle as I have stated it: Taney was sitting on circuit and the Supreme Court did not review his decision or Lincoln's refusal to enforce it.

8. A federal court sitting in diversity presumably can, and indeed under the *Erie* decision must, invalidate a state statute if it is clear that the state supreme court would do so on state grounds as those are defined by the state.

9. See *United States v. Lopez,* 514 U.S. 549 (1995). Justice Clarence Thomas's concurrence indicated a willingness to reconsider the New Deal decision, but no other justice joined him, and Justice Anthony Kennedy's concurrence, joined by Justice Sandra Day O'Connor, was clearly intended to repudiate any suggestion that *Lopez* undermined Congress's power over the national economy.

10. *West Virginia State Board of Education v. Barnette,* 319 U.S. 624, 642 (1943).

Conclusion

1. E. L. Doctorow, A Citizen Reads the Constitution, The Nation 208–17 (February 21, 1987). The essay is reprinted in E. L. Doctorow, Jack London, Hemingway, and the Constitution 117–38 (1993).

2. Mao, Speech (November 6, 1938), in 2 Selected Works 224 (1965).

INDEX